# A HOUSE OF STRAW

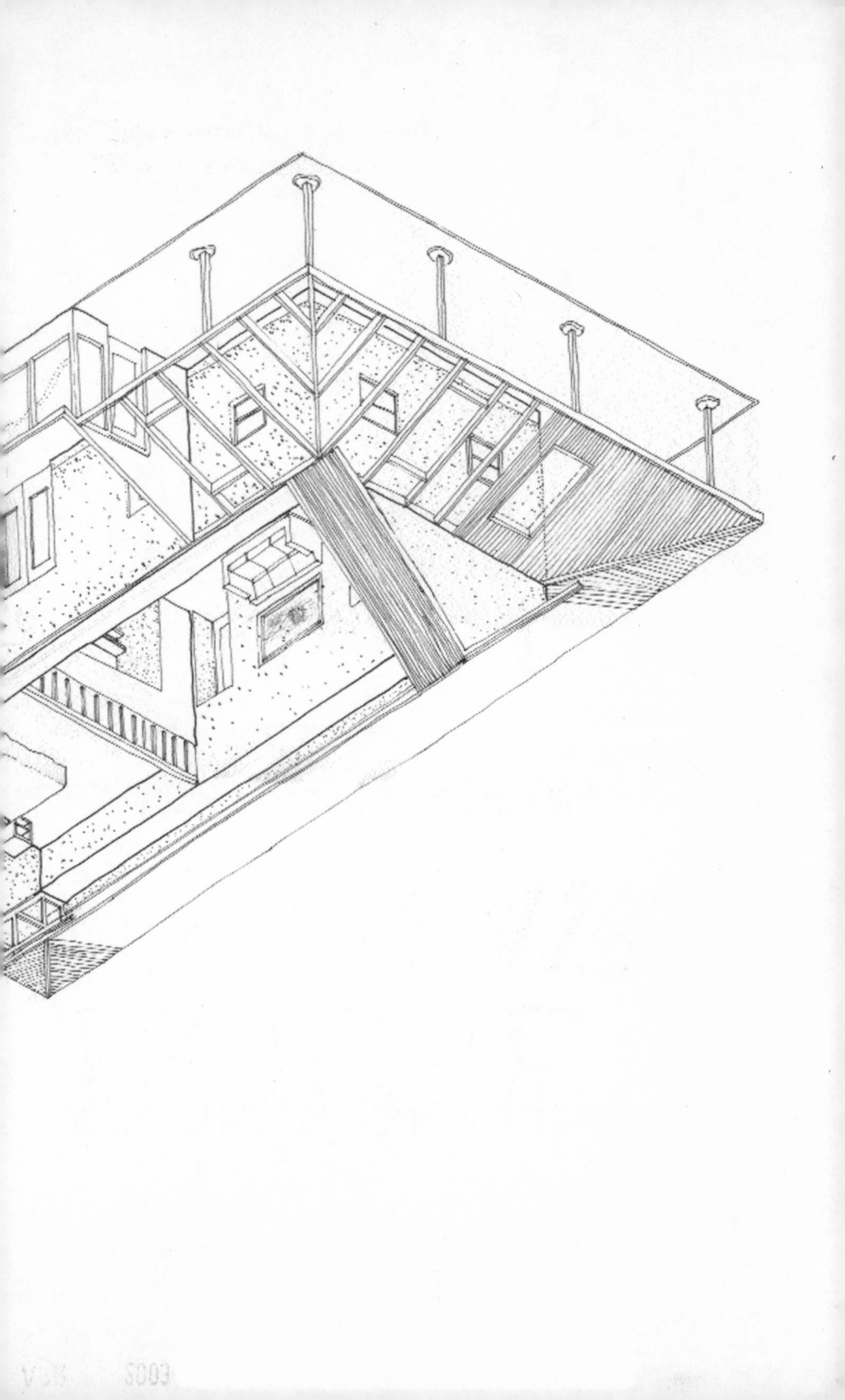

# A HOUSE
# of STRAW

## A Natural Building Odyssey

## Carolyn Roberts

CHELSEA GREEN PUBLISHING
WHITE RIVER JUNCTION, VERMONT

*Designed by Dede Cummings Designs*

Printed in Canada.
First printing, April, 2002.

05 04 03 02      1 2 3 4 5

*Library of Congress Cataloging-in-Publication Data*
Roberts, Carolyn, 1950-
A house of straw: a natural building odyssey / by Carolyn Roberts.
       p.          cm.
Includes bibliographical references.
ISBN 1-890132-30-6 (alk. paper)
1. Straw bale houses--Design and construction. 2. Roberts, Carolyn, 1950---Homes and haunts--Arizona--. I. Title.

TH4818.S77 R63 2002
693'.997--dc21                    2002022626


Chelsea Green Publishing Company
P.O. Box 428
White River Junction, VT 05001
(800) 639-4099
www.chelseagreen.com

*Ever keep your goal shining before you . . .*
*The things that happen to you in life don't matter,*
*What you become through them, does.*

—Sri Gyanamata, *God Alone*, 1984

For my sons, Andrzej and John-Jozef,

my parents, John and Kate Roberts,

and my Consultant in Shining Armor, Jon Ruez

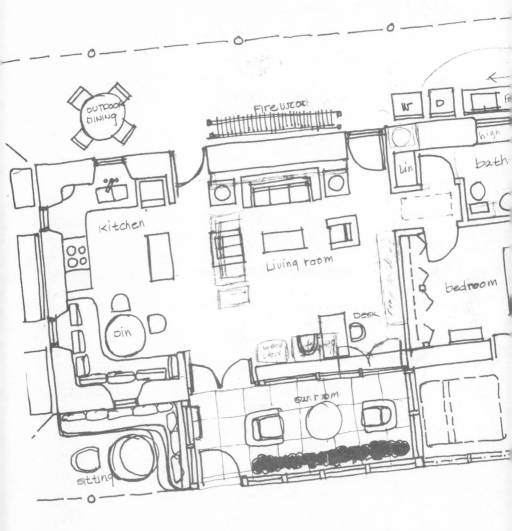

# CONTENTS

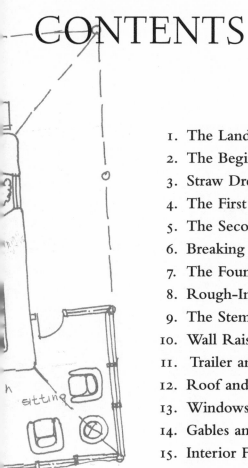

# A HOUSE OF STRAW

*Chapter One*

# THE LAND

*To live content with small means; to seek elegance rather than luxury . . .*
*to listen to stars and birds . . . to bear all cheerfully, do all bravely, await*
*occasions, hurry never, in a word, to let the spiritual, unbidden and*
*unconscious, grow up through the common, this is to be my symphony.*

—WILLIAM HENRY CHANNING, "My Symphony"

THE afternoon sun baked in a cloudless sky as I stepped out of my sedan
onto the sandy road. Summer heat enveloped me in dusty aromas and hazy
pastels. Slinging a water bottle over my shoulder and placing a wide-
brimmed canvas hat on my head, I peered down the road. A silvery lizard
with rainbow stripes raced toward me through the heat waves. As I moved
my foot, he stopped, camouflaged against the desert sand.

There were no cars in sight; that was good for both the lizard and me.
I wiped my brow with my fingers, but no moisture appeared. My sweat
evaporated faster than it could dampen my skin. Taking a deep breath, I
grinned. Perhaps the lizard and I had sprung from the same amoeba in
our distant past.

I loved the open desert, even in the middle of June. There was something primal, majestic, yet serene about the spacious land and distant Tucson Mountains, with cactus and shrubs more bizarre than my children's
kindergarten drawings. This is where I would put down roots and stay,
like the tall saguaros reaching for heaven.

I had arrived at the property early, on purpose. I needed time alone to
make sure this felt like the right place for the next phase of my life—to
make sure it was right for my straw bale house. I was going to build it
myself. I was very clear that this was no small undertaking. I had built a
house once before, hiring out most of the work that time, and still I was

so frazzled by the end of it that I swore I'd never do it again. Yet here I was, ready to give birth to another house, and excited about it. Building is kind of like childbirth that way.

This time, I wasn't going to rush my decisions, no matter how enticing they seemed. I would analyze this project from every angle to make sure there was no room for failure. I would consult several knowledgeable straw bale organizations and consider their input, but the ultimate decision would be mine. I would move steadily forward with faith, not fear, listening to my true, inner voice and learning from the mistakes in my past. Well, those would be the goals, anyway.

The location was good, within fifteen minutes of my sons' high school and the freeway, with only a short block on a washboard dirt road for my city car to drive (I had no plans for an SUV). What really pulled me to the property, however, was the sweeping view of the mountains to the south. The layout of the lot was perfect for the south-facing, passive solar home that was formulating in pencil sketches on my desk; the low winter sun would beam through the south windows to warm the house, but the high summer sun would shine only on well-insulated roof.

Marking my territory, I strolled eastward around the perimeter of the two-acre, north-south rectangle. The realtor, Kathy Lindstrom, had already faxed me the plot map and deed restrictions. Across the dirt road, to the south, lay a wide open parcel, forty acres maybe, of pristine state land. So far it was undeveloped and hopefully would stay that way.

After my version of extensive research, having friends call friends, I had been told the land was deeded in a trust for the state to use for revenue to improve the schools in the area. Every now and then the state got an idea to sell it to a developer, but local people had successfully fought that, so far.

A home and horse stables lay across a sandy easement on the east side of the property. Not the most attractive corrals, but I could plant trees to cover the view where needed. It would be fun to have horses next door. My younger son, J.J., loved animals of all kinds and both boys liked to ride. Maybe the neighbors had teenagers, maybe girls. That might encourage my sons, now fifteen and seventeen, to help with building. To the north stood a tidy home with oleander bushes and a grass yard enclosed by a chainlink fence. Maybe they'd like my lawn mower, which I planned to give away.

The owner to the west had built very close to the property line, and it looked as if she was using a driveway that cut through "my" property. Some trees would definitely need to be planted alongside her home. Big ones.

This would be something to bring up with the real-estate agent. I didn't need easement hassles with my neighbors before I had even moved in.

I strolled across a barren patch of land about thirty feet in diameter, which had obviously been scraped by a tractor. When the desert is excavated, it doesn't grow back for years. Even then, it will most likely produce only creosote bushes and other low shrubs. The stately saguaros and handsome cholla cactus take decades, even centuries, to reach a mature size.

A mound of gravel bordered the scraped area. I kicked it with my sandaled foot. Had someone begun to build here once? The land rose slightly as I approached the center of the lot, the most natural building site. Heavy monsoon rains, which build in late summer afternoons and explode out of dark clouds to flood every crevice of the land, would drain away from the house.

Instead of returning down the driveway to my parked car, I approached the mound. Two startled quail scurried beneath the creosote bushes before me, their knobby plumes bobbing whimsically. I'd love having quail for neighbors, with their gentle cooing. Nothing is cuter than baby quail in the spring, waddling in an orderly row after their parents.

Stepping carefully through the shrubs at the building area, I avoided, for their protection and my own, the tiny hedgehog cacti that were barely emerging from the sandy soil. Fallen nubs from the cholla cactus were even more dangerous. They are sometimes called jumping cactus because they appear from nowhere and poke themselves into any uncovered flesh.

Two sentry saguaros guarded either side of the rise. I stood on the mound, enthralled by the view and trying to feel my future. Excitement welled up inside me. A glow spread from deep in my being to my face, ending in a huge smile. I clenched my fists and spun around with glee. Yes! This place was perfect.

This would be a home that would reflect my love of the desert. It would be made of the Sonoran sands and clays, blending with the desert's light hues and delicate textures, using nature's own elements to protect my family from the harsh extremes. It would be a home built of my enthusiasm and sweat, with the assistance of my two teenaged sons whom I loved dearly, and with friends who build straw bale houses because they love them and all they stand for. It would be a home to embrace and inspire all who pass within its doors.

It was also a financial necessity. If I could build this house with a minimal mortgage, I could afford life with my two sons on the income I currently made as an office manager. The straw bale insulation would cut my heating and cooling costs to a minimum. In fact, given the costs of running my current household, I couldn't afford *not* to move out to the desert. If there were order in the universe, this house would be built.

Deed restrictions by the land's owner required that any building be on the north acre, where I stood, with the southern acre left natural as desert habitat. That gave me real respect for the owner and guaranteed me a wonderful front yard, protected from the occasional road traffic.

Maybe I'd put a nice walking trail in the southern area with a couple of benches. Wispy mesquite trees and the distant mountains of Saguaro National Park would be visible from the south-facing living room and bedroom windows. From my bedroom on the east side, I would look behind the horse barn to Sombrero Peak. To the west, I'd have a sweeping view of the sunset.

Thank you, I said silently for the future I was glimpsing. Thank you for getting me this far, where this home is more than merely a distant dream, an idea I sketch in idle moments, or stories of homes other people have built. Now it's my turn.

Why were my hands trembling? My mind kept reviewing all the myriad details that could go wrong, the stress and exhaustion, the costs that appear from nowhere, the incredible amount of work it takes to pull together a house, meeting all the official codes as well as the standards we set for ourselves. And this time I was on my own. I didn't have finances to hire out much of the work. My desk was covered with books on plumbing, wiring, basic carpentry, straw bale designs . . .

"Could I please have a sign?" I continued in silent prayer. "Show me a vision, something unmistakable that tells me this is where my future belongs; that You will make sure the house reaches completion and becomes a beautiful, friendly, functional home, an example for anyone else who wishes to do this. That I have all the money necessary to build it, my back will hold up, and my children will look at me one day and say, 'Wow, Mom, you really knew what you were doing, moving us out into the desert and building with straw bale. Thanks for making us help build it.' May my walls be so sturdy and strong that I won't have to listen to Big Bad Wolf jokes for the rest of my life."

No inner vision appeared. I opened my eyes, looking for an outward sign. Shrubs and cactus spread before me, as before. The only blinding light was from the sun. Quail cooed in the distance and a rabbit scurried across the clearing.

I strolled into the southern acre and examined the building mound from a distance, visualizing the one-story, Southwestern-style stucco home that lay in sketches on my desk. The straw walls would give it informal, rounded edges and a welcoming appearance. An earthen plaster exterior would blend with the desert sands, except for touches of bright Mexican tile around the windows and doors. Above the walls, a pale green metal roof the color of the mesquite trees would protect the house and gather rainwater for my garden. The south side of the house would be graced by a serene courtyard with a low wall, adobe pots of bright flowers, and straw bale benches, or bancos, for friends to gather upon on long, summer evenings. With eyes wide open, I placed the house onto the land with all my being, as if willing this home into existence.

A dark green Ranger barreling down the dirt road snapped me out of my reverie. Followed by a trail of dust, the car pulled into the lower portion of the driveway. It had to be Kathy, the realtor. A tall, thin lady, perhaps in her midthirties, stepped out of the car in a sundress and black sandals. Her blond hair fell loose and free around her shoulders, her face had very little makeup, and she greeted me with a broad smile. I liked her instantly. I was already sold on the property, but I didn't want to appear too eager.

Strutting ahead of me with legs that seemed about twice as long as mine, she led me to a metal pin marking the northeast corner of the property. It was even farther west than I had imagined. We stood at the corner and eyed the property line. I asked her about the bare patch.

"Oh, the utility company came in when they installed that other house and scraped away a huge area by mistake. I arrived just in time to stop them before they did more damage."

"I could make that my garden and plant some trees," I suggested. "That area with the two saguaros looks like the best building site to me."

She agreed, then added with a note of caution, "Have you read the deed restrictions?"

"Yes, I don't have a problem with them. It says something about no fences, but I would like to fence my garden, to keep the rabbits out and my cats in. Cats and coyotes don't mix well."

She smiled. "I'm sure that won't be a problem. I'll check on that with Frank, the owner. He's a really nice guy, an environmental writer. He owns some land right down the road now, but he doesn't live there yet. His writing takes him all over the world; he just got back from Malaysia, I think."

"Oh, really? I used to be a writer." He sounded like someone I'd enjoy meeting. "Well, he might like to know that I'm planning to build a load-bearing straw bale house. I'm going to do a bunch of the work myself."

"Oh! He'll be so excited to hear that!" she exclaimed. "I'm building a straw bale bed-and-breakfast down the road. I just sold my house. What a coincidence!"

"Are you building a load-bearing?"

"No, I'm going to do a post-and-beam house, steel-framed, and fill in the walls with straw bale. Have you contacted the Women Builders group here? They'll help you with anything you want and they lend tools. Or they offer consultation for about twenty dollars an hour."

I stood silent for a moment, stunned. In three years in Tucson, I hadn't met another woman interested in a straw bale project; in my two years as a realtor I'd never met another realtor the least bit interested in straw bale, and here was Kathy, soon to be a neighbor, launching into straw bale building herself.

"Thank you!" I exclaimed. "No, I haven't talked to them, though I know they exist. That would be a big help. I have so many questions!"

"When we get back to my car I'll give you their number. They also gave me a list of architects and draftsmen who are familiar with straw bale."

"I've already been working with someone, but thank you."

Letting my eyes sweep over the land in a very professional manner, I added, "This land would work well, because I want the house to face south. Since the owner only allows building on the north acre, that gives me the other acre for a buffer."

"Oh, Frank's into all that passive solar stuff, too. I'll have to tell him."

"Do you know what they're planning for that state land across the street?"

She didn't. She said she'd look into it.

We finished walking the property, and I asked a few more questions. She answered my main question for me. "Frank's not absolutely fixed on that price. He'd be happy to take an offer contingent on the sale of your house, also. Would you want to write up the offer, or would you like me to?"

"Oh, I'll go ahead. I think I remember that much." I still had my real-estate license, though I hadn't worked as an agent for a year and a half. "I would like to sell my house and work out a few details before I put in an offer, but I'm definitely interested. Please let me know if anyone else contacts you about this property in the meantime."

"Oh, I sure will." She smiled and climbed back into her SUV.

I calmly strolled back to my car. I kept my professional cool, but inside I was exhilarated, filled with that indescribable "knowing" that this house was to be a reality and it would be on this piece of land. Okay, I would give birth to a house just one more time, let the labor pains begin!

## Chapter Two

# THE BEGINNING

*Nature's peace will flow into you as sunshine flows into trees. The winds will blow their own freshness into you, and the storms their energy, while cares will drop off like autumn leaves.*

—JOHN MUIR, *Our National Parks*, 1901

I COULD barely contain my excitement after finding the land and knowing, deep inside, that it would be the site of my future home. My current house in a crowded subdivision of northwest Tucson had been on the market for six months with no offers and hardly any showings. As far as I knew, it would be months before it sold. Real estate moved slowly during the hot summer months. But in the meantime, I had so many things to learn that I couldn't stand still.

An e-mail about a weekend workshop on earthen floors flew across my computer screen. My boys were in Hawaii visiting their father, so I signed up. I glanced through the various do-it-yourself books on my bookshelves, trying to decide where to begin. I figured I'd read each one as that part of the house was upon me. There was far too much to store in my memory bank—I needed hands-on experience to learn all this. I had been studying alternative homes for seven years; why had I waited so long to take a workshop?

My quest for an alternative home had begun in the fall of 1993, while I still lived in Port Jefferson, New York. I had been scanning the TV schedule one Thursday evening, trying to take my mind off the stress of running a photography studio. My husband had gone to bed early, but I was wide awake. A half-hour PBS show entitled "Earthship" with Dennis Weaver roused my curiosity. I slipped a tape in the VCR to record the program.

I sat spellbound as Weaver told his story of building a solar home made of recycled tires filled with dirt in the Colorado mountains. Before then, I had looked at houses as attractive and somewhat functional places to live, selected largely by their shape and appearance. The thought of a house as a living entity that worked with the elements and blended with the land was completely new to me. The idea of a house that could be built at least partially by regular, unskilled people like me and my friends appealed to my independent and thrifty nature. I was not necessarily an environmentalist; I had been too busy raising kids and trying to pay bills to think about it much.

I had always loved nature in its many forms. Even in my early childhood years in New England, I felt most at ease while wandering alone through the forests. I spent many happy hours building fairy gardens from moss, twigs, and acorn tops.

I clearly recall the day in fifth-grade science class when I learned that plants take in carbon dioxide and give out oxygen, and humans do the opposite. Suddenly I looked at life as more than merely an accident. In my youthful innocence, I discovered a balance between the basic needs of humans, plants, and the elements—the many herbs to heal, plants to provide a wide variety of food, sunlight to warm, rain to water, soil to provide nutrients, as well as trees for shade and wood, metals in the ground. We really were being given everything we needed and more, for only the price of taking care of the land.

That year, when I was eleven, my parents moved to Hawaii, where houses opened to the trade winds and weekends were spent at the beach, hiking, or enjoying the fresh air. Nature's abundance was an inherent part of life and too magnificent to be ignored. Pale beaches embraced turquoise seas. Morning mists clung to the lush mountainsides, spawning rainbows in the rising sun. Bright perfumed flowers permeated the neighborhood yards.

While Honolulu seemed a large city compared to the town in Massachusetts that we had come from, the native Hawaiian culture balanced the bustle with joyful music and relaxed living. I wore simple cotton dresses with sandals to school and on rainy days we could go barefoot. The weather was rarely inclement, so every holiday was celebrated outdoors with feasts that included abundant fresh fruits and exquisite flower leis, gifts from the earth. Soothing Hawaiian music flowed freely at every party, exalting the beauty of the land, the *'aina*, as a source of life.

I continued to perceive a very loving Order that balanced human needs with those of Nature. As a critical teenager, I scrutinized society to see whether it was making decisions in harmony with that Order, or in oppo-sition to it. Most often, I determined we were moving in opposition, and that didn't make sense to me.

While I dreamed of a life of joyful simplicity, that was not the experi-ence of my school years. My natural curiosity and eagerness to please had given me the label of being an excellent student. My teachers didn't care much about my love of the outdoors, nor did I think that worth sharing, but everyone poured praises on me for my good grades. Responding to the accolades, I worked most weekends and late into the school nights to keep those grades ahead of my peers. I began to identify myself with my test scores. If they sagged, my sense of self-worth plummeted.

I graduated from Punahou School somewhere in the upper ranks of my class, earning admission to Stanford University in the fall of 1968. How-ever, I was tired of studying and completely confused as to what career I should choose. There wasn't a single vocation that interested me. Physics was fascinating, but after one advanced Calculus class I knew I didn't want to major in Physics.

In college I was surrounded by some very bright minds and fellow overachievers. I had never earned a C grade in my entire life, so I pushed myself late into the nights to maintain what I considered to be a respectable grade-point average. Halfway through my freshman year, I collapsed in exhaustion and ended up in the infirmary attached to an IV. As I lay in my stark hospital room, I began to see education as a big trap. The more I achieved, the more pressure I felt to excel further. If I struggled for a degree from Stanford, I would probably be rewarded with a stressful job that locked me in an office ten hours a day and sometimes on week-ends. Why would I want to do that?

After completing my freshman year, I dropped out of school, stayed in northern California, and pushed my friends away. Taking a job as a secre-tary to pay the bills on a small apartment, I began life on my own terms. I wanted to see who I would become if I followed my inner guidance, rather than the many outer pressures.

Mostly, however, I battled loneliness as I realized that I had no sense of myself. I had lived to please my parents, teachers, siblings, friends, and school standards. Inside me sat a dark void that I wanted to light.

As the months rolled by, I passed my weekends by taking long walks around a nearby lake with a notebook in my hand, writing whatever came to my mind. The quiet lake and my notebook became my best friends, patiently listening to my confusions, meandering muses, and raw attempts at poetry. I also joined an international meditation group, Self-Realization

Fellowship, which instructed me to still my mind and reach my inner depths. If I could listen to those depths, perhaps I could heal them.

Responding to a nagging pressure to focus on a career, I decided to return to Honolulu in my midtwenties and study journalism at the University of Hawaii. I loved to write and couldn't think of what else to do with that desire. For a year I attended classes, waitressed at night, and wrote every spare minute for a magazine called *Islands*. Finally, I sensed some direction to my life. Then the magazine went bankrupt, and I found myself close to exhaustion once again.

Honolulu had become a bustling, concrete-paved metropolis that didn't feel like home. When I was offered a news internship with a local TV station, I hesitated and flew to Kauai to visit my older sister.

I had never been to the outer islands and I immediately fell in love with the slow pace, friendly people, and beautiful beaches. Hanalei Bay enchanted me with its horseshoe of sand surrounding gently rolling surf. Mists enveloped the far half of the bay, while the beach beneath my bare feet basked in sunlight. Long, thin waterfalls cascaded from the lush mountains surrounding the bay. As I walked down the empty beach into the fog, a lone fisherman hand-tossed his nets into the choppy waters. I swam in the serenity of the warm rain, listening only to small waves hissing against the sand.

I couldn't return to city life. Turning down the internship, I moved to Kauai to rest for a year. I shared a small house near the beach, worked evenings as a waitress at a nearby seafood restaurant, and wrote a few magazine articles.

My sabbatical expanded into several happy years romping in the surf, napping to the sound of the waves, working on my writing skills with a correspondence course in creative writing, and studying Hawaiian slack key guitar.

Creative writing was a new and very different challenge from journalism, as I had to formulate characters and plots from within. There was no outer subject to research and nobody to interview. It was difficult for my mind to create, so my stories ended up stiff and shallow. I made writing a personal challenge to open up my inner core, find those personalities inside myself, and bring them to life.

As time went on, friendships formed and sunny afternoons of playing in the gentle surf melted into evening bonfires with guitar music and light conversation. I was very happy. In 1980 I married Rick, a surfer and roofer who shared my love of a simple life near the ocean. We lived in a small beach house along the shore of my beloved Hanalei Bay.

Our first son, Andrzej (which is Polish for Andrew and pronounced like Andre), was born on Christmas Day in 1981. I loved him from the depths of my being, as a long-lost friend, from the moment I laid eyes on him in the hospital. I had never known that I could love so deeply.

He had large, kind eyes, and as he grew he showed a gentle wisdom and sense of humor far greater than his tiny years. Any time that adults were joking, I could see Andrzej at the edge of the crowd, eyes twinkling, as he tried to absorb whatever was making us laugh. Music, likewise, enlivened his being from the moment his voice was mature enough to sing and his legs were strong enough to dance. On rainy days, I would play my guitar while he strummed his little ukulele.

John-Jozef joined the family in May, 1984, kicking a hole in my waterbag and zooming into the world a month early with an adorable, impish face and unbridled energy. My love wasn't divided in half, but expanded to encompass both beautiful children. Strong-willed from his first days, J.J. let his desires be known with loud screams. Beneath his defiant energy, however, was a sensitivity that continually reached out for hugs and quietly studied this new world he had entered. He would contentedly play in his playpen if it was in the backyard or on the beach but howl unceasingly if I caged him indoors. This made it a difficult to get any housework done, but fortunately I loved the outdoors, too.

J.J. was an energetic morning child and Andrzej was a late-night child, so I didn't get much sleep, but I didn't care. I loved both of them incredibly and enjoyed every moment of being their mom. When J.J. woke up early, I'd carry him down to the seashore to watch the sunrise over the ocean. In the evenings, I'd leave Rick's dinner in a warm oven and take both boys down to the beach, where I marveled at the ever-changing sunsets as the boys splashed in the edge of the surf. Followed by a warm bath, the evening beach session would usually, but not always, cause Andrzej to drift off to sleep at a reasonable hour.

As the boys grew older, we became highly advanced sand castle architects and wave riders. I sat their chubby little bodies on the front of my boogie-board with my arms wrapped around them while we rode small waves onto the beach.

Life definitely had its wonderful moments, but Rick's work was inconsistent and paradise was being discovered by the wealthy, causing prices to soar. Our beach rental was put up for sale in the mid-1980s at a price we couldn't even dream about, so we were forced to find other housing. Since rentals were scarce, my parents offered to use the equity in their home to loan us cash to build a house in the neighborhood of Kilauea, about fifteen minutes from Hanalei.

Both boys were in school by then, Andrzej in first grade and J.J. in pre-school, so in an attempt to save money, we decided we had enough free time to be our own general contractors. Since Rick was a roofer, he knew many people in the construction trade who might work at a discount or trade their labor for his roofing labor on one of their houses.

This was my first introduction to construction and a genuine learning experience. I felt as if everything that could possibly go wrong, did. But at the end of a year, we had our very own house and a great respect for general contractors.

One day while J.J. and I were driving between Hanalei and Kilauea, his cherub voice piped up from the backseat. "I just don't know if I want to take care of babies when I grow up."

"Well, you don't have to," I responded. "You don't even have to get married."

"Oh, I want to get married," he replied in earnest. "I just don't know to who."

Maintaining my composure, I said, "You have a long time to decide that. You want to be sure to marry the right person, too. You don't want to marry someone who yells at you all the time." There was silence for a few minutes. Then he said, "You didn't get the right one, did you Mom?"

I loved my life on Kauai so much that it was hard for me to face my unhappiness with my marriage. While Rick had always been somewhat fiery, the strain of moving away from the ocean and supporting a family seemed too much for him. His temper flared frequently and each explosion seemed to grow more intense.

I spent my days scurrying around to keep the boys quiet and the house tidy, because even crumbs on the floor could send him into a rage. His temper also focused at the boys, pushing them to become disciplined surfers when they just wanted to frolic with their friends, and pulling them away from me, because I let them simply play. Even going to the beach became miserable.

One day, after enduring a scary and embarrassing tantrum, I gave Rick the ultimatum: either attend counseling sessions with me or I would leave and take the boys with me. He agreed to counseling and we ended up in the office of Thomas Weinberg. For the first time in my life, I was in a safe territory where blame was not allowed and communication was encouraged. Thomas was not the sort of counselor who sat back, analyzed us, and told us what we should do differently. He assisted us in understanding our own difficulties and discovering solutions.

I began attending sessions alone as Thomas escorted me back through my childhood to confront old fears and disappointments and then regain the parts of my being that I had left behind. We held discussions with the different parts of my personality to uncover my many motives in life, whether they were fears or joys. Then he gently guided me as I decided which inner voices I would choose to follow.

Thomas was the first person in my life to tell me I had not only a right but an obligation to take care of myself. How could I be a good mother if I was falling apart at the seams? He said that the greatest gift I could give my children was to stand strong and refuse Rick's abuse. They would discover their own strength by watching me.

After two years of counseling and one too many rages from Rick, I determined to leave with the boys, though I had no career. I had attempted to keep up my writing when the boys were little, actually completing two book manuscripts, which were returned over and over from many publishers. Discouraged by the lack of response and too busy because of the house construction, I had given up. Writing really didn't pay much for all the hours of work that went into an article, anyway, I rationalized.

I decided I would like to become a teacher so I could work the same hours as the boys and take care of them over summer break. If I could return to Honolulu for two years, I could complete my education and get a teaching certificate. Then I could return to Kauai and teach elementary school. Rick's business was booming and we should have enough money for me to do that, I estimated.

Rick opposed my leaving and adamantly opposed the boys coming with me. With the assistance of a mediator, we shared care of the boys while we negotiated a separation over the summer of 1989. Rick refused to consider any option except that of my leaving the boys on Kauai while I attended school.

The thought of leaving them carved a hole in my heart, but I figured I could visit them every weekend and vacation. We continued to discuss the separation while I sent in an application to the University of Hawaii for January of 1990. As December approached, Rick still refused to sign every separation agreement that I presented to him and likewise refused to present me with his own version of the separation. I did not want to leave without an agreement that gave me the money to survive and put the boys' happiness as highest priority.

In mid-December, through reliable sources, I found out that Rick had been talking to a divorce attorney and was making plans to seek full custody as soon as the boys and I were separated. I was willing to endure almost anything except losing my children, so I said my prayers and formulated a plan.

I couldn't stay on Kauai because Rick was moving out of his rental and back into our house, where I had been living, on January 1. His mother was planning to move in, also. Most of the available jobs in the area paid minimum wage, which was why I had decided to leave in the first place.

Our verbal agreement had been that the boys would accompany me to Honolulu, then fly back to Kauai when my classes began. Rick agreed. I gambled that my signature was still good on our joint checking account, though I had been using a different one during our separation. With trembling hands, two days before I was due to fly to Honolulu, I wrote myself a check from our joint account for several thousand dollars and turned it into traveler's checks. The boys and I flew to Honolulu the day after Christmas, secured an apartment, and I filed for divorce. Thus began our bitter divorce process, which put untold pressure on the boys for years.

I was frightened but very determined to make a new life. Tossing my hopes of finishing school into the wind, I took a job as an administrative assistant at the Hawaii Community Foundation while my parents helped take care of the boys, and life moved forward.

Instead of hating office life, I actually enjoyed working with so many intelligent, interesting women. The foundation managed many charitable trusts and funds, working with both the public and the board members of each fund. While my duties were fairly routine, I found that the advent of computers made desk work far more interesting than I remembered from my previous secretarial jobs.

Over the summer of 1990, when the foundation needed a photographer, I remet an old friend who had taken photos for *Islands* magazine. Unfortunately, his name was also Rick. We began having lunches together, then began dating several months later.

Rick II was gentle, kind, and very creative. I knew he would never burst into uncontrolled rages, so I felt safe with him. However, his photography business had fallen apart and he was in debt. Advertising agencies, his source of work, had been the first companies to fail when the stock market took a dive in 1989.

He was considering moving to "the mainland" to manage a franchise of Headshots "glamour photography" studio. A former assistant of Rick's had created glamour photography: she analyzed women's faces, then adorned them with appropriate makeup, elegant hairstyles, fluffs of fabric, and silk flowers. In the photographs, they look like professional models. She opened a booth at Ala Moana shopping center and business took off so fast that soon she had moved to Texas to open franchises across the country.

I was having trouble making ends meet in Honolulu, where our dingy basement apartment cost me $1,000 a month and the courts kept cutting my child support. As much as the boys and I enjoyed Hawaii and my work, I couldn't afford to stay. I considered moving anywhere with a lower cost of living.

My share of the equity in our house on Kauai would come to about $60,000. This would barely make a dent on a family house in Honolulu, where prices began at $300,000. It seemed logical for me to invest in a business rather than a house, and Rick II's photography experience seemed to blend with my business experience into the perfect solution.

Rick II and I were married in May of 1992 and agreed to buy a Headshots studio on Long Island. It was very far from Hawaii but the only franchise available at the time. The boys, then eight and eleven, were unsure about this new Rick in their lives and unsure about leaving Hawaii, but eager to experience real snow.

I hung on the hope that the business would bring me a livable income, so I could offer the boys a stable home. The schools in Port Jefferson were supposed to be some of the best in the country, and I looked forward to showing the boys autumn leaves, spring lilacs, and the finer points of tobogganing.

Oh, what an idealist I can be! When we arrived in New York we were greeted with people dressed in black leather, fake fingernails, and teased hairdos. New York City depressed me completely. How did people breathe? Couldn't they see the homeless on their streets and the haze in the air? Didn't they want to do something about it? No, they worshiped the city as if it were the center of the Universe. It didn't make sense to me.

I was also horrified at what we had to spend on heating oil during the winter and electricity to run the air conditioner over the summer. In Hawaii, we only used enough electricity to run the lights and the computer—no heating or cooling was needed, as temperatures hovered near eighty both day and night. We simply opened louvers under our windows facing the trade winds and that provided all the cooling we needed. In the winter, we closed them.

With the photo studio, we now took home enough to pay our bills, but the strain was ruining us both. The future of the studio seemed constantly to hang by a thread. Glamour Shots was spreading across the country, imitating Headshots's photography style. Glamour Shots opened a studio in a neighboring mall on exactly the day that we opened ours and competed with every sale we ran, forcing us to keep our prices at a bare minimum.

Our studio construction had cost about four times what we expected, so we had large payments to make each month in order to break even. Bankruptcy loomed like a black cloud with no silver lining. Open seven days a week, Headshots had me at the constant command of my pager and cellphone. Employees called in sick, camera equipment jammed, money disappeared from the register, and customers needed me at all hours of the day and evening. The huge volume of money that came and went each month seemed beyond my control.

To make matters worse, I never fully believed in the work. Of all the women in the world who love working with hair and makeup, it had to be a joke of the Universe that I had ended up hiring and training cosmetologists in these arts. Given my choice, I'd photograph people in freckles and denim.

I was definitely not on the simple, joyous track I had intended for my life. But this was the life I was leading the night I happened to see Dennis Weaver's Earthship on television.

As I sat spellbound before the TV that evening, I felt a new hope. My mind flashed back to my simple life on Kauai and forward to a life with less pressure; perhaps even a life without a mortgage! God, I hated knowing how much a house would really cost after thirty years of payments. Who was getting all that money? With forever-climbing electric bills on top of the mortgage, I couldn't see how to survive with less strain in my life.

The house on the TV screen, called an Earthship, required no conventional power lines, collected rainwater and then recycled it from the sinks and showers, worked with the angle of the sun to keep the house at an even temperature—and was beautiful. More than beautiful, it was like a garden or a tree—part of the rhythm of life.

I raced eagerly into the bedroom, ready to share my new vision for the future, but my husband was sound asleep.

Chapter Three

# STRAW DREAMS

*Twenty years from now you will be more disappointed by the things you didn't do than by the ones you did. So . . . Explore. Dream. Discover.*

—Mark Twain

After a night of tossing and turning, I assailed Rick with my enthusiasm over breakfast. He nodded silently, which I figured was some sort of approval. He wasn't really much of a talker, anyway. My checks were in the mail by 9 A.M. for books on how to build one of these Earthships.

When the books finally arrived, I devoured them; reading about the thermal mass of earth-filled tires that maintained an even temperature, building into hillsides for insulation, interior walls from recycled soda cans and mud plaster, earthen floors, refrigerators opening to the frigid night air, solar ovens embracing the sun, indoor gardens providing clean air and filtered water, and so on. It made sense!

A year later, I flew to Taos, New Mexico, to stay in an Earthship bed-and-breakfast and glimpse these homes firsthand. My husband came along too, swept up by my enthusiasm, or so I thought. I saw some magnificent completed Earthships, along with a couple of half-built ones for sale, where the builders had run out of money before they were completed. That gave me the shivers. I learned that these homes were no less expensive to build than an ordinary home, but they could be independent of outside utilities. During that trip, I read my first article on straw bale houses in a little Taos newspaper. The article didn't really explain much, but my curiosity was aroused.

Business continued to decline and we realized that we couldn't survive for very long the way things were going. This incessant moving was exhausting for me and emotionally destructive for the boys, but Long

Island was so expensive that I couldn't survive if I had to go back to secretarial work. Closing the store would mean moving again.

I could not accept the fact that life would bring me a bankruptcy and another move, so I dug deep inside me and tried every technique I could think of to keep the business afloat. I even added a new business traveling around to Price Clubs to photograph children in antique clothes and print the images in sepia tones.

Rick moved to Phoenix to study graphic design and pursue his own photography career. It wasn't really a separation; he just decided he wanted to leave, so he left. I was stunned, but I realized that my life wouldn't be all that different with him gone. I sensed he was very unhappy, but he wouldn't tell me why. Instead, he spent most of his spare time in the bedroom reading magazines.

Our relationship improved over the phone, so after a few months I flew to Phoenix to visit him. I loved the airy, light feel of the open desert

*Saguaro with straw bales—a house waiting to happen.*

but disliked the metropolis of Phoenix. One day we drove to Tucson, a city smaller than Phoenix, nestled in the mountains. With its elevation, it was also cooler. The bright sunshine felt exhilarating after a long, gray winter on Long Island.

When I returned to New York, I had a vision of where I would like to live if the studio failed, though I hated discussing another move with the boys. Perhaps Rick II and I would get along better in a different environment.

We had lived on Long Island for four years now. The new climate, different culture, and challenging school system had been a difficult transition for the boys. A renewed custody battle and long, whiny phone calls from their father telling them how much he missed them and how beautiful it was on Kauai hadn't helped, either.

But they had made the transition and now had good friends who stayed up late at night with them playing a tabletop battle game called War Hammer. They had come to love the snow, hoping each winter day that school would be called off and they could go sledding.

I'm sure that beneath the surface they bore me some resentment for all the turmoil in their lives, but they didn't show it. They told me they were fine and enjoying New York. As far as I could see, they were adjusting well. They made friends easily, did well in school, and participated in the village soccer club. Zej had found a guitar teacher who let him bring CDs with his favorite rock songs to the lessons. He not only learned to play the songs but acquired some of the theory behind the music at the same time.

As often as I could, I turned off my pager on weekends and joined them for a hike or sledding trip. We also shared some joyful vacations skiing or camping in New England's fall colors. I talked to them as openly and honestly as I dared, to let them know that despite the many outer changes, my love for them was a constant they could always count on. In their own way, they likewise showed me that they loved me despite everything, and that's all I needed to know.

I vowed to be cautious in whatever move I made next, so that I didn't bring the boys continual turmoil. If they would forgive me for one more move, then I needed to promise them that this would be the last. I researched Tucson's cost of living and found it to be among the lowest in the country. The area was growing rapidly and jobs were plentiful. I already knew I would love the desert and its surrounding mountains for hiking. It seemed as if I couldn't go wrong.

Rick II returned to New York to help me survive the Christmas and Hanukkah season with both businesses in full swing and me on the verge of exhaustion once again. The holidays were my only hope to pay the past-due bills that were piled all over my desk. I made a good dent on the mound, enough to keep us going, but then January put me back into the realm of borrowing from one account to pay the other. Huge winter blizzards that closed the mall for several days didn't help matters, either.

As spring arrived, bankruptcy loomed more real than ever. No buyers for the studio had surfaced and time was running out quickly. Rick left again for Tucson to open a photography studio and find us a home in case I had to close Headshots.

Desperately, I prayed for a new chance at life. With my vision of an alternative home, I felt as if I could pull our life together. I just needed one more chance.

At the end of May 1996, my resources were exhausted and my debts were impossible, so I closed the Headshots doors and filed for bankruptcy. The Headshots corporation was essentially nonexistent now, and most of the other franchises across the country had sold or closed with the increasing competition.

As Andrzej graduated from eighth grade and J.J. graduated from fifth, we piled our furniture into a huge rented truck and drove my car, filled with our guinea pig in his cage and the house plants, onto a trailer behind the truck.

Andrzej was in tears at having to move again, and I couldn't do anything but apologize and hug him. I felt terrible for doing this to him, but I also felt exhilarated to be rid of the incessant pressure of Headshots and free to start over. I would never, ever again invest in a business with a high overhead.

We said our good-byes and chugged out of the neighborhood, trying not to destroy any mailboxes or stop signs as we made right turns. Rick's parents had given me a credit card to pay for gas, food, and lodging while the boys and I drove across country. They had also put a down payment on a house for us. It wasn't an alternative house, but I couldn't care less right then. It was a lovely two-story house with four bedrooms in a neighborhood filled with kids. It would be home. They even offered to make the monthly payments of $850 on the house until we could afford to do so.

As the boys and I left the crowds of New York behind us and headed down the open freeway, I began to breathe deeply for the first time in several years. Life was going to get better. If I had also known that Tucson was a center for straw bale building, I would have been grinning from ear to ear.

Rick's photography studio was off to a slow start, but he brought in enough to pay our basic bills while his parents paid the mortgage. I could have run out and gotten a job, but I refused to support the family. It was

Rick's turn. Besides, what was I going to do with a background in glamour photography management when the sight of a studio gave me a nervous twitch? I just wanted to be at home when the boys returned from school each day, to help them through this transition. When it became obvious that I really needed to bring in some money, I decided to train in real estate. That way I could work from home.

What I didn't understand is that the people who do well in real estate are the ones who have lived in a city for a while, know the layout, and have lots of friends as contacts. None of that applied to me and after a year of working seven days a week with little income, I decided to get a Monday through Friday office job and disconnect my pager once and forever.

The boys had not only survived their first year in Tucson, but they had friends within biking distance of our house. Money was still very scarce, so I felt we had arrived at a place where bringing in some extra money was more important than my being home. Rick heartily agreed.

After leaving applications all over town, I was hired by the University of Arizona Department of English to oversee the front desk and update their Web pages. I had learned a little about Web pages from working with digital photography and peering over Rick's shoulder.

I enjoyed being around English professors and writers, people who wrote and philosophized. As I copied the articles for their classes, I would glance over the short stories and essays. If I found one that looked particularly interesting, I borrowed a copy to read during my lunch hour. I also took a few classes on campus to learn more about computers and how Web pages are constructed.

The job lasted only six months, however, and I was laid off. Rick's photography studio was blossoming now, so he paid the bills while I enjoyed some mountain hikes and looked for another job. After a couple of months, I found a job as an office manager at StarNet, an Internet service provider owned by Tucson's Newspapers, which also put the *Arizona Daily Star* online.

I had landed in the midst of another group of writers, this time journalists, so I felt right at home. After running my own business I felt overqualified for this front-desk job, but as I watched the strain that the managers endured, I was happy to be exactly where I was. When 5 P.M. rolled around, I got up from my desk, locked the door, and forgot about work.

All seemed well on the surface. The boys were actually enjoying Tucson and we were paying our bills, but Rick was growing silently restless. He worked seven days a week, ten hours a day, and rarely came home.

When he reconnected with a wealthy old friend in Phoenix, he felt ashamed of our neighborhood and our old furniture. He met his friends at restaurants instead of inviting them to our house.

To the contrary, I continued my fascination with alternative building, aspiring to a simple life with a low overhead. I loved nature far more than any fancy neighborhood.

When I noticed an advertisement for an inexpensive straw bale workshop on a Saturday in the summer of 1998, I couldn't resist. Once again, I sat completely captivated by what I heard and saw. Straw bale is not like the thermal mass of rocks, earth, or adobe, which absorb and distribute heat. It is insulation—more than most houses have in their roofs and far, far more than they have in their walls. Here were real people who worked with this beautiful medium all the time; who considered the whole big picture of life as they made decisions for construction.

Straw seemed much more suited to the hundred-plus temperatures in the desert. It didn't take much to convince me that straw (not hay, which has blades rather than hollow stalks) bales would be a whole lot easier to stack than earth-filled tires. Bales could be covered with handmade earthen plasters that I could make myself, instead of cement stucco. Tucson had actually adopted a straw bale building code, so these houses could be built within the city limits. Once again, my enthusiasm was sparked and I had new books on my coffee table, straw bale books.

I had kept my real-estate license active, so every now and then I researched property for sale around Tucson. I fantasized that I would scrape together enough money to build a tiny straw bale cottage in the country where land cost about $5,000 per acre. Over the years, I would add solar panels and a well. By the time we were ready to retire, we'd have the perfect home to relax with "a piece of quiet" as the boys used to say.

In August 1998, Rick flew to Honolulu to cruise the islands with his mother. With my limited vacation time, I couldn't have gone even if I had been invited. He came back distant and disdainful. My discussions of alternative homes received cold snubs. When my conversation turned to compost toilets he announced his departure.

He planned to rent an apartment in a more elegant part of town and buy all new furniture. I could keep the old stuff. He would try not to move too far away, so that he could still visit us on weekends; he'd also be available for excursions and vacations. He assured me that this would be a friendly divorce.

All I really heard was that since he was earning most of the money that supported our family, he wanted to keep it. He wasn't the boys' father, so he wouldn't owe child support. The fact that I hadn't received support payments from Rick I in four years was not his problem. I would get some amount of money in the divorce and be on my own to support the two boys. I calculated that my income as an office manager would pay our monthly bills and basic groceries, but not those bills plus more than a few hundred dollars of a mortgage. There was no way I could keep up the payments on our current house, which meant we would have to move again.

Rick left on November 1, 1998. I waited until we had negotiated an agreement that gave me a third of the equity in the house and payments equaling half the value of his photography equipment before I informed him in no uncertain terms that he was not welcome on weekends nor any other time. This could not be a friendly divorce because friendship involved both parties recognizing the other person as a feeling, thinking human being with a desire for self-expression and genuine affection. He couldn't possibly be my friend in his present state of self-absorption.

I had never been one to dwell on my past, and now both Ricks belonged there. I decided that some of the happiest times of my life had been when I was alone or with my boys and that my life would be a whole lot better off if I could figure out a way to afford it on my own. I planned on having nothing to do with men beyond a few casual dates every now and then.

Through the chaos of my mind as Rick walked out the door, I glimpsed another door opening for me—the opportunity to build a straw bale house and the financial imperative. I would take my portion of the equity in our house, maybe $27,000 if the sale went well, and about $30,000 in back child support that Rick I owed. I would hire an attorney to collect it by forcing him to refinance the house we had built on Kauai. Together, those payments should be enough to build a straw bale house for me and the boys, a future with a minimal mortgage and only light dependence on electricity. My dreams were becoming reality faster than I had imagined.

The only part my brain kept skimming over was the part about doing most of the labor to build an entire house. I guess I had just sort of figured that I'd handle that when I came to it. And now I was there. Smack dab in the middle, with divorce payments to cover the rent for a few months, but not forever.

I estimated I had enough money to buy materials for the house, but not enough to pay for much labor. I didn't really know how much money I would have, nor how much the materials would cost. I was simply guessing from the bare figures I'd been given at one short workshop.

Even my best friends didn't understand why I had to do this. Why not get a small mobile home and relax? But how could I turn my back on something I had wanted so badly for so long? I wanted this divorce to be more opportunity than disaster, and I somehow felt that the path would become clear as I took each step forward.

When I was in high school in Honolulu, as I was becoming bored with being a perfect student, I took up skydiving. My parents gave me permission, though I think they later regretted doing so. My first jump on my sixteenth birthday was so exhilarating that I spent my entire allowance on making one skydive each Sunday.

After I'd been diving for about a year, I joined an exhibition jump over a carnival at the edge of a lagoon. We left the plane and pulled our ripcords over the ocean, with a clear downwind path to the protected pool of water. I was a very petite teenager, too small for my parachute, so I had continual trouble landing on targets, especially when there were warm updrafts. My chute would barely come down. But over the cooler ocean, I had a chance to prove what I could do in front of everyone.

As I drifted down, the crowds around the lagoon were little dots, but I knew my parents were somewhere among them. I desperately wanted to make a perfect landing in the edge of the lagoon and see them beaming with pride. Maneuvering my chute carefully, I pulled attentively on one toggle line and then the other. Floating closer and closer, I noticed a few jumpers land in the lagoon and a few turn back out to sea, so they didn't hit the rock wall that separated the bodies of water. Sighting the lagoon between my boots, I felt confident. I could do this. Hold steady. Just a little farther. Release some air, turn a little to the right. I pulled on my toggle lines and kept heading toward the lagoon.

A skydiver in front of me barely missed the crowds of people. Then the one below me quickly turned out to sea to avoid the rocks. I looked back between my boot toes and instead of water, I saw rocks. Frightened, I jammed my right toggle line all the way down, spun my chute around and turned out to the open ocean. No crowds cheered as the cool water flooded my boots and jump suit. Disappointment flooded through me.

As soon as I had turned around, I instinctively knew that if I had kept my course, I would have landed safely in the lagoon. Instead, I had panicked. My parents waited patiently at the dock until a boat picked me up and brought me to shore. There were polite congratulations, but I felt that I had truly let everyone down—especially myself.

This time, I promised myself intently that Sunday in June 1999, after I had seen the land, there would be no turning back and no panicking. Big things could be accomplished one step at a time, as long as the steps kept moving forward. Houses could be built one weekend at a time. I would listen to my mind, but I would follow my heart and my beliefs. Obstacles would arise, but I would not give up.

*Chapter Four*

# THE FIRST
# FLOOR PLAN

*We act as though comfort and luxury were the chief requirements of
life, when all that we need to be really happy is something to be
enthusiastic about.*

—CHARLES KINGSLEY

I BEGAN designing my house as soon as Rick left. It gave me a focus for
the future and a sense of independence to be able to make the decisions, all
by myself. Finally, I could use the information I had been storing away
for so many years. And yet, the process overwhelmed me.

With a few swipes of a pencil, I could design my future home; lines
would become eight-foot walls requiring analysis by the draftsman, the
county building department, and the inspectors before they became hours
of labor. If I drew too large, I could be overbudget and overworked. If I
drew too small, I might dislike the house and feel cramped.

Once built, this was where I would live and stay for many years—where
my children would bring their children; perhaps where my children would
raise their children and on into grandchildren. The house would be a legend, built by Grandma—a happy legend! I didn't want to look back at
what I had decided with regret, though it was probably inevitable that
someday I'd think of how I'd do things differently.

Hesitantly, I picked up a pencil and stuck it in the sharpener. The sharp-
ening coils groaned and hesitated against the wood, then found their
strength and whirred into action. I took a deep breath. My main purpose
was to build this house myself and build it inexpensively, without a big

mortgage. Also, it should be designed to utilize the elements of Nature, so I would have minimal dependence on utilities in my future. I wrote "Keep It Simple" on a piece of paper and tacked it on the wall behind my desk.

Slowly, my mind also began to whir. Whatever I built would have to be single story; two-story homes are miserable in the desert heat. I loved the simple plantation houses in Hawaii, with metal roofs that extended over surrounding decks known as *lanais*—long summer evenings spent rocking in the porch swing, strumming ukuleles, sipping guava juice, and talking story, as the locals would say. Metal roofs are inexpensive, easy to install, light enough for straw bales to support, and clean enough to collect rainwater. But a deck might be too much work. Okay, so I had the roof.

What about the house? I knew that I wanted a load-bearing straw bale house, which meant it didn't have wooden or metal supports; the roof rested right on the bales. That would be the easiest method for me to build, with friends to help raise the walls.

Tucson had a building code allowing such construction, but care had to be taken that the house shape was geometric, so that the roof settled evenly on the straw. A rectangle seemed trite, and I wasn't sure that a long expanse of load-bearing straw bale wall would hold up in high winds if it weren't supported by posts.

Designers of dome houses talked about their energy efficiency and strength. What about a round house? The monsoon winds would swirl right around it, instead of impacting a long wall. I searched through my straw bale books and saw a photo of someone bending bales for a round house. It didn't look that hard. But what about a round roof? Round roof plates? Round walls for kitchen cupboards? It was probably all possible, but I needed simplicity if I were going to construct this myself.

How about an octagon? That would have all the advantages of a round house, but several straight walls. Could I work the necessary rooms into that shape? There was one way to find out.

I sat up straight in my chair, raised my ruler and traced a dinner plate to form a circle on the graph paper. I inscribed eight flat sides.

Something I had always wanted was an indoor garden with a soothing little waterfall. Maybe I could filter water beneath the planter, as the Earthship homes did. The octagon lent itself easily to a center planter. I would light it with a solar tube, a tall skylight that reached from the roof down to the inner ceiling over it. This would allow full-spectrum light but very little heat to enter, with no electricity required.

I drew a master suite on one side, two kids' rooms and their own bathroom on the other side, and a nice large living space with a kitchen in between. The walls from these rooms would also serve to support the outer bale walls.

This was good. The planter separated all the doorways, giving everyone privacy, but the octagon would circulate the heat evenly. I smiled and laid down my pencil. It was sturdy, simple, beautiful—and unique. During the next few days I refined the design a little, moving a few rooms around, changing shapes, adding closets.

When it was as complete as I could imagine, I eagerly called Dan, a draftsman familiar with the Pima County building codes and straw bale construction. I had met him at my first straw bale workshop. Dan had built the first straw bale house in Tucson, to code, but had later sold it to move near the downtown area, where he could conduct his business from his home and do many errands by bicycle.

Dan greeted me and led me through his small rectangular home with bright turquoise trim to the porch on the north side. There on the patio perched a bathtub, sheltered by palm fronds to the north and west for privacy. Dan proudly showed me some new rainwater cisterns on the other side of the porch that he had recently made from large steel drainage pipes with cement foundations. After offering me a natural soda, he led me down a meandering path through his backyard garden to his office, a straw bale outbuilding half dug into the earth for insulation.

Large south-facing windows kept the office warm on the cool November day that I met with him. Dan looked over my sketch politely and said gently, in his slight southern accent, "You could take it to the building department and see what they say. There's never been an octagonal straw bale house in Tucson, so they might want an engineer's stamp. You might want to consider a rectangle; a passive solar rectangle."

I made some more polite chitchat, asked a few questions, then thanked him and left, feeling only mildly discouraged. This octagon house still made sense to me, so I took it to the county building department the next day during my lunch hour. They agreed that it would probably be more durable than a rectangle in monsoon winds. However, since they had no building codes for octagons, they would require a structural engineer's stamp to verify that the house would withstand hundred-mile-an-hour winds. Dan was right.

I then proceeded to call every structural engineer in Tucson. Only two would even talk to me about straw bale houses, and one of them had no time for about six months. One agreed to glance at my plans. So, on a Saturday morning in December of 1998, only a month after Rick II had left, I walked into Desert Engineering with my sketches under my arm.

Large tables strewn with roll upon roll of house plans and blueprints greeted me instead of a receptionist. Several men in khaki pants huddled around a table in an intense discussion. Finally they glanced up and noticed me. One broke away from the group to offer assistance.

As I described my plans for an octagonal, load-bearing straw bale house, he peered at me over the frame of his glasses. After letting me finish my explanation, he proceeded to describe how the roof would push out on the walls of the octagon, so that they would require large posts at each corner, extra bracing for the roof, and possibly supports in the center. All in all, the shape would raise the cost of construction considerably, not to mention their charges of about $3,000 to review the plans. I said thank you for their time and left. Sinking into my car, I was now thoroughly discouraged.

Good thing I hadn't tried for a round house. Look at tipis and yurts all over the world. They didn't require structural engineers!

Why is it so hard to do something original in our society? I seethed silently as I wound through the downtown traffic. We shop at the same stores, in the same strip malls and shopping plazas, which carry the same products. We all use the same credit cards and run up the same debts, which we pay to the same banks. We watch the same shows on TV, the same movies, drive cars that vary slightly in their color and interior but are essentially the same. We eat the same food from the same chain restaurants, or bought from the same national line of grocery stores, manufactured by the same huge companies with different labels.

Soon after we moved into our current neighborhood in Tucson, my son was biking home from a friend's house one day and got completely lost. All the streets, and all the houses along the streets, looked just the same.

Okay, maybe I was overreacting, I told myself as I loosened my vice grip on the steering wheel. Work within the system, here, or this house will never happen. Dan was right; a rectangle is a better passive solar design. The roof axis would run from east to west, so the long sides of the house would face north and south. The hot afternoon sun would blaze on only the narrow west side, whereas in an octagon it struck a broader side of the house. If I put large windows on the south side of a rectangle, the low winter sun could heat most of the rooms. Keep It Simple. Okay. I was on a budget, so someone with more money than I would have to push the octagon issue.

Arriving home, I went straight to my desk, pulled out the graph paper, and drew a rectangle. In my years as a real-estate agent I had seen many floor plans, and a few designs came to mind as a good use of space. I would put the boys' bedrooms on one end of the house and my bedroom on the other end; there would be the quiet side of the house and the rock music side. Then I'd have a big room with an open kitchen in the middle. We'd need one extra room for computers and television.

About 1,800 square feet would be a reasonable size. In his class on straw bale codes, Dan had said that it was possible to build a house for as little as $25 per square foot if the owner did most of the labor and built very simply. A more realistic price was $35 per square foot. That meant I might be able to build this design for between $45,000 and $63,000 if I did the labor. If my house sale and child support collection went well, I'd have $57,000. I'd just plan on doing the labor, then.

I wanted a pantry. Kitchens were never large enough by my standards. I drew lines, measured my furniture, erased lines, drew again . . . on into the evening. Finally I had something workable, but it had extra niches and wasted space that I still didn't like.

My house plans sat for several months while I waited for my divorce to finalize and my subdivision house to sell. For tax reasons, Rick wanted to wait until January to file the divorce. Life was comfortable; days passed easily with work, gardening, household chores, movies with friends, and hikes in the great Tucson mountains. Rick's divorce payments covered the mortgage after the divorce was finalized, so I didn't have to worry about money.

But deep inside, I was anxious to move ahead with the straw bale construction. I'd waited seven years for this to happen, and each day that passed without any progress made me wonder if my dream would ever materialize.

As I put my boys on a plane to Hawaii in early June to visit their father, a distinct feeling spread over me that my time had come. A few days after that, I found the land and with it a feeling that this house was on its way. I still had to sell my subdivision house, however. Six months on the market and nothing very promising had happened, so it could still take months.

The next week brought my earthen floor workshop at Canelo, the home of Bill and Athena Steen, two of the coauthors of *The Straw Bale House*. This book had been my main inspiration to build with straw bales, answering many questions and filling in my gaps of knowledge after one brief workshop.

The book reassured me that a straw bale house would last for generations if properly built and cared for. The first bale homes were built around the turn of the century in Nebraska and they are still standing. In the early 1900s, bales were easier to build with than sod and readily available from the harvest of grains and meadow grasses. While some of these early structures were considered temporary at first, they were soon plastered as permanent houses because they offered durable protection from the winter and summer extremes.

A 1973 article by Roger Welsh entitled "Baled Hay" chronicled these Nebraska houses and initiated a revival of bale building. Several other articles followed, as a number of people built their own straw bale houses and reported on their discoveries. The revival kept growing from there and hasn't stopped. Bale walls are not only beautiful but are great insulation, fire-resistant, and can absorb the shock of an earthquake. I envied the Steens, who had been working with these natural methods of construction for more than ten years.

Finally I would get to meet them. On Saturday morning I literally hopped out of bed, fed the cat and the birds, tossed my sleeping bag, notepad, and overnight bag into the car, and took off. I estimated a two-hour drive to Canelo. Soothing symphonies from my car radio greeted the peach-hued sunrise as I watched housing developments and warehouses morph into chollas and creosote bushes. Rolling down the windows, I let the wind mess my hair and rustle the papers in the backseat. As I began climbing, desert cactus turned to open meadows with billowing grasses and evergreen bushes as the road grew narrower and bumpier.

Then my doubts began to surround me. Was I being overly idealistic again? Would I meet exciting new people full of ever-changing ideas, or would this be like one of those business seminars where I was handed some manufactured format by folks who churn out the same data every weekend with false enthusiasm? Life had handed me so many disappointments that I barely dared hope for anything more.

I so desperately wanted to build my future with meaning and texture, starting with straw bale walls. No more processed, manufactured, imitation pastimes to consume my days and numb my mind. Excitement, yes, but not the kind of thrills from games that scream for more quarters, more batteries, more upgrades, and more money. Always more money.

As I drove, I silently prayed. Please let my future hold such thrills of discovery and joy as when I hike to the top of a mountain and sing at the top of my lungs, stand under a raging waterfall and let it pound on my bare shoulders, or when I find myself along the trail staring wide-eyed at a newborn deer with its mother. Thrills that come from deep within me and deep within Nature—when I let the two blend. That's what I would like this house to be. Let me meet other people who feel the same way.

As the sun rose above the mountains, I wound my way through the foothills, following the directions I'd been given. Finally, a roughly drawn sign perched against the roadside fence pointed out the entrance to The Canelo Project.

I was a little late; the drive had taken longer than I expected. Grabbing my notepad, I joined a group of about ten people crowded around a lovely, commanding woman with shoulder-length salt-and-pepper hair in a long, navy blue jumper.

She was carefully explaining the features of a smooth, brilliant blue wall on the end of a straw bale shed. Her voice was strong and self-assured. Her deep tan spoke of many hours in the desert sun. She had strong shoulders and bare feet, which skipped easily over the earth and rocks. I knew this must be Athena Steen.

After giving us a tour of the various workshop sheds and projects, Athena led us toward their lovely home nestled into the hillside and introduced us to Bill, who would be conducting the workshop. There was genuine warmth from the Steens and a casual atmosphere to the entire surroundings that assured me this would be no artificially manufactured business seminar.

Bright turquoise and purple paints trimmed the front door as we entered an expansive living room floored with orange and rust-colored Saltillo tile. I couldn't resist walking over to the deeply colored, thick walls and running my hands across the rough earthen textures. One dividing wall was a beautiful peach shade with shiny mica flecks throughout. When I asked Athena what sort of paint had created such a magnificent wall, she answered with a wave of her hand, "Oh, we just did that from the clay. We keep a lookout wherever we go for colors in the clay soil. We keep a bucket and shovels in our car. Then we stop and get some. You don't need much."

Our first day was focused on cooking with prickly pear cactus pads, or nopales. Bill Steen was as much a master of the kitchen as of earthen plasters. We spent most of the afternoon seated around outdoor tables, scraping the spines off nopales, then sampling Bill's creations as he sautéed, grilled, boiled, and chopped them into delightful concoctions. And while we scraped and nibbled, we chatted.

Many of the others in the group were already building straw bale houses or additions and were much further into their planning than I was. Conversation drifted to their projects, dilemmas, solutions, or latest discoveries. Absorbing every tidbit of information that I could, I frequently put down the nopales and picked up my paper and pencil. There were so many details that I hadn't grasped from the books.

I learned that there are builders who serve as straw bale construction consultants, as opposed to general contractors. For an hourly rate, they oversee the details, are available for questions, and will usually drive to the site to help out as needed. I got the names of a few who were recommended, especially Jon Ruez, but I was told he was very busy and needed months of notice. He was working with several people at the workshop already.

At the mention of Matts Myhrman, author of *Build It with Bales,* which also graced my coffee table, my ears perked up. I didn't know much about him, but the general consensus was that he was the master of wall raisings. He would also consult for the entire home construction, and he lived right in Tucson. I would most certainly ask him if he'd consult for my house, when the time came.

After a delicious homemade pizza dinner cooked in the Steen's outdoor earthen bread oven and a slide show of their work in Mexico, where straw bales are catching on as an inexpensive but reliable building method, I crawled into my sleeping bag. My head buzzed with questions. Everything I learned brought up five more questions, but I was so tired that I drifted quickly to sleep and awoke to roosters crowing at dawn.

After a breakfast of prickly pear pads chopped in scrambled eggs and rolled in a tortilla, we gathered in the living room and began the earthen floor portion of the workshop. Bill Steen gave us names for suppliers of clay, natural pigments, and oils for floor sealers, as well as a brief description of the many layers that comprise an earthen floor. Then he led us outside so we could make our own earthen floor squares.

Every step was new to me, and I jotted notes in between tossing shovelsful of sandy soil sifted through large, framed rectangles of fine hardware cloth similar to window screening but made of metal instead of nylon. The forms were propped diagonally so that the coarse sand would slide down the front and the finer soil would sift through to the back.

We scooped the sifted soil from behind the screen, along with some finely sifted clay soil and chopped straw, into wheelbarrows for mixing. After blending it well with a hoe, we took samples and threw them on the ground to see how they held up, so we could determine whether they had the proper clay content.

I quickly surmised that a person couldn't possibly learn how to make an earthen plaster, whether for a wall or a floor, from reading a book. Only by feeling the soil could I understand when the mixture was just the right blend of sand and clay for its purpose. Each layer of an earthen floor has a different purpose, to bind or drain or be the smooth surface layer that repels water. I could not write down exact formulas, because I found that every soil has a different ratio of clay and sand—and every clay absorbs differently.

We each worked on our own small samples of floor to see how metal trowels and wooden floats perform very differently on the damp mixture. Metal brings the water and clay to the surface, which you don't want on the sublayer. So metal is only used at the very end, and the rest is done with wooden trowels or floats to keep the mixture blended evenly.

While we were smoothing the finish coats on our square earthen floor samples, black thunderheads formed over the mountains behind us. The clouds were a relief from the stifling summer heat, even though Canelo was about ten degrees cooler than Tucson.

Thick drops of rain splattered in the wet clay, pitting our artistic endeavors. Booming claps of thunder echoed through the foothills around us as we dashed into the straw bale "bus stop" that had been built by a previous workshop. Bright darts of lightning streaked through the black, menacing clouds while the heavens unleashed torrents of water upon our projects. But no matter; we all had learned what we came for and much more.

As it became clear that the rain was here to stay, a few folks danced in the welcome shower, but I sensed sadly that it was time for me to begin my drive home and prepare for my Monday morning work routine. I thanked the Steens and bolted for my car.

It was the first rain of the summer after a long, dry winter, and I felt my life changing with the weather. The weekend workshop had been everything I could have possibly anticipated, and more. As I wound my way carefully through the puddles in the dirt road, I ran through all I had learned. I was excited and yet, in the pit of my stomach, an uncomfortable knot was telling me I was taking on far more than I could handle. Whatever happened, I couldn't let myself end up like those people in Taos who had put thousands of dollars into half a house that they couldn't finish and couldn't sell.

During the workshop, I had been fairly quiet about my building plans, mostly out of insecurity. I had the distinct feeling that if I opened my mouth too much, someone would tell me that what I was planning was impossible. Most of the other participants seemed far more knowledgeable than I. As far as I was concerned, my physical and emotional survival depended on getting this house built. Somehow, it had to be possible, and I couldn't stand to hear otherwise.

But as I drove home, Athena's words of warning haunted me. Somewhere in the middle of one of the casual discussions, Athena had looked firmly at us all. She said, "I can't stress enough how much work this is. Nobody understands until they've done this. It's going to take way longer and cost three times more than you think it will. Whatever you do, design a house with the minimum amount of square feet that you can live in. These people that think they're going to build 1,800-square-foot houses don't understand what they're getting into!"

She had picked the exact square footage of my house. Well, if I ran out of money, I could do the bare minimum to get my final permit, then finish the rest later. But then again, maybe I could get away with a few less square feet. Maybe I could take the design down to 1,500 or 1,600 square feet. Anything smaller than that would make me feel cramped with my boys' rock 'n' roll music right on top of me. They would be embarrassed to have friends over, and the house would never sell if I had to move. I had learned that from real estate. People like lots of space.

As soon as I returned home from the workshop, I dropped my overnight bag at the front hall, walked straight to my desk, and pulled out the floor plan. By moving the kitchen off to one side and removing a few closets, I took the floor plan down to a very comfortable 1,500 square feet. Actually, I liked the plan better this way. I still had my pantry and nice master suite. I grinned. This would work.

That night, I also decided to build Web pages about the construction of the house, logging costs, hours of labor, and detailed photos to share with future builders. I'd keep a journal of whatever I learned, too. There had to be some other people planning to do what I was doing. I knew I wasn't the only person struggling to support a family, nor the only one who desired a simpler life.

Two days later I still had a knot in the pit of my stomach. Why? Probably because I still didn't know how much money I would have. I had an offer pending on my house, finally. But it was several thousand dollars less than I had expected. I would net closer to $24,000 instead of $27,000—and I still hadn't collected on my child support. I could never rely on the boys' father, and here I was, trusting that he would come through with $30,000.

I thought briefly about getting a construction loan. I had met several people at the workshop who had taken out construction loans even though they weren't using a general contractor and were doing much of the work themselves. But they went to the bank with lots of building experience, which I didn't have. I didn't have great credit, either, after the failure of the photography studio.

Anyway, I couldn't do that; I couldn't afford the payments on a construction loan or a mortgage. I might as well live in a subdivision or buy a mobile home if I were going to do that. This house was supposed to be about reducing my monthly payments and building it myself. My brain was spinning and my body was exhausted.

I closed my eyes. God, are you listening? This is the smallest house I'll consider, so please figure out how much money I will need to build it and make sure it works out, okay? I'm willing to work hard on the weekends and evenings, too, if there's anything I can do after dark.

Just make this happen. Please. You know how long I've been planning this. If I'm on the wrong track, then show me the right track. Okay? Thank you.

*Chapter Five*

# THE SECOND
# FLOOR PLAN

*Look not mournfully into the past. It comes not back again. Wisely improve the present. It is thine. Go forth to meet the shadowy future, without fear.*

—HENRY WADSWORTH LONGFELLOW

MY house sold a month later, on July 4, my birthday. Soon I would have to move, since the buyers wanted to close in three weeks. My joy was followed quickly by terror as I assessed the project before me. The entire weight of the house I wanted to build seemed to rest on my small shoulders, threatening to crush me in a mass of straw and lumber. My mind buzzed with details. I was going to build a whole house, myself, on weekends? Was I crazy?

Perhaps, but one way or another I would do this. I determined once again not to let the fear that was surging through my veins stop me from following the path that had lain before me for so many years.

I slowed myself into the most immediate decisions. I needed to secure a three-bedroom rental within my budget. I had promised my sons that after moving them six times in the past ten years, I would stay in the same neighborhood for at least a year until Andrzej graduated from high school.

I spent July 5 searching the classified ads and driving all over the neighborhood looking for rental signs. Only one house was available in our area—a depressing place, with bright pink carpet and a tiny backyard that would barely fit a table, much less our trampoline. As trivial as the need for a trampoline might appear, for us it was critical. It was our social centerpiece, where we bobbed as we talked with friends and each other. It gave us joyful, stress-busting breaks from our routines of housework and homework. So I hesitated. I wasn't even sure I would be able to afford a one-year lease, since my payments from the recent divorce would end in seven months.

The next weekend, I helped my good friend Denise move. She lived about two blocks down the street in a house with almost exactly the floor plan of the one I was leaving. It had a large backyard and had been up for sale, but hadn't sold. Two days later, she called me to offer it for rent, month by month. Heaving a joyous sigh of relief, I accepted. There was Order in the Universe, I assured myself.

I had no word on the $30,000 of child support, though my attorney was working on it, but I still had a strong feeling that my straw bale house would happen, somehow. If I took the first few steps, the next ones would become clear. Faith. I'd have to move forward on faith. Not necessarily my favorite way to work, but one with which I was becoming increasingly familiar. I went ahead and put a down payment on the land and agreed to close escrow, finalizing the sale, on August 16, 1999.

The next step was to hire Dan to begin drawing up house plans. I hadn't had the money to do this before now. When I phoned him to check on his schedule, he announced that he was leaving town for three weeks at the end of July. However, he had time to draw up the plans before he left. That very afternoon, I took Dan the plans for my 1,500-square-foot house and gave him a deposit to begin drawing.

He began by asking me questions about every little thing. Would my appliances use propane or electricity? Was I going to build an earthen floor or concrete slab? Where would I put the water heater? What method of plumbing was I going to use? Was the land in a sheet plain area that might flood during the monsoons? How big were the windows? Who was going to oversee the project? and on and on.

Why hadn't I spent my time the past few months working on all this instead of hiking in the mountains and relaxing in our community pool? I tried to keep calm and handle one decision at a time over the next few days as I researched the house, packed up my belongings, and prepared to move.

Friday night, one week after I accepted the offer on my house, I lay down on the couch, exhausted. I was still excited about the house construction, but the worried knot in my stomach just wouldn't go away. Overwhelmed, I sat in front of the TV, barely seeing what crossed the screen, not sure whether I wanted to cry or celebrate. Mostly, I wanted to cry. I stumbled into bed and fell sound asleep.

I bolted awake into silent blackness, knowing it was long before dawn. The clock said 3:07. I tossed off my sweat-soaked sheets and let the cool night air sweep over my belly. Memories of past construction disasters churned through my mind as fast as my breath.

After Rick II and I relocated the entire family to New York to open the photography business on a limited budget, the architects had turned out to be only draftsmen who couldn't complete the drawings. We had to hire architects in New York, at great overtime and rush expenses.

Then the contractor turned out to be on the brink of bankruptcy. He took our money, paid his past debts rather than his subcontractors, and split. The construction cost about four times the estimates, leaving us with a huge overhead that we never overcame. We opened the store with construction liens, workers screaming, and the attorney's bill mounting . . .

And the house on Kauai! Rick I and I had ordered our materials from Oregon, since lumber is scarce in Hawaii. It took two weeks to get every shipment and often the material was the wrong size or missing. Once, some very expensive lumber had been stolen off the docks. Our main carpenter quit from the delays all this caused and the inconsistency of his work schedule. I swore I'd never do anything like this again. And now I was doing it again!

I turned on the light. This was different, I promised myself. I was doing this simply; I would be the subcontractors; I would show up on time every weekend.

I promised myself that the next day I would sit down and begin a realistic materials list for the house, then research costs for everything on the list. I would pray and meditate every day, regularly. It would work out— things always did one way or another. Finally, I switched off the light and drifted back to sleep.

About a week after I was in the rental, I received the title report on Rick I's house from my attorney. It listed all the money he would need to pay before the house could be sold. I had hoped that he could refinance to pay the $30,000 he owed in child support. But the house had so many tax liens that there was no way he could refinance, nor could I foreclose. I knew that tax liens took priority over everything else, including child support.

So I had $24,000 instead of $52,000 to build my house. The boys' father was offering to make monthly payments of $1,000 on the past-due amount, but that sure hadn't worked for the past five years.

Time to give up? Part of me thought so; the part of me that had turned around when I was skydiving, the part of me that I was trying to overcome.

But this time my boys refused. They'd rather live in a partially built straw bale house than an old mobile home. If we put our money into a mobile home, they insisted, we might never get the chance to build a straw bale house.

But how could I build this? Even at $35 per square foot, the house would cost $52,500. I paced back and forth in front of my desk. No solutions offered themselves.

I wanted to know that straw bale houses were within the reach of ordinary people like me who didn't have lots of money, who didn't have extensive construction experience, who had to work for a living, and who needed to live within the city limits and commute to work. But maybe they weren't. If they were not for ordinary folks, then who did they benefit? Perhaps they were only suitable, after all, for Mexicans, yuppies, and the independently wealthy who could live in rural areas with no building codes. Perhaps they were just another fashionable fad for rich hippies.

As I planned my house, I kept in touch with Bill and Athena Steen about a possible article in the *Arizona Daily Star*, where I worked. I hadn't shared my dilemma with them, but as they sent me an e-mail about a series of workshops they were giving, they also offered to assist with my house plans. I knew what they'd tell me—that my house was too big.

"Okay," I replied, "as long as you don't tell me I have to live with two teenage boys in 800 square feet!"

"We have an architect, Wayne, living with us," Bill told me in a return e-mail, "who has been looking at ways we can live in less space, consume fewer building materials, and be perfectly happy. Houses have tripled in size since the 1950s and much of the space in them doesn't get used."

I had to agree with that. My boys' bedrooms had served as receptacles for dirty clothes and beds. They weren't used for much else. Our formal living room housed the fancy furniture, while we all hung out in the little den off the kitchen. And as for a formal dining room—every time I had people over to eat, we gathered outside around the barbecue. The holidays seemed to be the only time I needed a large dining table. I would be willing to rearrange the house for that.

But my pantry and my master suite!

"Smaller houses won't sell, if I have to move," I replied. "I know that from being a real-estate agent."

"Houses need to be seen as more than investments," he replied. "If you can build something for $30,000 then you can sell it and move on easily. There is a growing market for smaller, less expensive houses."

He had a point. While a smaller house might not appeal to everyone, I had seen plenty of clients who would buy a smaller house if the mortgage payments fit into their budget. "Okay," I agreed. I had no strength left in me to object to anything. "I have to relook at this whole project, anyway. I'd like to come out and see what Wayne is doing."

I recalled an article by David Eisenberg entitled "Sustainability and the Building Codes," which stated that only one-third of the world's population lives in modern buildings, but these homes are so resource-intensive that they consume one-fourth of the world's wood harvest, two-fifths of its material and energy usage, and one-sixth of all fresh water usage. In the past one hundred years the level of carbon dioxide in the atmosphere has risen 27 percent, one-quarter of which has come from burning fossil fuels just to provide energy for buildings. During the same period, the world lost 20 percent of its oxygen-creating forests.

Building a smaller house would not only ease my construction workload and lighten my financial strain, but do minimal damage to Earth's ecosystem. If I could find a way to live in a smaller house and still meet the needs of my family, I would consider it.

So, that Friday in late July, after work, I once again found myself on the road to Canelo, hoping there would be a miraculous solution to all my doubts. Clouds rolled over the Santa Rita Mountains to my right, while brilliant bolts of lightning pierced through the blackness. I breathed deeply of the musty, damp desert air. As I neared the foothills, thick drops of rain spattered on my windshield and occasionally in my open window. I left it open, enjoying the coolness of the spray. Thunder exploded over the mountains to the west, which were now engulfed in dark mists. My breath slowed automatically as my little car and I became engulfed by the awesome magnificence of the thunderstorm on the empty, open highway.

As the storm subsided, I maneuvered down the driveway to Canelo, feeling energized and renewed. Wayne, Bill, and Athena were very polite as they rolled out my plans on their kitchen table. Knowing my stubbornness against reducing its size, they searched for ways to reduce the amounts of expensive lumber and concrete. Even so, their estimate of construction costs was between $50,000 and $100,000. And they didn't figure there was any way I could do the labor on weekends within a year. We talked briefly about construction loans, but they felt the same way I did. Without prior building experience, there was no way to get around the bank's requirements for a general contractor and the subsequent limits of how much work I could do myself. I wouldn't be able to afford a loan, anyway. The evening grew late and the prospect of a mobile home was calling me louder and louder.

Athena led me to their little straw bale guest house to sleep. I woke at 3 A.M. with the realization that, like it or not, I had to reduce the size of my house. Maybe I could cut out the computer room, reduce the main room and kitchen, shrink the bedrooms a little . . .

When I wandered back into the main house at 7 A.M., the Steens were both at their computers and Wayne sat at his drawing table with some plans unrolled before him. He beckoned me toward him, showing me the drawings.

"The Steens and I have been tossing around ideas for efficient use of space in smaller houses," he said. "This is a design we've been working on. It's for a guesthouse in Utah—an 800-square-foot rectangle, with a sleeping loft and surrounding covered porch. The porch would be far less expensive to build than the finished core of the house and would serve as alternative living space." He had drawn in an area of the porch that was screened for summer sleeping, another portion as a south-facing sunroom for winter passive solar heating, then more room for outside dining and storage cupboards.

Memories of Hawaii's plantation homes with surrounding *lanais* flashed through my mind. All my objections melted away as I listened in fascination. "My wife and I are looking at reducing our possessions and building this house ourselves, doing all the labor, for under $30,000."

That was all I needed to hear. A solution! Athena chimed in, "You can have storage cupboards for kitchen appliances out on the deck. All those things that you use once or twice a year—they don't need to be in the kitchen. And then after you build this and know what you are doing, you can build a little guest house for your teenager while he goes through college. I lived in a tiny house when I was first married—I even took care of a baby in there."

My mind was so overworked that it barely comprehended what I was hearing, but I knew it all made sense. The covered deck could be alternative dining, laundry area, storage area, perhaps even a place to sleep. I loved being outside and watching the sunsets or thunderstorms and had often wondered why Arizona homes didn't utilize porches more often to spare the house walls from the intense summer heat and pelting thunderstorms.

The porch wouldn't have to be much more than a surrounding roof, really. I could probably just lay flagstone or brick for flooring. As I drove away from Canelo that morning, I had a small sketch of the new house plan on my passenger seat—a gift from the Steens and Wayne. The Steens had even offered to help Dan redraw my plans.

I had a few ideas for small changes I would make on the house, but all in all, it felt like it was made for my family. I wasn't sure how my boys would react to this, since it meant they had one sleeping loft instead of separate bedrooms. But then, I could give Zej hope for building his own guesthouse where he could blast rock music late at night, after we built the main house. I'd let him quit work and offer to pay his car insurance so he could learn how to build with straw. Then he could largely build his own cottage. What a great experience!

Hope for my straw bale house flickered anew. The former alleged mansion that threatened to topple over and crush me had become a friendly cabin that I could imagine building. The knot in my stomach was gone.

When I arrived home about midday on Saturday, both boys were engrossed in the computer, where they had virtual lives in the realms of Everquest. Zej was a Dark Elf and J.J. was a Troll. I'm not sure of all that goes on in the game, but they meet their friends on this Internet site, disguised as Elves, Barbarians, Dwarfs, and Gnomes. They pursue careers, go adventuring, earn money to buy spells, and form guilds to hunt Dragons. It took up a good portion of their spare time—well, okay, all their spare time.

When they were younger and I was busy in the kitchen, constantly barraged by "Mom, come look at this," "Mom, where are my socks?" "Mom, there's nothing to do!" or "Mom, can I punch my brother?" My brain automatically filtered out many of the questions and I often replied with my subconscious, "Uh, huh." "Sure." "That's nice."

Now, it was my turn. I pulled up a chair next to the computer with the rolled house sketch in my hand. "Hey, guys! I had a great night at Canelo!"

"Where were you?" J.J. asked as he tapped on the keyboard.

"I spent the night at the Steens. Remember? I told you about three times and wrote the phone number on the message board?"

"Oh, I guess I didn't hear you."

"Well, I have these new house plans that I'm sure we can afford to build. It's really cool, with a *lanai* all the way around it and a sunroom. It only has one bathroom, but I figure we can share."

"Yeah." Their minds were drifting back to Everquest Elfland.

"The sunroom's on the south, so we can still get the passive solar heating in the winter. And there's a sleeping loft for you guys to share. Is that okay?"

"Uh, huh."

"Great. I figure Zej could quit work and help build the main house. Then when we really know what we're doing, we could build him a separate little house with a sleeping area and a bathroom."

"Uh, huh."

"Okay, great, then. This will be much easier! I'm excited."

"Yeah, okay."

And so it was set. The new house plans were adopted and my e-mail to Bill Steen on Sunday contained heartfelt thanks for getting me to listen; it hadn't been easy.

During the next two weeks I familiarized myself with the new house design, measuring furniture once again and going around to yards that had recycled building materials to find doors and windows. One of the nicest yards, Gerson's, was about five minutes from work, so I could zip up there during lunch hours. It was fun—like thrift shopping. I poked through piles of doors and windows and began finding just what I wanted: some French patio doors for the living room, large 6 x 6-foot windows with a small slider at the bottom for the sunroom, some great double-paned windows that matched for most of the house.

It was a little scary since I didn't have official house plans and had to estimate window sizes. Recycle yards don't take returns like regular stores, either, so I had to be careful not to buy something that wouldn't work. I also made some trips to retail stores to compare prices, so I would know a good deal when I saw it. Sometimes, the newer recycled items were priced as high as those in a retail store, I noticed. All in all, I'd say I purchased the doors and windows for about half of what I'd pay at a regular store, about a quarter of what I'd pay for elegant wood-framed windows.

The only problem I later ran into is that the building codes require that all glass in external doors be safety glass, and some of mine were not. Gerson's was kind enough to give me exchange credit for those doors. The code also required that external windows be double paned. Fortunately, that was the only kind I had considered.

My garage quickly became a workshop as my power tools accumulated. First I bought a circular saw and a power drill/screwdriver, along with some sawhorses. A carpenter friend gave the advice to lean into my cuts so the saw wouldn't bounce back: approach the work with confidence, he said, as everything else. I read the manuals and did everything I could to prepare for the construction while I waited for my permit and to finalize my land purchase in mid-August.

Fear still churned in me every now and then, but with each step I had one less thing to worry about. I would have to make the entire house be a series of small steps: study and gather materials during the weekdays on my lunch hours and evenings, then do my best to complete a task each weekend.

I had asked Matts Myhrman, the Tucson author of *Build It with Bales,* to be my consultant and he had agreed, but in the meantime his wife had become quite ill and his time was consumed in caring for her. It usually took about three weeks for me to get a reply to any questions I asked. So, for now, there was really nobody to rely on but myself.

*Chapter Six*

# BREAKING GROUND

*Whatever you can do, or dream you can, begin it.*
*Boldness has genius, power and magic in it.*

—JOHANN WOLFGANG VON GOETHE, *Faust*

ON August 16, barely a month after my house sold, I completed the purchase of the land. It was now mine, with $6,000 paid from my checking account and the former landowner, Frank, carrying the rest. I would make payments to him each month, which I would roll into a mortgage loan when the house was completed. I wanted to save as much of my cash as possible for house construction.

Kathy, the realtor, was out of town, so Frank celebrated with me over iced chai at a nearby coffeehouse. He was interested in helping with the construction and learning all that he could so he could build his own straw bale house in the future. I clung to the hope that he would be one of a few people who might consistently help on weekends.

As I imagined myself living in this smaller house, I noticed a change come over much of my activities at home. I started to simplify everything. I followed my urge to purge my closet of all the clothes I'd been hanging onto just in case I might want to wear them someday. If I hadn't worn it in a year, I put it in a bag for the homeless. I looked at the art on my walls with a new eye. My new house wouldn't have much spare wall space. Which ones did I really like? Which ones gave me a lift when I looked at them and which ones were just there because they'd always been there? I took those to the nearby thrift shop.

Then I started going through the pots and pans, visualizing myself fitting into a much smaller kitchen. I didn't need three one-quart saucepans. I only used one at a time. Nor did I need five frying pans; one large, one small did the job. Although I didn't carry these things around on my back, I already felt lighter and freer without them.

I even simplified our dinners. We didn't need gourmet meals every night. I left fruit out to munch, then started creating dinners from the many cans I had in my cupboards. Our staple dinners became baked potatoes and salad, rice with melted cheese and salad, or pasta and beans with salad. Suddenly, my evenings were free to study do-it-yourself manuals, log my expenses from the day, make phone calls to prospective helpers, write, meditate, or go to bed early if I felt tired.

Awakened energy surged through me. I didn't need caffeine to keep me awake in meetings at work. I greeted each day with enthusiasm for what I would learn and whom I would meet next. The house was becoming the joyful project that I had intended it to be. But of course, I hadn't begun the hard physical labor yet.

It seemed strange when I looked at it, but much of my desire to be successful was to impress my kids, because they had to impress their friends. When I realized that they were okay with the smaller house, and would probably benefit from realizing how simply they could live, I relaxed. J.J., then fifteen, asked me once, "Is this going to be a hippie house, Mom?"

"Well, yes, I guess it is," I replied with a smile, not exactly sure what fit that definition.

However, I later asked him what he meant by that and realized he was concerned that it would be something akin to a tent or propped-up bales covered by a tarp. Once he started helping me with construction details, his fears of living like a hippie diminished. This was a real, solid house being built.

As one carpenter said to me, "Those two words, 'simplify' and 'straw bale,' should always go together." And so they should. The texture I was seeking in my life wouldn't come from merely having straw behind the stucco of my home. It would come from changing something inside me and the choices I made each day.

Within two weeks, on September 8, Dan had the new house plans completed. Eagerly, I made copies and spent a couple of lunch hours walking them around to the various divisions of the county building department—addressing, zoning, grading, and floodplain. There, I had to sign a paper saying I wouldn't sue the county if my house flooded after they granted me a reduction in the floor height from eighteen inches to twelve inches. I had no intention of suing the county, anyway. I left my blueprints in the hands of the building department for scrutiny, which I was told would take up to a month.

Dan warned me that the county might object to a few things, such as the pull-down ladder to the loft and the loft itself, since two-story straw bale homes weren't allowed. Also, framing the large sunroom opening could be seen as making this a hybrid house, part straw bale and part wood-framed, also not allowed.

They might also object to external pinning and tie-downs for the walls. Pinning strengthens and supports the walls, while tie-downs connect the roof assembly to the foundation. The Pima County code called for internal pinning, which is accomplished by pounding long metal rods down through the center of the walls. For tie-downs, the code required a rod of all-thread, a long steel shaft whose entire length is threaded like a screw, running every six feet from the foundation through the center of the bales all the way to the roof assembly.

Instead, we were requesting to put two rods of all-thread or bamboo every six feet on the outside of the bales. This exterior method would be stronger, easier for wall-construction, and much simpler if I ever needed to remove a bale from the wall. But again, this wasn't to the building code and therefore might not be permissible. I couldn't figure out why—just rules. I was learning to flow with them a little.

While I waited for the outcome, I moved ahead with whatever details I could. Since there was no sewer system in the area, I would need a large, underground septic tank. As much as I had wanted to try a composting toilet, codes required at least one flushing toilet in the house.

The septic tank required a separate permit, so I could proceed with that. After phoning around, a tractor and septic company near the lot gave me a reasonable quote. The owner, who called himself Dakota (I wasn't sure if that was his first name or last name), met me at the land and explained that first he would do a perk test and then install the septic tank.

The perk test involved digging several very deep (about ten feet) holes, then having an engineer pour water in them and study the drainage. That would determine how large the leach fields coming out of the septic tank needed to be. I didn't even know what a leach field was, but Dakota drew me a diagram: a series of long pipes with holes all along them, set into a field of large gravel that allows the septic water to drain into the land.

I gave him a deposit and let him do the work. That would be one of the few things I would just hire out to someone else, I figured. It took him almost a month to finally install the septic system. It's a good thing I wasn't in a rush.

While I waited for the septic completion and the building permit approval, I gathered supplies for the foundation, which would be my first major construction project. The foundation would consist of footings, more commonly called footers. My footers would consist of concrete poured into trenches dug about one foot into the ground and two feet wide. This would take the weight of the walls down to really solid earth, rather than letting the house rest on looser surface soil. The drain plumbing would have to go beneath these footers on its way to the septic tank, and on top of the footers there would be a stemwall, also two feet wide, made of two rows of concrete blocks with holes in them, called cement masonry units (CMU blocks). The holes would be filled with concrete and would have attachments that went up into the bales.

Where we put the foundation would, of course, determine where the house would sit, so I would have to measure carefully, make a perfect rectangle with ninety-degree angles, and situate it exactly where I wanted the walls. I had been studying how to do this in my do-it-yourself foundation book, *Foundations and Concrete Work: The Best of Fine Homebuilding*.

First, I purchased CMU blocks for the stemwall, a low concrete wall that would raise the bales a foot above ground level. Since the footers and the rising stemwall had to be two feet wide to support the bales, I would need one row of eight-inch-wide concrete block on the outside of the wall and one row on the inside. The inside row would be largely covered by the raised floor, but the outside row would be very visible.

Bill Steen recommended that I use earth-colored, split-face CMU block to match the earthen plasters on the exterior walls. CMU blocks are concrete blocks that measure eight inches high by eight inches wide and sixteen inches long. They are shaped like figure eights with two holes in each block, so they can be filled with concrete. Split-face blocks are poured two at a time and cracked in half, giving one surface a rough appearance.

I finally tracked these down at a brickyard near my work. Whereas most companies had told me they would special order them only if I needed at least a thousand, this lot had several hundred left over from another job. But if I wanted them, I had to pay for them right away and haul them myself. They didn't deliver such small quantities.

There was something scary about buying building supplies without a contractor to tell me I was buying the right kind in the right amount, especially when it cost hundreds or thousands of dollars. Waiting wasn't going to help that however, so I double-checked my figures and wrote the check.

For the next two Saturdays, J.J. and I rented a trailer to pull behind Zej's truck, loaded up the 260 bricks I had purchased, which weighed thirty pounds each, drove them forty-five minutes to the site, and unloaded them one by one. My sacroiliac has been known to give out every now and then, especially with heavy lifting and bending, but aside from a few aches and pains, it held up pretty well. J.J. and the ten-year-old truck also survived the hauling in fine shape.

I think the task gave J.J. a renewed sense that this wouldn't be just some hippie house, but indeed would be set on a firm foundation! After a congratulatory high-five as we unloaded the last brick, we headed home via Burger King to return him to his virtual life in the land of Everquest, where lightning-fast reflexes and high-speed Internet lines are more important than strong backs.

On Saturday, September 18, I packed up my tape measure, orange plastic ribbon, string, stakes, a saw, scissors, a hand mallet, and a large covered pail of water and headed out to the land. It was time to mark the area that should be cleared before construction could begin; an area that I already knew by heart and that was quite well defined by two large saguaro cacti to the south and west.

It was still hot in the desert, close to one hundred degrees. I dunked my white shirt in the pail of water and slipped it over my tank top. Using the saguaros as markers, I estimated what would be a right angle and found the corner where my first stake would go. Of course, it was in the midst of creosote bushes and adorable hedgehog cacti that sprout rings of sweet little purple flowers in the spring.

I loved the desert foliage and wanted to do only minimal damage to the environment in building this house. The thought of moving some of the cacti out of the building area had crossed my mind, but then again the thought of grabbing a cactus to move it was too painful to consider. I'd just say good-bye to them and let the tractor do its work.

I dug a little hole and filled it with water, letting that soak down to loosen the soil while I stuck the end of my tape measure under the rock and headed due east, measuring out sixty feet.

Fortunately, this area was only sparsely vegetated. I looked at the plants to the north of my line, mentally thanked them for being there, and warned them that within the week their time would be up. Somehow I figured they'd want some warning. Maybe they would just shrivel up voluntarily before the tractor arrived. That sure seemed simple enough in this heat!

When the corners were marked with stakes that had orange ribbon on top and a string connecting them, I stepped inside the rectangle and walked around. I had to step carefully between the cacti; I hadn't let go of my Hawaiian habit of wearing sandals.

Now I could really see where the house would sit. It looked much larger than I had previously imagined, since the *lanai* was included in the space to be cleared. I strolled to the area of the sunroom and gazed at my sweeping view of lush desert bushes, ocotillo, and palo verde trees against the distant mountains. The site was absolutely perfect.

The view to the northeast of Sombrero Peak was likewise magnificent. I decided to call the peak Diamond Head, because it looked very similar to the Honolulu landmark. I determined to leave the north porch open for dining at sunset, when the mountain reflected purple and the moon rose dramatically in the eastern sky. Estimating where the front door would go on the north, I imagined a lovely courtyard with pots of flowers leading into the front door and wind chimes ringing gently from somewhere in the distant desert.

On September 29, I finally got a call from the county that my plans had been rejected and I could pick them up to make changes. Since I had pretty much expected this, I phoned Dan immediately. He picked up the plans the next day and said they had rejected just about everything he had wondered about. The all-thread had to go in the center of the bales, I needed a spiral staircase instead of a pull-down ladder, and they were calling the loft a second story. I would also need to create a huge, wooden buck like the ones I had around the other windows and doors to support the bales over the sunroom opening, rather than use traditional framing. This way the entire house would be considered a straw bale structure, not a hybrid.

Dan made the necessary changes on the plans and managed to get the loft approved as a mezzanine. I was very thankful for all his work, as I got a call the next week that my plans were approved and I could begin construction—after I wrote the county a check for about $2,000 and signed a paper that I would install either sprinklers or a fire hydrant on the property. I also had to pay an impact fee of $1,500 before I could get my final permit. When I picked up the plans, the cashier handed me the rolled blueprints along with an inspection sheet, listing the twenty-four inspections that I would have to pass before I could live in the house. Whatever: I was on my way!

With some trepidation, I phoned Dakota and told him he could come clear the land during the week. I instructed him to clear only the area inside the stakes and strings because I had purposely left a few large bushes and cacti outside the tractor area.

After the land was cleared, I would need to mark the foundation on the ground and then install batter boards. Batter boards establish a level plane for the concrete, since the land is uneven. They are comprised of

any strong board or metal stake pounded into the ground several feet outside each corner of the house, with a horizontal board attached to them
at a level plane all the way around. Small nails pounded into the tops of
each horizontal board mark where an extension of the line of the outer
wall will meet the board. When strings are attached to those nails, they
mark exactly where the foundation and walls will go. I figured they were
called batter boards because wet concrete looks much like a nutty cake
batter and these boards' ultimate goal was for accurate placement of the
foundation concrete.

By now, I had outlined a rough schedule of what I needed to accomplish each week in order to have the wall raising by late November or early
December. Matts wasn't available past that time and I really wanted him
to oversee the wall raising. Not only had he worked with straw bale for
years, but he seemed to be a very pleasant person with a jovial twinkle in
his eye. I looked forward to working with him and learning some of his
deep knowledge about straw bale building. From what I had heard, he
was one of the first people to discover this building technique in Nebraska,
and he had been leading workshops to teach straw bale building for more
than twelve years.

The weather was still sweltering as J.J. and I headed out to the land in the
middle of the morning on Saturday, October 9. With 2 x 4s from the recycle yard sharpened into points for batter board supports and 1 x 4-inch
crosspieces, I was ready to attempt the first phase of construction. I had to
bribe J.J. with soda, chips, and promise of a trip to Burger King on the
way back—which was becoming our standard fare. Andrzej had decided
that he wasn't ready to quit his job yet, because he really wanted to save
up money for another stage-worthy guitar amplifier. He also enjoyed the
companionship and friends he had at work. So I let that be. J.J. would be my
main assistant, and maybe Zej would join us after he bought his amp.

As we neared the top of the dusty driveway, I gasped. A gaping hole sat
in the desert, at least three times the size that the house would require!

"What did Dakota do?" I moaned. "Look at that!" My heart was
pounding.

J.J. jumped in quickly. "It's okay, Mom. He cleared away the house area,
just like you asked him. You need extra room to work. You can't work right
next to a cactus!"

"But he went beyond the stakes! I'm sure the tractor killed a couple of
prickly pear plants that I meant to keep and there was supposed to be a
bush over there. Where are the stakes? He just plowed right over them!"
Angrily, I dashed out of the car.

But as I ran my tape measure over the open area, I realized the tractor hadn't gone far beyond my marks; the overturned ground just seemed like a huge, gaping wound. And J.J. was right: a few extra feet for working wouldn't be bad. I didn't know it then, but as the work progressed I found that I used every inch of the cleared area for tractor room, plumbing, and electric conduit trenches. It was all dug up at one point or another.

For practice, J.J. and I decided to begin by marking the rectangle that would become the sunroom, leaving a large saguaro at its corner. I didn't want the cactus to end up right outside my bedroom door or to block the sunroom's view. With a couple of tent stakes in one hand and the hundred-foot measuring tape in the other, I headed for the towering guardian. We measured a few feet to the north of the saguaro and pounded our first stake.

Placing the compass on the ground, we scratched long lines for the north-south and east-west axes with a broken stick. I wanted the house to face south as much as possible. Doing my best to stay parallel to the east-west line, I measured sixteen feet to the west and planted another tent stake. This wasn't so hard! I handed J.J. the other end of the measuring tape while I held onto the existing corner. We guestimated a ninety-degree angle, measured seven feet, and J.J. pounded in the next stake. After tying nylon string to all three stakes, we measured to the fourth corner, drove in a stake, and fastened the string.

According to my book, the way to tell whether we had a rectangle or a rhomboid was to see if the diagonals were the same length. They weren't. We were about two inches off. So we undid the string, moved one of the stakes, and retied and remeasured the diagonals. This time *they* were the same, but now the side wasn't the right length. We did this about four times and finally had what I considered close enough to a perfect rectangle.

Then, measuring out from the inner corners of the sunroom, we marked the southern wall of the main house. This time we didn't tie any string. We just pounded in four stakes and adjusted. The fourth wall came out way too long—by about three feet—so we moved it in and then made some adjustments to get the diagonals the same. But somehow the wall was still about two feet too long.

It took me a few paper and pencil sketches to figure out which corners needed to move, but within half an hour, we were staring at a perfect rectangle, with string at its perimeter. This would be the house. Proudly, I let J.J. run a line of red spray paint over the string to mark the dirt so the trencher would be very clear where the lines were. Then we pulled up the string. It would get in his way. As long as it didn't rain before the tractor arrived, we'd be okay.

By this time, the midday sun was baking us both into extreme dehydration. We had already soaked our shirts a couple of times and they had dried out thoroughly. Since J.J. wasn't quite as motivated as I was, I decided to keep him in a good mood and take him home. I'd find some way to continue on my own.

After a brief lunch and cool-down back in our air-conditioned house, I returned to the land and resumed work by digging three small holes for the batter board supports about five feet past the corners of the house. I then pounded 2 x 4 posts into each hole. The desert ground was fairly soft from recent rains, but I still found it impossible to drive these posts very deep. Gripping the mallet with both hands I pounded with all my strength, then poured water around the posts and let it soak in. I did this at each corner, then returned to my original corner and pummeled the stake some more. After a while, the wood at the top of the post began splintering from my blows, still without going deeper. My mouth was parched, my head began to pound, and sweat was pouring from my face and neck.

I took a break in the narrow shade of a saguaro and surveyed the progress. It didn't look like that much for all the toil, and I realized I hadn't made batter boards for the sunroom corners. I'd have to go by the lumber store and pick up some more boards on my way home.

Finally I pounded the posts solidly enough to let the soil dry around their bases overnight. The sun was sinking in the sky, and a cooling afternoon breeze blew through my hair and across my baked skin. With spray paint, I marked a stick at two feet, the width of the foundation, then laid it flat on the ground and worked my way around the perimeter, marking the inside of the footing with spray paint exactly as it should be dug. Exhausted, I decided that was enough for one day.

With no energy left to cook anything, I headed home via the pizza shop. All I could think of was a cool shower or perhaps a long soak in the tub.

I woke before the sun the next morning and tossed and turned, my mind churning about batter boards and work details. Sunstroke, probably. I tried to go back to sleep, because I knew I needed all the rest I could get. But my cat, Toonses, heard me rustling the sheets and began meowing for breakfast. Our birds, Merlin and Arthur, joined in the chorus, until I gave up and got up.

Toonses had moved with us from New York. She was a sweet tabby who needed constant care because a pellet from a gun was lodged in her skull, giving her seizures. If she wandered outside the house, she couldn't find her way back. In the subdivision this was no problem because we had a fenced yard, but I knew that a cat yard would have to be constructed at the new house before we moved in.

Merlin was a white cockatiel that I had found in the desert shortly after my Tucson divorce. I had been strolling along a trail near my work during a lunch hour for some fresh air. When I returned to my car, he was sitting right in the middle of the paved path. He must have been dazed from the hot, dry weather, because he let me pick him up even though his wings weren't clipped and he could have flown.

I put him in my car, drove to a nearby discount store, bought a cage and some food, and took him back to work with me. I ran an ad in the paper, but nobody claimed him. I didn't think he'd enjoy being in a tiny cage with no company, so I bought a larger cage and Arthur from a local pet store at a discount. Arthur had been pulling out his feathers from what the store workers thought was loneliness. Sure enough, as soon as I put him in the cage with Merlin, he stopped plucking and filled out into a very handsome gray cockatiel.

Merlin could sing at the top of his lungs and Arthur could screech. According to my bird book, this meant that Arthur might be a girl, but nobody was sure. Screeching or squawking, they knew how to get me out of bed.

Taking just a few moments to do my morning exercises and a brief meditation to attempt to calm myself, I dressed in my usual tank top and shorts. After cooking up scrambled eggs and toast, drinking a cup of green tea, and hanging a couple of loads of laundry, I entered my garage/workshop and sawed some lumber into the proper size for batter board supports, sharpened the ends, and loaded up the truck again.

I asked J.J. to come for a few hours to help me with the leveling as we attached the horizontal batter boards to the posts that we had installed the previous day. I bought more soda and chips on our way out to the site, the price of a half-day's labor.

For this day's work, we brought along a water level, a fifty-foot-long piece of plastic tubing, about a half-inch in diameter, tied to tall wooden handles at the ends. These handles are marked identically with inch measurements. The tubing is filled with water and since water always seeks to level itself, the tubing can be stretched long distances, traveling over bumps and crevices, but will still give accurate measurements of whether one point is lower or higher than another.

Once at the site, we began by pouring water through a funnel into the tube of the level until it was almost full. To make the water line more visible, we dropped in quite a bit of blue food coloring on one end and green on the other, just for fun. By the end of the day, a great deal of the food coloring had worked its way onto my face.

Beginning at the southwest corner of the house, we measured sixteen inches up from the ground, the height of two rows of CMU block, and marked the boards. I nailed a horizontal 1 x 4 across the posts. To my great pleasure, the posts barely wobbled as I nailed in the crossbars. Being rather new to carpentry, I promptly smashed my thumb with the hammer while I was trying to hold the crossbar in place and pound a nail into it.

I stuck my thumb into the remaining ice at the bottom of J.J.'s soda. From then on, J.J. ran to my rescue and held the board in place, using a carpenter's level, while I nailed, or vice versa. Then, to run level strings, J.J. stayed at the southwest corner, while I took my end of the water level to the southeast corner. We let the water settle down and then he told me his blue water was at the twenty-one-inch mark. My green water was at the twenty-three-inch mark.

That meant that the ground where I stood was two inches lower than where J.J. stood, so my water had to compensate by going higher. I always had to say this out loud to get my brain to register. Even though I'd done it a few times with my garden, it still seemed backward.

I measured eighteen inches from the ground—two inches higher than the sixteen-inch mark at J.J.'s corner—and made a mark for nailing 1 x 4s. That went well, but somehow as we measured the last two corners, we got off. Nothing was coming out level and we were getting different readings from the water level each time. Hmmm.

I had faith that gravity was still at work, so it must be our water level that had a flaw. Air bubbles, most likely. Examining the tube, I saw that somehow we had gotten quite a few air bubbles inside, probably at the tube connections. After chasing all the bubbles to the ends of the tubes, we tried again.

Now we got consistent readings. While I double-checked the level, J.J. pounded in the supporting posts at the corners of the sunroom. Swinging a mallet was more fun for him than marking little lines on a board. But the thermometer was pushing into the hundreds again, and J.J.'s patience with all these details was running low. I decided I could finish the work in the afternoon by myself.

Sighting straight down the red lines painted on the dirt, I tacked a small nail into the top of each cross board where the red line intersected. Then, using a special knot called a twist knot (formed by wrapping the string around the nail, pulling it very taut, and then twisting the loose end around the tight string five or six times so that when the loose end of the string is pulled back toward the nail, the tension pulls the twists into a knot that is easy to undo and redo at any time), I attached a nylon string to each nail and ran it down the perimeter of the foundation.

It took a couple of trips around, checking and rechecking all the strings, until I felt confident that they were exactly level all around the house and exactly perpendicular to the red lines below them. I didn't have to be told that a level foundation and square corners to the walls were very important.

Then I untied the strings. They would be destroyed by the tractor when it came to dig the footers, so their only real purpose was for accurate placement of the nails on top of the batter boards. As long as the tractor didn't bump into the batter boards and as long as the nails didn't fall out, I could retie the strings later to continue the foundation construction.

By now I was tired. My trips to the water bottle were becoming very frequent. My shirt seemed to dry out every ten minutes. I wanted to sit down, but there was still much to be done: I had to mark the deck perimeter and all the foundations for the supporting deck posts. I would sit down when that was done.

As I gathered the measuring tape, scissors, and sledgehammer, I fantasized about standing in a cool shower at home, then relaxing with a tall iced tea. A wave of anger jolted through me, thinking of my friends who were spending their weekends with spouses or mates, relaxing, hiking, swimming, eating at fine restaurants, and going to concerts. They just paid someone money and were given houses! Why did I have to be out here slaving away for mine? I hadn't had a moment of leisure in three months.

Because this is what I chose to do, I reminded myself. There's no time for self-pity. I did my best to let that wave of anger pass right through me and out the other side. Then I proceeded with my work.

My measurements for the deck post foundations weren't quite as precise as for the main house. I had no instruction book on how to do this, so I just did my best: stuck metal rods called rebar into the ground where I figured each post should go, tied an orange ribbon around the top of them and spray painted a two-foot square around it where the hole should be dug for pouring concrete.

As I was finishing up the last markings, I paused to survey the open patch of desert that had so recently embraced bushes and cactus. Now it was prepared to be carved into the foundation of a house with very detailed and professional-looking marks. Through my fatigue, I felt a sense of accomplishment. One more step completed.

As I stood there Rudy, my neighbor with the horses, strolled over and offered me a cold beer. Now, on a full stomach I can handle about two sips of alcohol in any form before my nose goes numb. I could barely imagine how incapacitated I'd become if I drank a beer after a day of labor in the desert sun. Visions of lying face first in the dirt almost made me laugh.

Politely asking if I could trade the beer for a soda, I accompanied him over to his yard next to the stables. He resumed peeling recently roasted chilies—a gift from relatives in New Mexico. We chatted about gardening and such. Never had a cold soda fizzling over frosty ice tasted so wonderful. Sitting down in a chair felt like the ultimate luxury.

Rudy was very friendly, offering water, shovels, whatever I needed. Just come ask; we're neighbors. He'd even help me if I told him what needed to be done. When was the last time I had sat down to chat with my subdivision neighbors, or offer them help? Never, that I could remember. My new life was beginning.

## Chapter Seven

# THE FOUNDATION

*If you have built castles in the air, your work need not be lost; that is where they should be. Now put the foundations under them.*

—HENRY DAVID THOREAU, *Walden*

WHEN I arrived home that Sunday night, I called Don, a local backhoe operator, to tell him I was ready to dig the foundation trenches. Dakota was too busy. Don had been recommended by Lonny, a neighbor down the street who was also a foundation professional and who would be filling my footers with concrete. Don said he'd meet me at the property at 6 P.M. on Monday, after work.

Uneasiness crept through me as I drove to meet him. I hadn't realized the land wasn't level until I completed the batter boards. I couldn't get a clear mental picture of how he would manage to level the land now that we had the surface marked and batter boards at the corners. I just hoped he wouldn't tell me that I was supposed to have him come level it *before* I built the batter boards. But I couldn't have done that either, because I was required to build above the highest grade of the land, not level it down.

But when Don arrived, he shook my hand and surveyed the building site with a silent pensiveness. Sure enough, he told me I should have leveled the lot before I did the batter boards. There was no way he could level it now. The county wouldn't let him build up the low part of the land, either, unless we compacted the soil and had an engineer test it. My heart sank, but if I had to take down all the boards and put them up again, I figured I could do that. It was bound to be easier the second time around.

However, in all reality, we were only talking a few inches. While using the water level, I had realized that the land at the highest corner was only about six inches above the lowest corner. There must be some way to deal with that.

He did agree that he could dig the footers slightly deeper on the high side and shallower on the down side. Then I'd have to make forms for the concrete on the low side, where it would come up higher than the ground. I had been hoping that wouldn't be necessary, since Lonny told me he could pour the concrete right into the dirt.

I could see that there would be no option other than to build forms to hold the concrete in place as it dried. I had books at home that explained all this, so I ignored the pit in my stomach and pretended I knew how to make forms.

I gave Don a deposit and he said he'd have the footers dug in a couple of days. He'd also dig a trench from the septic tank toward the house and from the water meter up to the east side of the house. The deck post foundations, I'd have to dig myself—or get the boys to dig. Okay, sure, we could do that, I agreed uneasily. The soil was rock hard.

After driving home and making a quick chili and rice dinner, I checked my e-mail (I was now on the straw bale listserve), then roughed out a grocery list and did my grocery shopping. Normally, laundry and grocery shopping were leisurely weekend tasks, but now they had to be completed in the evenings. The store was only about fifteen minutes from my house, so that was okay.

That evening, I began to obsess over the forms for the concrete. How much would they cost? What kind of lumber would I use? How did I get them to stand up straight? A few batter boards had taken me all weekend—how long would an entire set of forms take?

As I made my rounds in the grocery aisles, I started to get a picture. I wouldn't need wood that was too thick, because the trench would largely support it. I could probably use half-inch plywood or oriented-strand board (OSB). OSB comes in 4 x 8-foot sheets made up of wood chips melded together with some conglomeration of chemical glues. The result is something very heavy yet inexpensive that doesn't warp as plywood can.

If I cut the boards in twenty-inch widths, I could reuse them for the top plate. The top plate, or roof-bearing assembly, is comprised of long slabs of wood twenty inches wide lying on top of the bale walls like the twenty-four-inch-wide foundation underneath. The box sides are made of 2 x 6 planks, while the top and bottom are made of plywood or OSB. There are other ways to make a roof-bearing assembly, but this method is approved by Pima County and was on my plans. The all-thread rods from the foundation run all the way up through the bale walls and through the top plate, where they are bolted down.

Bales are usually about twenty-two inches wide, and one of my books said that the top plate should be slightly narrower than the bales, so I figured that twenty inches would be about the right width. I could push the base of each board against the trench walls with short rebar stubs pounded into the ground. Rebar, short for reinforcing bar, is an inexpensive steel rod with ridges that is used most commonly to strengthen concrete. It can be cut or bent and is sold in sizes from a quarter inch around and a foot long, to shafts large enough for building a bridge. I would use the small, foot-long variety to brace the forms.

After putting the groceries away, I made a diagram of the forms and a list of supplies I'd need. During my lunch hour on Tuesday, I took the blueprints to a lumberyard to get estimates on premade roof trusses. These wooden supports looked like huge upside-down Vs and would connect the roof to the top plate. They were generated by a computer program that considered the slope and shape of the roof, the slope of the ceiling, the size of the house, and whatever engineering is required to make that all hold together.

My real-estate agent, Kathy, e-mailed me with an update. She was becoming a friend. Her house was progressing on just about the same schedule as mine; she happened to be phoning for estimates on trusses at the same time as me, so we could compare. Her boyfriend, Denny, who was a straw bale builder from New Mexico, was coming down to build her house soon and she wanted me to hire him too, so he could stay longer. As much as I would have loved to do that, it wasn't in my budget. Rick I had made a few payments against his back child support by now, totaling about $5,000, and that really helped keep the project going, but I had no spare money anywhere in sight to pay for labor.

Kathy had also been calling around for bale prices and found we were pretty late in the year to get them. Some farmers had not kept them covered during the summer rains. If water soaks into the center of a bale, and is unable to dry quickly, the straw will turn to mildew and disintegrate. Kathy had a good lead from a farmer in Casa Grande, halfway to Phoenix, that she would work on. Thank goodness for Kathy, I thought as I dug into the stack of papers on my desk.

Tuesday evening I finished the laundry, went through the pile of mail on my desk, paid several bills, and decided I should buy insurance on the house now that construction was well underway. I already had an estimate from someone at the farm bureau. At about 8:30 P.M., I drove down to the hardware store and spent almost $200 on eight sheets of OSB, eighty rebar studs, and some 2 x 4s to brace the forms. I felt as if I must be spending about $100 per day on one thing or another. Better not think about that.

I had a lunch meeting the next day, so I took only a quick break to drive over to the lumber store and pick up the blueprints and their computer printout for roof trusses. The cost would be more than $2,000. It seemed high to me, but what did I know?

Once home that evening, I sat down at my computer and checked in with the listserve. One guy, Mark, was talking about how much he wanted to come to Canelo and experience the workshops, but didn't have the money. I sent him a reply, telling him to just stay positive and create his life the way he wanted it. He e-mailed back that he felt like he'd met his mental match, for this was just the way he thought. I smiled inwardly; I hadn't heard many kind words lately. A wolf whistle from my cockatiels was about the most I could hope for.

On Thursday morning, I had a voice mail from Kathy at work saying she had found a great price on roof trusses from another lumberyard near my work. Her house was about the same size as mine, but her trusses cost only $1,000, and she also had a better price on metal roofing from a local company than the price I had from a company in Texas. My shopping bargain genes clicked into gear.

At lunch, I drove over to Kathy's lumberyard and dropped off my house plans. They would not only give me a price on the roof trusses, but on the metal roofing also. That made sense, since then I could be sure to get the roof to fit the trusses. As I was talking to them, in walked Kathy to pick up her blueprints. She had more great deals to tell me. Denny, her boyfriend and builder, was hard at work on her foundation while she was scouting deals. I tried not to turn green with envy.

She gave me the name of the farmer in Casa Grande with good straw. The farmer would deliver for $4 per bale and he had four thousand bales, so there was no rush. I only needed about two hundred. With renewed enthusiasm and one more peanut butter and jelly sandwich stuffed into my mouth between errands, I headed back to work.

That evening, Don called to say he had finished digging the footers and septic trenches, and while I was talking to him the insurance agent showed up at the door with the construction/house insurance contract for me to sign. Meanwhile, I completely forgot I had put dinner in the oven. The boys were very kind about letting the charred food sit for a few minutes before opening the oven door, so we didn't set off the smoke alarm.

The boys put a new set of frozen french fries and chicken bits in the oven to try again. They must have seen the strain showing on me, for they weren't usually very adept in the kitchen. Dinner and insurance forms were completed by about 9 P.M. I checked my e-mail. I shot off a few questions to some builders who were willing to help me through my befuddlement. By now, I had a pretty good conversation running with my "mental match," Mark, who wanted to visit around wall-raising time and do what he could to help. He was planning to build a straw bale house in Missouri, where he had lived most of his life, and was likewise interested in all I was learning.

On Friday, Kathy called to tell me about the great deal she'd found on rebar. Someone would deliver a ton, or a bulk, of twenty-foot rebar for about two-thirds the price of Home Depot's. I hadn't calculated everything I would need yet, but Kathy needed about half a bulk, so she offered me the other half. I had been wondering about using bamboo instead of rebar, but I couldn't even think any more. I just said "sure."

My brain was definitely on overload. Work at StarNet was very busy right now, as my coworker had been promoted and I was essentially doing two jobs. My body and mind were worn out, but at some deeper level I was in awe at the workings of Whomever oversees the details of life. Between Kathy's great shopping services and all the straw bale builders with e-mail answering questions for me, everything I needed was being given to me at exactly the time I needed it. I even had Mark for cyber-conversation. I unloaded my construction burdens on him, and his light sense of humor always made me smile.

On Saturday, it was 96 degrees already when J.J. and I arrived at the construction site in Zej's truck loaded with twenty-inch strips of OSB. It was time to build the forms for the footers. The place was all dug up; trenches with mounds of dirt piled along their edges cluttered the site, making the house area look very small. The sunroom looked barely large enough to hold a chair. Just as Don had predicted, the trenches were shallower on the southeast corner, but the batter boards in the northeast corner were knocked over. I could still see the original holes for the stakes, so I thought it wouldn't be too difficult to rebuild the boards and rerun the strings.

The strings were back up and measured again by about 10 A.M., so I began placing the OSB forms under the strings and bracing them with rebar. I had thought this process would be simple enough to finish by early afternoon, but it took the whole day to get about half of the boards in place, even with J.J. helping. Plus, I needed more boards. I must have calculated wrong.

So, after a quick shower, I went back to the lumber store and got five more 4 x 8-foot OSB boards. They were huge and heavy to handle, but I struggled them into the truck and then into the sawdust-coated garage, where four sawhorses awaited them.

I cut them on Sunday morning, before going out to the land and had most of the boards in place by the afternoon. As I was nearing completion, Kathy's boyfriend, Denny, stopped by and let me know as gently as he could that there was no way rebar and OSB would hold up under the weight of concrete. These forms were sure to "blow." I would need to brace all around the top of the OSB with 2 x 4s.

"How can I do that?" I asked, pointing to the imitation plywood. "I can't even pound a nail through this stuff!"

"You screw them together," he replied with a grin. "Then you just unscrew them after the concrete is poured."

It would take me into the following weekend to brace them and I still hadn't formed the sunroom side of the house. But if that's what had to be done, then I'd do it.

By 5 P.M., I was again running out of both OSB and water. My love of the desert heat was oozing out of me as fast as my zeal for building this house. I wasn't having fun. My head pounded from two days in the 99-degree heat. What had I been thinking? Me, build a whole house? People study these trades for years, and I thought I could read a couple of books, attend a couple of workshops, and throw this thing together.

I felt like quitting and joining my old friends at the pool. I asked myself: If I fell apart in complete exhaustion, sat down right here and cried, would a Builder in Shining Armor drive up on his backhoe, wave a wand over the foundation and have it completed, along with all the utilities?

No, so get back to work. You have quit too many times in your life and you're not going to quit this project. You promised you wouldn't.

I began looking at the rough-in plumbing situation. I'd have to dig under the footers to run the drainpipes, so I figured I'd better go ahead and dig up the footers before I braced the forms for good. The desert earth was like rock, I was tired, and the septic trench needed to be three feet deep. I couldn't imagine pickaxing all the way from the house out to the tank. That would be an entire weekend unto itself.

How on earth was I going to do this? And who would help me? Frank, who had sold me the land, stopped by to check on the progress for a few minutes. He was still willing to help, he said, but he had a backpacking trip planned next weekend along with some other hikes in upcoming weeks. He was also fighting a hernia. It was becoming obvious that J.J. wasn't as fascinated with this project as I was and about half a day per weekend was the most I could expect from him. All these other builders who had been so kind to answer questions did this for a living. If I bugged them with questions for months, I was bound to push them beyond their limits and lose friendships. Matts, the wall-raising expert, was too busy taking care of his wife to consult for me. Sunset Books' *Basic Plumbing* really didn't cover what I needed to know about roughing in a foundation either, as if that information were reserved for contractors.

Silently, I let the tears roll down my cheeks and splat in shiny drops on my dusty, sunburned legs. What was I going to do? The house loomed like a huge black void ahead of me—endless weekends of tasks I didn't know, mistakes I could make that would double the cost and delay construction.

I allowed myself to cry as the sun dipped below the horizon. The tears began to cleanse my fears as the darkness spread over the land, and slowly a light flickered inside me. It couldn't be that bad. Small steps. I could do this in small steps. Just don't look at the whole thing at once. I remembered Lonny saying he knew some workers who would dig trenches. It was time to put out some money and have someone else do some work. A couple of hundred dollars would definitely be worth it.

Slowly, my mind came up with solutions. I would go back online and find a plumbing book that was meant for home construction. There had to be one. I would find a laborer who would work with me on weekends, not just for digging trenches, but for everything. There must be someone available. The weather had to get cooler. And I had time. The wall raising was set for December 4 and this was only October 17.

Once I was ready to raise the walls, I'd have Matts to oversee it, and then I'd hire some carpenters to build the top plate. I'd hire someone to apply the roofing, too. I'd hire an electrician at whatever cost, and then the earthen plasters I would do with joy, all by myself if necessary. My only deadline on completion of the house was when my rental sold. My parents had generously offered to pay my rent until the house was completed, so I wouldn't have to work under such time pressure.

I stood up with a new determination. I could do this. One step at a time, one day at a time, one weekend at a time. If I had to postpone the wall raising, so be it. Slowly, in the darkening twilight, I gathered myself together, as well as the tools scattered around the job site, and bid the land farewell.

As the week went along, I recovered slowly, both from the heat and from the panic. At my meditation group on Wednesday night, I managed to settle my mind. On Wednesdays, I often joined the meditation group in downtown Tucson for a two-hour meditation. It was much less distracting for me than trying to meditate at home (which I tried to do for an hour each day, though these days I was so tired that my meditations were dwindling to about fifteen minutes, if anything). Meditation usually filled me with a deep feeling that everything was in Divine Order, even if it looked like chaos on the surface. However, when my days were hectic and my time was in great demand, I had trouble convincing my mind that two hours could be better spent in meditation than running errands.

On Thursday, I purchased the lumber I needed to finish the forms and had long, twenty-foot 2 x 4s delivered to the site. On Friday evening, I went back into the garage to cut stakes and braces for the forms.

As I pulled out my power saw and set up the sawhorses, I found myself smiling. Power tools were becoming fun. Sure, I could be at the movies, but this was exactly where I wanted to be—where I chose to be. I still had years ahead for movies and dinners, but this year I was building my own house from the ground up. One day it would be completed and beautiful. I didn't even get discouraged when I sawed through my power cord; I just found some splicing caps and put the cord back together. Nothing to it!

Early on Saturday, I headed eagerly to the job site, determined not to let this project overwhelm me. The desert was far too serene and beautiful. I knew what I had to do: screw the long 2 x 4s around the tops of the OSB forms so they wouldn't "blow" as Denny had warned me, and then brace as necessary into the ground. How hard could that be? I had all weekend.

I pulled my wet overshirt over my parched arms. Even though it was only in the 80s now, by midmorning we'd be pushing into the upper 90s and my skin would need it. One of the form corners looked crooked, so I fiddled around straightening and measuring it, laying strings across the inside lines of the sunroom walls, and securing the last couple of sheets of OSB. I had to hack away at the walls of the trenches to get the boards straight. The parched clay and sand crumbled into dust as I poked at it. Sometimes it broke off in large chunks.

The OSB boards were too long for me to move easily, so I used C-clamps to hold one end of the board at a time, until I had it positioned perfectly. I used a level to make sure the boards were vertical. I probably should have imbedded them into the dirt so that the tops of the boards were level, but that seemed like an impossible amount of work. I didn't want to cut the boards, since I planned on reusing them for the top plate. Instead I used a magic marker to draw a level line along the inside of the boards. I hoped the concrete guys could just use that to level the footers.

This was still time-consuming work, requiring me to walk back and forth, adjusting each board. By now, however, I had trained myself not even to think about how great it would be to have a helper. I simply tried to be thankful for figuring out a way to do it myself.

About midday, which I could tell from the shadow of the western saguaro, my neighbor, Laura, who lived in the mobile home nearest to my building area, invited me in for cold water. I accepted eagerly and relished not only the liquid, but the air-conditioned interior. She offered water any time I need it and electricity from her exterior outlet.

So far, I'd done all my wood sawing in my garage, but I assured her the electricity would be a wonderful help soon. As we chatted, she mentioned that she was a nursing student at the local community college. That seemed like a perfect career choice. Kindness emanated from her being and gentle voice. I was sure that someday she would make a great nurse.

After cooling down and enjoying her friendly conversation for about half an hour, I went back into the desert sun to complete my forms. I still had to line the sunroom trenches with OSB, and as I measured some of my forms, they weren't quite twenty-four inches wide. Maybe the dirt was settling behind them and pushing them in, but at any rate, I had to pull them out, hack away some more dirt from the sides of the trench, and replace the OSB.

Time flew by as I became completely engrossed in my work, forgetting even to take a lunch break. Soon, I noticed a coolness in the air, and glanced up to see the shadow of my sundial saguaro aiming toward me as the sun settled below the horizon. There was still much to do, as I needed to replace each area of the forms at least once, because it was crooked or not wide enough.

Sunday was a continuation of bracing the forms. Sometime around midmorning, Frank showed up with an eager smile beneath his Sherlock Holmes shade hat. His backpacking trip had been canceled. Boy, was I glad to see him!

Immediately, we went to work, placing the OSB, wedging it into place with short rebar stubs, measuring the depth and width of the footer, then screwing the 2 x 4 braces into place. I felt thankful for his soothing presence.

It was 5:30 when we secured the last piece of lumber. I was beaming with pride at having gotten so far on the foundation, regretting only that the sun was too low for a photo. Next weekend I could move along into the plumbing and then fill the trenches with rebar. This would strengthen the concrete in the footers. There were codes on exactly how to do this, but I already had a diagram of how to place the rebar and a bender/cutter reserved at a tool rental shop. That had to be easier than building the forms!

Frank drove me over to Kathy's job site, where bales were stacked at least fourteen feet high, waiting for her walls to be raised. I wanted to take one bale and put it on my job site for Matts to see, if he came by. But there was no way we could climb that high to get one. But I measured the bales with a sigh of relief: they were twenty-two inches wide, which meant that my twenty-inch OSB for the top plate would be perfect. And a twenty-four-inch-wide stemwall would also be just right, allowing for two inches of earthen plasters.

I could see it all taking shape! With joy in my heart and dust all over me, I gave Frank a big hug and thank-you. He said something about how it was the highlight of his week, since he spent the other days writing at a desk. I laughed and grimaced playfully, because this was hard work, but deep down I knew what he meant.

## Chapter Eight

# ROUGH-IN PLUMBING

*Success is going from failure to failure without loss of enthusiasm.*

—Sir Winston Churchill

With the forms somewhat secured, I was ready to install the underground plumbing drainpipes from the foundation to the septic tank, or "rough-in" the plumbing. I purchased a great book by Peter Hemp called *Plumbing a House*, sent out a few e-mails asking how to get the pipes under the footers (dig up the dirt under the footer, lay the pipes down, then cover them back up), how to cut the big, black pipes (with a handsaw), and so on. After drawing myself a detailed diagram of how all the pipes would connect from the kitchen and bathroom drains, off I went to the plumbing store with a list of the many little connectors I would need.

I had put in a couple of lawn-watering systems in the past, so I didn't think this could be all that difficult. It looked like making a Rube Goldberg contraption. I get all the pieces, cut them to fit, and then glue them together.

During the week, on a recommendation from Kathy, I lined up two laborers, Alfonso and his nephew (whose name I never understood), to dig trenches for the plumbing. Don's tractor had dug a trench parallel to the north side of the house, about ten feet away, that ran into the septic tank, but I needed side ditches that went from the main trench into the house exactly where the plumbing fixtures would reside, turning at precise angles to match the pipe connectors. These trenches seemed too small for Don's tractor to dig, so we would need to dig them by hand.

I might have been able to find workers for $6 an hour, but I just couldn't see paying that little for hard physical labor in the hot sun, meanwhile nobly giving money to charities. I felt better just paying them more money.

Alfonso was quite a jovial talker, with good English. Originally from Mexico, he'd been in Tucson since 1985 and had taught himself English from listening to rock 'n' roll stations. I had to enjoy a guy like that! He had a radiant smile and marvelous sense of humor.

It had been about two months since we'd had any rain and the desert sand was turning to rock. Alfonso and his nephew took turns pickaxing, soaking the hole with water, shoveling out the dirt, and resting while the other one pickaxed. I worked on the forms, back-filling the outside of them with dirt and dampening it so it would pack solid.

About midday Lonny stopped by on his all-terrain vehicle. Years of spreading concrete in the desert sun had left him with a body and tan that most weight lifters would envy, but he still looked like an overgrown kid with scraggly blond hair, rosy cheeks, and a big, impish smile. He scratched his head as he wobbled the forms. They needed the dirt for bracing, but they would hold, he said. However, as he surveyed the plans, he noticed the loft.

"What about the supports for this?" he asked, pointing to the four corners of the loft.

"I'll attach them to the stemwall, won't I?"

"No, I'm sure the county wants you to pour these down into the ground, just like the house wall footers. You gotta take these supports down to solid ground, so they won't sink."

"Oh." I tried not to sound stunned. "You mean I have to jog the inner forms into the house in a two foot square beneath each loft support?"

"Heck yeah, I'm sure about that."

I groaned. Another full day's work. I would not only have to rebuild the forms in those areas, but pickax out the dirt. But if it had to be done, it had to be done. "It won't be that hard," I told myself. "And I'm a form expert by now. I can whip those suckers up and down in no time!" This was much better than finding out a few weeks down the road when the inspectors showed up. I thanked Lonny and told him I'd call him when we were ready for the concrete pour.

"Sure thing!" He flashed his grin at me and revved up his bike. "You've sure done a lot of work here. I could lay the rebar inside the forms for you. It's not as easy as it looks and the inspector will want it perfect. You're gonna need four shafts running along the trench. You can't let any of the rebar touch the dirt or the wood. It's gotta be at least three inches into the footer on all sides, so you need to hang the rebar from braces that stick out over the forms. You'll need verticals running up into the stemwall, too. You gotta be sure when you connect two pieces of rebar, you overlap them and tie them together just right, too. If it gets to be too much for you, just let me know. I'll give you a good price."

"Thanks. I might consider that." I grinned, wondering silently what he would charge, but not wanting to ask, not yet.

That day my mind was on plumbing, and I was in no mood to pull apart the forms. In my garage that night, I could cut the pieces of OSB for the loft foundation and install them the following day. Today, I would begin the plumbing by laying three-inch black ABS (acrylonitrile-butadiene-styrene) pipe. I had never worked with ABS before, but I had read about it in my plumbing book and I felt ready. I had a big can of black glue that would fasten the pipes together and an entire array of connectors. The back of Zej's truck was loaded with several ten-foot lengths, and I'd begin by laying these down the main trench—a nice straight run to warm me up.

From the plumbing book I learned that the pipe had to slope about a quarter inch for every horizontal foot. If it sloped less, the water wouldn't drain, and if it sloped much more, the water would run out too fast and leave solid waste behind. Though I had searched several plumbing stores, I couldn't find a level that marked this slope. So I decided to use the water level to estimate how much my total slope should be from the beginning of the house drains to the septic tank. If I ran all my pipe and the difference in height at each end was somewhere close to that total, I could assume my slope was calculated correctly.

I also figured that each ten-foot pipe should slope about two inches from one end to the other, and I could estimate that pretty well with a long, four foot level. I dropped two ten-foot pieces of ABS in the three-foot-deep trench and jumped in after them. I propped their ends up with rocks to keep the dust off and applied the black, goopy cement to one of them. I did the same to the inside of a pipe connector and easily pressed it over the end of the pipe.

With a new confidence, I gooped up the end of the second pipe. But as I went to shove it into the connector, it wouldn't go. The large pipe was heavier than I could handle with one hand, and since I was pushing at a slight angle, it refused to budge. The glue was drying rapidly, and if I dropped the pipe to get a different grasp on it, I'd get dust all over it. If I shoved it in only a tiny bit, I'd have a lousy, leaky connection. I decided just to let the glue dry and try again, this time enlisting Alfonso's help.

Happy to take a break from pickaxing, he joined me in the trench. With one of us on either side of the connection, my second attempt slid together smoothly. From then on, we worked our way down the main trench from one end of the house to the other, gluing together pieces of ABS but leaving a space where the pipes had to angle into the house. The trenches for those pieces weren't complete yet. Each connection got easier as we learned how to line the pipe up exactly and push it in with a little twist.

When we finished gluing pipes, I headed back to the far side of the house. I could see that the OSB boards, behind which I had filled in damp dirt, were warping and bending. The weight of the earth was too much for the meager propping I had done, and, with water added, the particle-board couldn't hold the weight.

Oh, it can't be that bad, I told myself quickly, before I could get discouraged. All I need to do is unscrew the support—that's easy, pull the forms out—that's easy, scoop the dirt out with a shovel—also no problem, then put them back. Then, increase the bracing of the forms and fill the trenches back in with dirt. Nothing to it. I have a few hours left today and all day tomorrow. We need to take some forms out for the loft post notches, anyway.

The main thing was to do this well enough to pass inspection. I picked up my shovel and began. Do one little thing at a time, I chanted silently, and someday I'll see something big.

We worked until dusk, then I drove Alfonso and his nephew home. After taking a long, cool shower, I once again sank into the couch, my mind a soggy lump of hot oatmeal. There was no energy left for anything but ordering out pizza. J.J. was equally exhausted from a day at the paintball park, so we relaxed together.

Too bad I didn't drink, I thought. A beer would probably be about right at this point. But I had no energy to go get one. I got up to catch up on my e-mail and then crawled into bed with Dave Barry's *Guide to Guys*, which Mark, my listserve buddy, had recommended. Some light, silly humor was about all I could handle. I fell asleep with a grin on my face.

At midnight I woke up, out of breath, my mouth dry. Somehow, I just couldn't get my heartbeat to slow down, nor stop the visions of plumbing pipes and bowed forms. My body was stuck in overdrive. How many weekends did I have left to get this done in time for the wall raising? I should check that out in the morning. I got up, drank some water, read a few more pages, and laughed out loud.

I dozed off and on through the rest of the night, waking up to drink water and try to slow down my system. At 7 A.M., I rolled out of bed, ate as much as my tense stomach would allow, took a couple of deep breaths, and headed out to pick up Alfonso.

The morning was much cooler—somewhere in the seventies at long last. Once settled at the job site, I directed Alfonso to begin digging the post holes for the porch roof supports, all fourteen of them. I went to work on the forms. Hours passed and I worked without resting. I needed to see this work completed so I could get back to the plumbing. I knew what I was doing now. Chipping away at the dry dirt to the exact measurement, I nested and braced the boards in perfect alignment with the strings. These would be forms that I'd be proud to show off.

Laura came over to offer me cold water, but I declined. Too much work to do. She suggested that I plug in the power saw to the electricity from their house, instead of cutting everything by hand. Good idea. After completing two of the notches for the loft posts, I began to feel faint. A little voice in me was not whispering but yelling through throbbing temples that I should be careful about pushing myself too hard in this heat. I could end up with sunstroke and dehydration.

Thoughts of a long, cool shower or maybe even a swim in the community pool pulled me toward the car, while the urge to complete my task pulled me back into the trenches. My decision was made by Alfonso; he wanted me to take him home early. So somewhere near midafternoon, I packed up my tools and headed home, stopping off for an ice-cold mango smoothie on the way.

When I opened my front door, I was greeted with a chorus of cockatiel squawks.

"Hi, Tweeters!" I called to Merlin and Arthur, "I'm glad to see you, too!"

The screeching continued at such a high pitch that I knew something was wrong. Racing to their cage, I noticed the door ajar and only one bird, Merlin, inside. Arthur had clipped wings from his previous owner, so I wasn't too worried about his escaping, except that our cat, Toonses, shared the house. However, she was so full of Phenobarbital to control seizures that she'd never taken the least bit of interest in the birds.

After a few seconds of trying to figure out the direction of the second set of squawks, I found Arthur waddling around the kitchen floor in quite a state of excitement. The birds continued to echo each others' chirps, like dolphins sending out radar to determine their distance from each other.

Toonses followed me into the kitchen, oblivious to all the commotion. Laughing at the mayhem, I carefully grabbed Arthur in my hand, enduring his mild bites of protest, and placed him safely back into his cage. I secured the loose door with a twist tie and laughed again at the chatter between the birds as they gossiped about this eventful Sunday afternoon. God, it felt good to be home!

I took an extra-long, cool shower, did some laundry, made a grocery list, and opened my e-mail. I began to feel human. With the groceries, I bought a beer—the first one I'd had in a couple of years, I think—and some kava-kava, an herbal relaxant. Anything to slow down my heart rate. Five days sitting at my computer in an air-conditioned office would also help, I thought.

And they did. After another week of recovery, I headed back to the site early Saturday morning, November 6, to finish up the forms and work on the plumbing. I knew what I had to do now and simply had to do it. This time I had to make all the little angled plumbing connectors fit into the trenches that Alfonso had dug.

To my dismay, the first trench, which was supposed to be at a horizontal forty-five-degree angle, was angled at more like fifty-five degrees. I had to get out the pickax and widen the trench, then push the pipes into the connectors at a slight angle to make them fit. Each connection required precision in measuring, then gluing at just the right slope. Each time I moved too fast or swung the pickax, dirt sprayed all over my face and glasses.

The weather was a little cooler, and as the weekend approached its end, my tasks also reached completion. I surveyed my work with pride while pink streaks spread across the evening sky. The forms looked straight and sturdy, almost professional. The plumbing twisted and turned in its matching crevices, sloping slightly up to just the right height beneath the footers. I still had a little more to do on the plumbing, but probably just one day and I'd be done. Then I could hook up the water supply and a hose so I wouldn't have to haul water any longer.

That would be next weekend. I had a month until the wall raising on December 11. But my nerves were shot and the thought of taking on the rebar the following weekend was too much for me. My brain simply couldn't handle a new task right now, especially one that had to please the inspectors. I'd call Lonny and take him up on his offer to do both the rebar and the concrete. At this point, I really didn't care what it cost.

Kathy had left me a "half bulk," or half ton of rebar. Lonny gave me an estimate to do the rebar the following weekend and pour the concrete for $500 plus the cost of the concrete. That seemed like a great price to me, and boy would it be wonderful not to have to strain my brain any longer.

On Sunday night, I left a message with Kathy asking if Denny could come by and check the slope of my pipes to make sure they looked like I'd pass inspection. On Wednesday, I got an e-mail from her that Denny said my ninety-degree angles in the plumbing were not up to code. Where the pipes went from vertical to horizontal, I was supposed to use ninety-degree connectors that made a longer sweep in the turn. My connectors made the turn too fast and might clog. Also, my cleanouts weren't right. Cleanouts are the pipes that angle to the surface so I could put a roto-rooter inside if the plumbing got a blockage. I had put in one pipe that angled out in two directions, but code required that two pipes rise to the surface, one angling each direction, so I would know which way my roto-rooter was heading.

How was I supposed to know these things? The local codes were different from those in the plumbing book. Well, again, good thing I found out before inspection day and not after. So, the next Saturday, November 13, I climbed back into the trenches, sawed out my 90 degree connectors and cleanouts, and replaced them with the correct ones.

I spent the rest of the day hooking up the water supply with half-inch white PVC (polyvinyl chloride) pipe. That was easy and familiar; I had used this white flexible pipe for lawn-watering systems before, so for once I knew what I was doing. I even attached a spigot near the southeast corner of the house with a hose that would reach around the entire construction area. By the time the pipe glue had dried the following day, we'd have flowing water.

I still wasn't quite finished with the drain plumbing, but I filled the area where the pipes had gone under the trenches so that Lonny could begin the rebar the following day. Lonny was going to be there at 7 A.M. on Sunday to begin work on the rebar, but I told him I'd show up around 9 A.M. after cooking the boys a decent Sunday breakfast. And so I did. When I arrived, Lonny was scratching his sunburned forehead.

"We have a problem," he said. "We shot these forms with the transit and they're at least six inches off square. The batter board level is perfect, but not the forms. And some of them are too narrow. That's the first thing the inspector's going to check for." He measured inside the forms, to show me. Sure enough. The weight of the dirt on the outside had nudged the boards in a couple of inches.

I stared at him blankly, my mouth frozen ajar.

"But heck, we figured out we don't really need most of these forms, anyway. You only gotta pour nine inches deep, then sink the stemwall the other couple of inches. You only need forms on the low side on the north, here. The other part, we can just pour into the dirt. But we'll have to take out all these forms and chip away some more dirt and that's gonna take some time. It'll cost a little more."

"How much?" I asked, still stunned.

"A couple hundred more. Seven hundred dollars total."

"Well, we gotta do what we gotta do," was the best reply I could come up with.

He sensed my grief. "But hey, you did a heck of a job for someone that didn't know what you were doing. Even this guy who lives down the road and drives by all the time has been watching you. He stopped by a while ago and said that, too."

My mind was rolling over the hours I had put into building those forms. Why hadn't God sent someone by to tell me I didn't have to do that? Oh, well. There was no sense grieving over it all. Just move on. I wrote Lonny a check and told him to do whatever he had to do. Actually, it was wonderful to have someone who knew what he was doing; priceless, in fact.

Lonny planned to leave the sturdiest section of the forms, where I had put braces and stakes, so I could figure that I had saved some amount of labor. As he worked, I completed the last plumbing connections— long ninety-degree angles and double cleanouts all in place. Ready for inspection! As we were wrapping it up at the end of the day, Lonny glanced at me.

"Well, aren't you going to fill the pipes with water for the inspector?" he asked.

"What?" I stared at him blankly, my stomach climbing toward my throat.

"Yeah, that's what we always do. You gotta give them the water test. Fill the pipes up with water, let them sit overnight, and then if the water level holds, the inspector knows there aren't any leaks."

"But if I fill it with water, it will drain right into the septic tank."

"Well, we cap it off before the septic, so it doesn't go in there. Ah, but don't worry about it," he replied. "Just call the inspector out here and he'll tell you what you need to do."

That night, I phoned all the builders I knew to see if I was supposed to set up some water test. No one answered, all I got was voice mail. I searched through my plumbing book, but there was nothing about water tests.

Finally, Denny called me back. He hadn't worked in Pima County that much and he wasn't sure, but he didn't think it was necessary. Relieved, I phoned in the plumbing inspection for Tuesday. Pima County had a voice mail system, where I punched in my job code and the specific inspection code so that the inspectors were notified for the following day. If I failed the inspection, I could always rephone it later at no charge. My third inspection would cost extra, I was told. Nobody was sure how much, and I hoped I didn't need to find out.

After work on Tuesday, I anxiously drove out to the job site as the sun was setting behind the peaks to the west. In the golden rays of the evening light, sat a note from the inspector—"Rough Plumbing Inspection Rejected—no water test, minimum 42″ above grade." My heart sank.

Wednesday morning, I put my work clothes in my car so I could set up the water test after work. I still couldn't find anyone who knew what this was about, so I paged the inspector and asked him exactly what I needed to do.

"Do I need to fill all the pipes with water and have all the pipes forty-two inches above grade?" I asked. From his note, I assumed he meant that this was how high the vertical plumbing pipes should extend for the appropriate water pressure.

"Well, you can, or you can have just one pipe that high and cap off the others. They'll fill up with air. It's not so heavy that way." I had to picture that a minute. As the water rushed into the pipes, some air would escape from the main pipe, but with all the pipe ends capped off, the water would eventually block the air from escaping from some of the side pipes.

"But won't the water come out the cleanouts?"

"No, it shouldn't."

"Okay, thanks. I'll do that." After hanging up the phone, I rephoned the inspection for the following day. I would have about an hour of evening light to work in. I'd go buy the test caps during lunch hour and do just what he said. How hard could that be?

After work, I sawed open the connection to the septic tank and placed a tight cap over the pipe. Then I placed smaller caps on the other vertical pipes, except the farthest one, which I extended to about forty-five inches above the ground and began filling it with water from the hose.

The water ran for at least twenty minutes. Nervously, I paced up and down the length of the pipes to see if I had some major leak somewhere. Nothing showed. The water kept running and running and running . . . probably forty-five minutes, now. Something wasn't right.

Suddenly, the lid on one of the lower vertical pipes blew off with a loud pop that sent me jumping back. I raced to shut off the water that was over-flowing the pipe. I must have bought the wrong kind of test caps. There had been several to pick from. As I examined the rest of the plumbing system, I could see a small leak on the very first joint I had made, which I sensed hadn't fit too well. That would need to be replaced. The pipes around the cleanouts were shiny and wet. The inspector had told me that wouldn't happen. Was I doing this whole thing completely wrong? Oh, what I would pay for someone who could tell me what to do!

It was already dark and I was working with a flashlight. I could race to the hardware store before it closed, and work until midnight out here, but it wasn't that important. The boys were waiting for dinner. I'd cancel the inspection and work the following night.

And so I did. I found no special test caps made for cleanouts, but the person at the plumbing store told me to wrap the threaded areas with Teflon tape and tighten them down really hard. The smaller test cap that blew off the lower pipe was supposed to be glued in place with the ABS glue. So, the following evening, with new connector and Teflon plumbing tape in hand, I once again climbed into the trenches with my flashlight.

After replacing the leaky connection, I threaded the cleanout caps and tightened them with my vise grips. I glued down the other test caps. My neighbor Laura, sweetheart that she was, came over and shone her headlights onto the work area. However, as I finished all that, I realized that I didn't want to pour water into a recently sealed joint. If I blew it out, I'd just have to do it all over again.

Discussing it with Laura, who was far less crazed than I at this point, I decided to save the inspection for the following Monday and finish up everything over the weekend. That way, if there were any other problems, I could fix them under the light of the sun with plenty of time to run to a plumbing store.

Arriving home that night, I made one more sweeping decision. If I kept up at the stress level I was now operating under, I would never complete this house. This work was far more complex than I had ever imagined. I needed a real consultant who knew all about construction and all about these inspections. Matts was too busy, but there had to be someone.

Jon Ruez came to mind. I had heard his name often, but I had also heard that he was extremely busy. Matts had mentioned him once as someone who could fill in for the wall raising if I picked a weekend when Matts was unavailable. I had Jon's phone number somewhere, and it couldn't hurt to ask. So that night, I picked up the phone and dialed.

The voice that answered was so deep and soothing that it almost made me cry. Without pausing, I poured out my dilemma and asked Jon if he could possibly find the time to consult for me. He wouldn't have to come to the job site too often, just let me phone him up every now and then with questions . . .

"Yes," he replied almost before I completed my many sentences. "How about Monday? I could meet you there about 5 P.M. and see what you're doing."

"Oh, thank you!" I gushed. "Monday? You mean you could come by this Monday?"

"Yes."

"Great. I get off work at five, so I can't get there until almost six, though. It's dark by then."

"Could you get off work a little early?"

"Yes, yes, I could. I could just ask to leave work a little early. That would be fine. I'll see you there at five. This will be such a great help. Thank you!"

"Okay, see you then." He sounded so calm and confident that I wished I could call him every day just to hear his voice.

On Saturday, November 20, I had nothing to do but get the plumbing right and haul some bales over from Kathy's house. It was the weekend before Thanksgiving and I felt festive. I began by refilling the pipes with water and watching the level drop and drop until drips showed around one of the cleanout connections that I had replaced during the week.

It had been a tight, awkward fit, and the various connections were so close that I couldn't remove one without replacing the whole section. Another trip to the plumbing store yielded about thirty dollars' worth of fittings and a special primer for ABS pipe that would help seal the joints. From here on out, I would leave at least six inches between every connection I made, so they could be replaced and repaired, one by one.

The primer melted the outer layer of the pipe, making the joints slide together so smoothly! In the future, I would use that on every joint. I wasn't worried that the repairs would leak, but I needed to wait until the glue in the joints dried before I refilled the system with water. Oh! If I had only known what I knew now when I had started the job.

J.J. was with me on Sunday, as I literally held my breath and once again dangled the hose into the raised plumbing pipe and turned on the spigot. It was another spectacularly clear, warm day, about eighty degrees and beautiful. Even with all the stress, I loved being out in the open air and sweeping desert. Even though there were houses nearby, all I could hear were the birds chirping in the nearby saguaros and occasionally a quail cooing from a distance. My unobstructed view to the south revealed graceful mountains arching against the brilliant sky.

J.J. and I paced nervously up and down the plumbing system as it filled, looking for any sign of shiny dampness on the sandy black pipes or darkened dirt from moisture near a joint. Nothing appeared as the sound of the water in the hollow pipes grew louder and higher, then suddenly burst over the top! I raced to shut off the hose, then ran back to see if the water level was holding.

With utter dismay, we watched the level inch slowly downward. We filled it up again and watched it continue to drop. What could the problem be? Air bubbles, we figured. It must be air bubbles rearranging themselves in the system. Give it a little more time and it will stabilize. The rate at which the water sank did seem to be diminishing, but nevertheless it kept going down. Watching it became pure torture.

Maybe if we ignored it, the water would settle at one place. After topping it off again, J.J. and I drove over to Kathy's to haul some of her leftover bales to our house. It was invigorating to be dealing with straw bales finally, a medium that felt familiar, even though I'd never done a wall raising. I had seen bales at a couple of workshops and practiced lifting them. The straw smelled musty and earthy. I could hardly wait for the day that I could move beyond rigid concrete and plumbing pipes to work with such a friendly, flexible material.

We unloaded the bales before wandering toward the pipes again, saying prayers on the way. Now J.J. was as wrapped up in the water test as I was. Frustration and inner dread gnawed inside me. If I didn't get this water level to hold today, it would delay the concrete pour and the entire foundation construction, then the wall raising. And if I delayed the wall raising, I'd have to put it off for about a month, past the holidays. By then, rain would undoubtedly be arriving, and I'd disappoint Mark, who was driving down from Oklahoma specifically to help with the wall raising.

"Please, God, let the water be at the top of the pipe."

Peering into the black tube, I let out an exasperated sigh. The water level was down about four inches! I raced up and down the maze of pipes looking for any sign of a leak. This time I spotted a tiny air bubble sputtering at a joint near the kitchen—near the section I had just replaced. If I cut out the joint and replaced it, I'd have to let the glue dry again, I thought, I wasn't sure, but how could I take a chance? I couldn't delay this inspection any longer. The inspector was coming tomorrow, and one way or another I had to be ready.

"Okay," I told myself out loud, "don't panic. At least we know the problem, there are still several hours of daylight, so we can find a solution."

I suddenly flashed on some plumbing repair tape that I had picked up at the last minute, just in case something like this happened. I didn't know if that would be okay with the inspectors, but why not? I opened the package of stretchy black rubber tape and wound it tightly over and over the area, saying more prayers. I used up almost the entire roll of tape on the one tiny air bubble, until I was quite sure no air or water could escape anywhere.

After topping off the pipe again, J.J. and I drove back to Kathy's for another load of bales. I felt cheerful and confident as we unloaded them and strode over to view the plumbing pipe again. The water level had held much better this time, but it was still down a couple of inches. Once more, we paced up and down the maze of black pipes. No shiny wet spots or moist ground was visible and by now these pipes had been filled with water for several hours. What could it be?

I stomped angrily over to the truck, my patience vanishing fast. A cool breeze swept across the foundation: signs of winter were finally arriving. I pulled on my jacket. As I stood there in complete perplexity, Lonny drove up on his ATV to check on the rebar and finish up a couple of details. His inspection, called the excavation/layout/rebar inspection, would also be tomorrow, Monday. I explained my dilemma, knowing full well he wasn't a plumber.

But as if he wore wings and had dropped from the sky, he flashed his magnificent grin and said, "Well, the temperature's dropped about twenty degrees in the last couple of hours. The air in those pipes has been shrinking up, I betcha. That'll make it drop."

I could have hugged him. Of course! Why hadn't I thought of that? It was eighty this morning and now it was approaching sixty degrees. Tonight was due to drop into the forties. It would still be cold when the inspectors arrived the next morning. Since I would have no time to top off the pipes in the morning, I'd leave them a note and some water to fill it up and hope for the best.

"Thank you, Lonny." I waved good-bye as he hopped back on his bike. "I'll see you out here after work tomorrow to see how we both did on our inspections. I'm also meeting a straw bale builder out here, Jon Ruez. I've decided I need someone who's familiar with these inspections as a consultant. This is just more than I can figure out alone."

"Yeah, you sure been working hard," he said. "Good idea."

Even though I drove home, slept, and got up on Monday and went to work, a large part of my being was wrapped around every one of those plumbing joints, holding them together through sheer willpower. Mentally, I tried to prepare myself for another leak, but I couldn't figure out any acceptable time frame for more repairs. I couldn't pour the concrete until I passed the plumbing inspection, and Lonny was leaving for the Thanksgiving holiday in two days. If I didn't pass, then I'd have to postpone the wall raising until after the holidays and tell Mark to postpone his trip. Uggghhh!

The day dragged on at an interminable pace, until 4 o'clock arrived.

With great trepidation I drove to the job site. I wished someone else would drive out there and report back to me; I almost couldn't bear the strain of facing those pipes again.

Pulling into the driveway area, I immediately spotted the inspection card on the top of the table with no white notes attached. Exploding from my car, I raced over. Both inspections—the excavation/layout/rebar and rough-in plumbing—approved!

"OOOOHHHH Yeeessss!" I screamed out loud, jumping into the air. The entire weight of those water-filled pipes lifted from my being. "Yes!"

I grabbed a shovel and began filling in the side plumbing trenches so the concrete truck could fit down the north side of the house the next day. Taking deep breaths, I let out months of tension as I worked. If I had dared spare the time to fall onto my knees, I would have. Lonny stopped by to make sure he had passed and told me he'd "try" to have the concrete truck there the next day. If he got too busy, could I wait until the following week?

I groaned. "My wall raising is in two weeks! I still have to build the stemwall and all the window and door frames. I need Thanksgiving weekend to work. The concrete has to get poured before you go on vacation. Please!" I literally begged.

"Okay," he smiled. "If I can't do it, then I'll have a friend do it. Don't worry."

But I was worried. Nevertheless, I continued to fill in the trenches, visualizing the truck driving over them the next day.

Jon pulled up at about 5:30 in a blue Jeep Cherokee. He looked genuinely friendly as he shook my hand with a firm grip. That wonderful voice was encased in a strong, compact body whose dark sun-tanned skin and brown eyes contrasted against a bright smile and graying hair. Something about him was very pleasant, as with most people I had met during the construction of the house; he was exactly the sort of person I had hoped to work with. Maybe the worst was over and it was all downhill from here, I thought with great relief.

Orange streaks spread across the darkening sky as a frigid north wind blew through the open valley. We didn't have much daylight left. Quickly, we unrolled the plans on the worktable, and I put my mind on the next phase of the construction. I had a couple of questions about the stemwall, but mostly about how to construct the window bucks.

- How big exactly did I make the window frames?
- Could I make them narrower than the bales, so I could set the windows in a bit from the edge?

- What kind of mortar do I use for the stemwall?
- Do I need to get a truckload of sand to mix with the mortar?
- Should I rent a mortar saw to notch the stemwall down at the doorways?
- What was the electric UFER inspection that was underlined on my inspection sheet?

. . . and on and on. He answered them all with great expertise, drew me pictures of how the windows fit into the box frames, and only charged me for half an hour, no drive time. I was amazed and pleased as I handed him a set of plans so we could confer over the phone in the future. With a slight smile, I relayed the story about how I had constructed all these forms and the concrete guys had charged me extra to remove most of them and pour the concrete into dirt trenches.

"Yes," he replied with an understanding smile. "I did the same thing on my first house."

Telling him how very much I appreciated him and his expertise, I said good-bye, then turned back to my shovel with a distinct feeling that the perfect guide had finally shown up to assist me through the rest of the construction process. What a great day!

A glowing full moon rose over Diamond Head to the northeast. I closed my eyes and let the pale golden light radiate through my Being.

Thank you, I said silently, letting the tears roll down my cheeks. Thank you.

# Chapter Nine

# THE STEMWALL

*Press on: nothing in the world can take the place of perseverance.*
*Talent will not; nothing is more common than unsuccessful men with*
*talent. Genius will not; unrewarded genius is almost a proverb.*
*Education will not; the world is full of educated derelicts. Persistence*
*and determination alone are omnipotent.*

—CALVIN COOLIDGE

WHILE I had been struggling with the plumbing inspection, I had spent my lunch hours and evenings ordering the straw bales, roofing, trusses, and preparing to construct the stemwall.

I realized I had asked Jon the wrong questions when I asked him how to make mortar. Reading my foundation book, I learned that mortar is what you put in between the CMU blocks to make them stick together. It is a smooth mixture of sand and cement, containing no gravel. I had decided not to put any mortar between the two rows of block, since it wasn't required by the county.

What I should have asked Jon was how to make concrete. Concrete is what you pour into foundations. It is a mixture of gravel, sand, and cement. Cement is the gray powder that makes it all stick together and stay hard. You buy that in bags from the hardware store, and it is very, very heavy.

Since the CMU block had holes in them, which I would be filling with concrete, it wasn't necessary for me to also put mortar between the blocks of such a low wall. "Dry-stacking" the blocks would be much easier than mortaring them and save me quite a bit of time.

As I had been forewarned, building a house was costing much more than I imagined. It seemed that every day I was running to some store for another hundred dollars' worth of supplies. These purchases were adding up, and my bank account was draining rapidly—too rapidly. I could see that I'd barely make it through the wall raising, and then I probably would not have money to pay carpenters to attach the roof. I wasn't too surprised that the payments from the boys' father had stopped arriving.

To compound the situation, the home I was renting had been sold. A very nice couple had seen the "For Sale by Owner" sign and offered to purchase the home at the end of February when their current lease expired. Both financially and physically, it would be impossible for me to complete the straw bale house by the end of February.

Could life perhaps bring me a few less challenges all at once? Apparently not! I have always believed that for every problem there is a solution if one looks hard enough, so my search began. After a couple of very restless nights, I decided to look for an inexpensive trailer to put on the land. It would have to be really, really inexpensive. And I would swallow my pride and ask my parents if they could assist me with construction costs instead of paying extended rent, as they had offered.

Asking my parents for money felt completely degrading. At the beginning of construction, I had told God that this would not be an option I would consider. My parents had already lent Rick I and me the money to build our house on Kauai. That had gone well and we had paid them back once we could get a mortgage. Then, when I was divorced and living in Honolulu, they had lent me money every month to pay my bills. My salary and child support just didn't cover our expenses.

When Rick II and I had moved to New York and opened Headshots, they had once again used the equity in their house to loan us the money to relocate and buy a house. As I filed the bankruptcy, I still owed them many thousands of dollars. Our relationship was very strained, and I hoped that my future would hold the means to pay them back, rather than ever again ask them for more money. But now I could see no other option.

I was numb from thinking, planning, comparing costs, coordinating schedules, reading instruction books, and working in the hot desert sun every weekend; not to mention my full-time job and the details of caring for the boys. I hadn't had a spare moment to spend with friends, relax, and socialize since July—six months now.

Friday evenings were spent at hardware stores and Saturday evenings found me semi-comatose in front of the TV, usually ordering out for pizza because I didn't have enough energy to cook or drive. My e-mails with friends were about the only thing that kept me feeling human.

I was beyond any sense of satisfaction from all this; I just knew that I had to complete what I had started, and I still wasn't sure how I was going to do that. The project seemed immense and I felt very small.

I left a message with Kathy, asking if she knew of any inexpensive trailers I could live in while I built my house. She knew lots of people and always seemed to have contacts for everything. The next day, she phoned back telling me she had just bought a two-bedroom mobile home from our mutual draftsman, Dan. She had been too busy to move it off his property. It was in really bad shape, hence she had only paid $150 for it, but I could have it if I would pay half the cost of moving it to my land, as long as she could have it when I was done. She might decide that she didn't want it, in which case she would sell it to me for a nominal amount.

"It's ugly, but it's functional," Kathy explained, "I'd live in it if I had to. I mostly bought it because it was cheap, but I don't have any plans for it. I might put it on some land after a while and sell it with the land. But I'm in no hurry for that."

"Thank you!" I chirped back, while waves of relief spread through me. "I suppose I should look at it, but I have no time. I'm just going to figure this is our next home and take your word for it."

"The only thing is we have to have it moved, which will cost $400. I'll split the cost with you, so you only have to pay $200. And of course, it needs some fixing up, too."

"No problem. I don't need it for a few months, so I can spend that time working on it after the wall raising. I know how to plumb now."

I broke the news to the boys, who looked up from their computers in disbelief. Was it not enough to explain to their friends how they were handbuilding a house out of straw, but now to live in an old, filthy trailer? Finally, after much conversation, J.J. decided it was okay as long as we had a real house under construction, so he could tell everyone the trailer wasn't really his home. Honestly, I didn't care what they thought or what anybody thought at this point. This was survival.

When Dan got the word that Kathy was giving me the trailer, he phoned me up very frustrated that Kathy had left it on his land for two months. He had his land for sale and needed it moved right away. So, there was no rest for the weary. Kathy's mover was unavailable, so she gave me the title and I agreed to pay the moving costs myself. The lowest cost I could find was $700 and permits were another $300, but it would be well worth the money in rent saved and reduction in my stress levels.

Amid all this commotion, I felt like a three-ring circus unto myself as I headed into Thanksgiving weekend. However, my parents had agreed to assist with construction costs, giving me $1,000 a month, and that was a huge relief. I knew they were retired, but the stock market was on an upswing, so they were kind enough to share their profits. Although I'd never taken much interest in the activities of Wall Street, I would cheer it on now, hoping this wouldn't be an inconvenience to my parents. They are good people who have helped me through many tight spots.

The mobile home would be moved out the Monday after Thanksgiving, the plumbing was roughed in, the footers were poured, and the wall raising was still scheduled for December 11. About twenty people had volunteered to hoist bales with Matts Myhrman leading the way.

Between now, November 26, and December 11, I had to build the stemwall, pass its inspection, have someone build window and door frames, have the straw delivered, purchase all-thread and round up many other wall-raising supplies. I had two weekends and my e-mail buddy Mark's volunteered labor the week before the wall raising.

Mark was in a transition between jobs and was able to take two weeks to drive down from Oklahoma to help do whatever was necessary. In return, he would gain experience that would help him build his own house someday—and of course, we would get to meet each other after many, many e-mails. We could have dinner a couple of nights, with any luck. And I'd have the company of a peer for the first time in months.

Thanksgiving, however, looked bleak. There was no turkey in my freezer, no yams in my refrigerator, Christmas shopping was nowhere near the surface of my conscious mind, and the Christmas decorations were buried deep in the garage somewhere.

One of my goals on weekends was to try to sleep as late as possible— maybe until seven or eight if I was lucky—before my brain clicked into hypergear about all the work I had to accomplish that day. Thanksgiving was no different. At about 8 o'clock, I clicked on the TV to catch a little of the Macy's Parade, cooked hash browns and eggs for the boys, and gleefully drove through the sunlit saguaros to remove the forms from the concrete footers. As he had promised, Lonny had poured the concrete before leaving for Thanksgiving vacation. I only wanted to work about four hours and get back in time to take the boys to dinner at the restaurant where Zej washed dishes. They were having a potluck turkey dinner for the staff.

Most of the forms came off with relative ease, but a couple of them had concrete poured around their ends and simply wouldn't budge. Lonny had left most of the strings from the batter boards intact. I remeasured them and found them to be perfect, to the half-inch. So I measured two feet inside them and ran another set of strings for the inside of the stemwall. After tossing a few shovelsful of dirt to refill more of the plumbing trenches, all four hours were up and I headed back home to spend some much-needed time with my children.

Since I was saving my vacation time for the wall-raising week, I worked at the office on the Friday after Thanksgiving. The boys kindly took some of their time that day to go out and shovel more dirt into the trenches. We were all amazed at how time-consuming it is to fill a three-foot-deep trench, shovelful by shovelful.

As J.J. and I drove out on Saturday, we had a task before us that again seemed much like playing with building blocks. We had to stack CMU brick around the edges of the footers, two rows high and two rows wide. We would place light gray ones on the inside of the wall, where they wouldn't show, and lovely rough brown ones on the outside of the wall.

We would notch them down two inches at each doorway, since I planned to have the interior floor two inches below the bottom of the bales. Matts had recommended this as a precaution, just in case the house ever flooded. Bales can handle some moisture in our dry climate, as long as that water can evaporate quickly. If straw sits in water, it will quickly turn black with mildew and transform from straw into powder.

J.J. and I worked well together that day, with him notching and me stacking. The two-inch cuts were tedious and difficult, however. The circular power saw jammed very quickly, so we rented a grinder, which is stronger than my saw. J.J. became the expert cutter, shaping every custom block I requested, while I stacked. The gray blocks were by far the easiest to lift and cut. They weighed about half of what the brown blocks did and with just a little cut of the blade, they could be whacked apart.

But not the brown ones. The grinder smoked and churned its way through those until J.J. was spending almost a half-hour per cut. I realized that wasn't going to work, and I would need a diamond blade, as Jon had recommended.

Despite the tedious cuts, we completed the entire interior wall by late Saturday afternoon, with the most difficult brown block exterior wall to go. I purchased a diamond blade on Sunday morning and promised J.J. he could work just half a day, since he had homework to do before Monday. The cuts went much faster, but it was still very difficult to make them exact enough so that the floor of the wide doorways was perfectly level. The brown blocks were still extremely difficult to deal with.

Somewhere through my stacking, I realized that the stemwall wouldn't show at the doorways. I'd have a stairway on the outside that would cover it, so why not make the doorway sections with the two-inch cuts out of the gray block? This sped up the day's work. J.J. had completed about half the doorway bricks by the time I drove him home for lunch. I had stacked only about a third of the outer wall, so I rushed back after lunch. No matter what, the stemwall had to be completed by the end of the day.

My back was feeling the strain of two entire days lifting and positioning these blocks, but it held up beautifully. I found myself talking to it and promising it there were only a few more blocks to go and then the stemwall would be complete.

The most time-consuming task was cutting the bricks as I got to each corner, but I was in hypergear and I had it down to a science. I'd mark the cut over the rough brown exterior with a magic marker. Then, snapping a pair of safety goggles over my eyes and lifting the brick onto the tailgate of the truck, I'd let the grinder whir as I leaned into the mark. I didn't let the cloud of dust intimidate me, and within a few minutes, the brick was divided by a deep gash.

With great care, I'd insert the chisel and say my prayers as I hammered deeper into the cut. Usually, the brick broke in approximately the right place. Sometimes it cracked in exactly the wrong place and I had to start over.

The sun was sinking fast on this late November day, so I couldn't take the time to cut the remaining bricks for the doorways, but I could keep the grinder for another day. I'd concentrate on getting the remainder of the wall in place before sundown.

By the time the golden sun was rimming the distant mountains, I was rounding the last corner of the house. Three hundred blocks down and about forty to go. With masterful efficiency, I loaded four into the wheelbarrow at a time, pushed it along the narrow dirt groove to the far side of the house, then hoped that the rebar sticking up from the stemwall would match the holes in the blocks. Sometimes it did; sometimes it didn't, and I had to run over to the grinder and make a notch.

Soon, I had a flashlight perched on the front block in the wheelbarrow to light my path around the house. Then, for the last few blocks I switched on my car headlights. By 7 P.M., the stemwall was stacked and completed, ready for concrete the following weekend.

Before driving away, I paused long enough to admire the straight rows of blocks lined under the strings, looking pretty darn professional if I did say so myself, and realized that when I drove out there the following weekend, I would have more help. Mark would arrive from Oklahoma that Friday and from then on it would be a whirlwind up to the wall raising, which was now only two weeks away. I was ready and eager.

*Chapter Ten*

# WALL RAISING

*Hard work spotlights the character of people: some turn up their
sleeves, some turn up their noses, and some don't turn up at all.*

—SAM EWING

MARK rolled into town on Friday afternoon, December 3, in the middle
of a dust storm that smothered Tucson and its surrounding mountain
ranges with a brown haze. This wasn't the way I wanted him to see the
Sonoran Desert, which was usually sparkling with sunlight and blue skies.
But then, he'd already made it known that his trip to Tucson many years
ago had not ended in a love affair with the desert; he much preferred his
rivers with water in them, his trees with broad green leaves, and grass
beneath his feet, not cactus poking his toes.

Fortunately, the weather had finally dropped below the nineties; now
the temperature was generally in the seventies, with nights dropping almost
to freezing. That should make him feel at home.

When his white pickup pulled into the parking lot at StarNet, out
stepped a stranger who was already a friend, dressed in white coveralls.
There was the deep, gentle voice with a slight southern twang and the
hearty laugh I had heard over the phone several times, wrapped in a rather
tall, gray-haired flesh-and-blood form.

After a quick tour of my office, I led him to the job site via the Saguaro
National Park West. This was the long but scenic route from my office to
my new home, avoiding the freeway. My office was in the newspaper
building in south-central Tucson, and my house was about a forty minute
drive northwest on either route. The dust lessened considerably to the west
of the Tucson Mountains as the setting sun turned the open sky to vibrant
swirling auras of orange and purple.

As much as Mark claimed to dislike the desert, I was sure he'd notice the glowing beauty of the grasses and teddy-bear chollas as the sun lit them from behind, transforming their spines into golden haloes. He was driving in a separate car, so I couldn't show him.

When we arrived, he quietly surveyed the stemwall and the surrounding lot, commenting that he had expected it to be more remote. But all in all, I think he liked it. A cold breeze blew steadily through the palo verde trees as the sun lowered to the Baboquivari mountaintops. After showing him the house and introducing him to the boys, we headed out to a nearby restaurant not only to eat, but to converse in spoken word rather than cyberspace. It was almost like a real date, and it felt wonderful.

I turned my office into a guest room for Mark and moved my computer into the living room. I promised him a free place to stay and possibly a home-cooked meal every now and then, if we got our work done on time. Being a chef by trade, however, he volunteered to do the cooking if we ever found ourselves home before dark and if I bought the groceries. That sounded like an even better idea to me.

Early the next morning, we were out at the job site, ready for a full day's work. This was our weekend to put rebar inside the stemwall and fill it with concrete. I now knew how to make concrete. Gravel companies sell concrete mix, a blend of sand and gravel, by the truckload. Don, the backhoe man who had dug the trenches, had left me a mound of concrete mix during the week. Today, he was meeting us with his tractor to scoop the gravel mix inside the stemwall, so we could later smooth and tamp it into a raised subfloor.

Again, what I thought would be a few hours of labor turned into an all-day event. We shoveled and leveled the gravel, prepared rebar for inside and above the stemwall, removed the last forms from the footers, built forms for the concrete doorway thresholds, and marked the top of the CMU block with different colors of spray paint for exact placement of the J-bolts and rebar stems.

J-bolts are long, large bolts with a threaded section on one end and a curved "J" on the other end. The J part would be imbedded into the concrete of the stemwall, with only the threaded portion sticking up. That part attaches with long nuts to four-foot lengths of all-thread that then connect together and rise all the way through the top of the bales and get bolted into the top plate, essentially bolting the walls to the foundation. That's the Pima County code, though many people prefer other methods of attaching the walls to the foundation.

The rebar stubs would stick up about a foot, anchoring the first row of bales in place. More five-foot lengths of rebar would also be pounded down through the top of the bales as we reached the upper courses, to give the wall stability. This again was according to Pima County building codes, but there are other methods to strengthen the walls.

Matts had instructed me on how to place the rebar stubs every two feet around the top of the stemwall, except where a J-bolt was placed. J-bolts were placed every six feet according to Pima County code. All of them needed to be about one foot into a bale, so they would catch the ends of all the staggered stacks of bales. If I placed them in the center of a bale, they would pass right between bales on the next row. I was also careful to place J-bolts every few feet around the outer walls of the sunroom, which would be framed in wood, like a regular house.

Mark seemed to have brought winter with him. Unless the sun was blazing high in the sky, the air was bitingly cold and very dry, with a humidity level below 10 percent. Despite carrying jugs of water around with me, drinking constantly, and lathering my lips with lipbalm, my throat was constantly parched and my lips formed a leatherlike coating. Calluses lined my worn hands.

That evening, we phoned Alfonso for assistance in pouring the concrete into the stemwall, arranged for rental of a cement mixer, and loaded Mark's truck with thirty-five bags of cement and a couple of metal trowels.

"Welcome to my world," I exclaimed, in a mixture of exhaustion and elation at having Mark's company and help. "Saturday nights in the hardware store." He looked very, very tired and a little shocked at the amount of work I had poured on him in one day. I'm sure he was reconsidering the construction of his own home.

Early Sunday morning, with J.J. along to help, we hitched a rented concrete mixer onto the back of Mark's truck and wove through the Tucson Mountains to the job site. Alfonso and his nephew (whose name I still couldn't understand), Mark, and I began mixing concrete by 9 A.M. The air was still frigid and dry. We huddled in hooded sweatshirts and work gloves, with thermoses of hot coffee. Alfonso had worked with a concrete mixer at some of his other jobs, so he was far more familiar with this than Mark or I. While I pulled out my foundation book to figure out which proportions of gravel, cement, and water we needed for our mixture, Alfonso revved up the gas turbine.

For the first batch of concrete, Mark poured a bag of cement powder into the large bin, then followed that with several shovelsful of gravel and sand. After adding water to this mixture, we had tight clumps stuck to the metal bin that had to be chipped away with a shovel. Alfonso explained to us, with his marvelous grin, that you have to put in the water first, then add some of the gravel, then the cement powder, then more gravel to make it just the right consistency. So we made Alfonso the master concrete chef, as the mixer chugged and clanged through the still desert air.

The rest of us lined up with buckets, figuring that the stemwall was too high to get the wet, heavy concrete mixture over the top in wheelbarrows. I only filled my bucket about half full—a lady's bucket, as Alfonso called it. After struggling across the foundation with the heavy bucket bumping into my shin, I watched this gray mush disappear into about one and a half holes in the CMU block stemwall. An entire batch of two bags of concrete filled about one brick on both sides and the area in between. The outer row of the stemwall was about two hundred CMU blocks long.

The blood drained from my face as I realized we had another huge task ahead of us—far greater than I had estimated. There was no way we would finish in one day. So, there would be more money spent on hiring workers the following day. Perhaps I should have just hired Lonny again. Oh well! Live and learn—nothing to do now but work.

Mark became the perfectionist concrete finish-chef, smoothing the surface with the trowel to just the right consistency. The rest of us formed the grunt work line. I could feel the strain on my shoulder from the heavy bucket and bruises forming on my right thigh where the rim hit me with each step, but my determination to keep the project on schedule overrode anything else, and I felt no pain.

Between concrete batches, I traveled the length of the stemwall with my measuring tape placing J-bolts and rebar, though the concrete pretty well obliterated the marks I had left the day before, and catching any gray drips that oozed over onto the outside of the brown bricks.

By the end of one long day of hard labor, we were a little more than halfway around the perimeter. We'd need to repeat this for one more day. Alfonso had to return to his regular job and J.J. had school, so we would need help. Alfonso recommended a labor company that employed his nephew and had workers available on last-minute notice.

At five Monday morning, I requested two workers for the day, beginning at nine, and took the day off work. After curling up in bed for one more precious hour, I rose to get the boys off to school and oversee the final phase of stemwall construction.

Pete and Bill showed up right on time, brimming with energy and a whole new perspective on how to pour concrete. The previous day we had used buckets to haul the concrete around the outside of the house because the top of the stemwall was too high for a wheelbarrow. Pete and Bill suggested that since we had a raised gravel subfloor on the interior of the house, we could probably fill the stemwall with wheelbarrows of concrete from the higher ground.

Removing a few blocks from the sunroom stemwall near the concrete mixer, we built a ramp over the wall and across the raised gravel of the interior of the house. After pouring half the first batch of concrete into a wheelbarrow, we pushed it up and over the ramp, then dumped the load with ease into a large portion of the CMU block wall. Mark and I shook our heads, wondering why we hadn't thought of that the day before.

As the work sped along at a rapid pace, I sat back and supervised. I measured for J-bolts and rebar stubs, smoothed the dirt around the foundation, and generally rested, enjoying the blue sky, cool breezes, chirping birds, and splendor of the open desert. By one o'clock, the entire foundation stemwall was completed. Pete and Bill really knew how to hustle!

As they were working, at about eleven, the farmer's truck with the bales of straw arrived. The golden straw glistened in the morning sun. The bed was packed with ninety-two bales, stacked ten bales high. In what is called a bale squeeze, the stack was laid on its side in the truck.

The driver skillfully maneuvered backward by the saguaro that guarded the west side of the house, and stood the entire back of the truck on end. The bale squeeze was like huge tongs at each of the four corners, gripping the whole pile together. He released the tongs and with a slight rocking motion set the enormous mountain of bales on the ground. It towered above us majestically like a castle turret made of gold. What a refreshing sight after months of dirt and concrete work!

The driver returned after lunch with another stack, which he set right next to the first. Like school kids playing on a dirt pile, we dropped what we were doing to set Mark's long ladder against the stack and scurry eagerly to the top. The view spread for miles and miles, north to Picacho Peak near Phoenix, west to the Baboquivari Mountains on the Tohono O'odham Indian Reservation, and east toward the Tucson Mountains that hid the city. What a spectacular day!

But I had hired workers and had no time to waste, so we climbed back down and got back to work as adults. We had an hour before Bill and Pete were being picked up by the agency van, so we had them shovel the remaining concrete gravel mix inside the stemwall, then level the subfloor with a long board. At 2:30 in the afternoon, we paid the driver and thanked Bill and Pete profusely for their great work.

As the wall raising became a clear possibility, I felt as if a great pressure had been lifted. Tuesday night, I made a lumber list for the door and window frames and phoned into the county for the stemwall inspection on Wednesday. I had no worries about that inspection. I had been very careful about my placement of the rebar and J-bolts on the top of the wall.

I had already scheduled a vacation day for Wednesday, so I got up early to supervise two carpenters plus Mark as we began the window and door frame construction. When we arrived at the job site at about eight in the morning, there was already a note from the inspector: "Stemwall inspection rejected because concrete was poured before the inspection."

Oh, my God! Would he make me knock it down? I had twenty people lined up for Saturday's wall raising, along with Matts Myhrman, Mark here from Oklahoma, and the holidays rapidly approaching. This couldn't happen! And I had no spare money whatsoever to buy more materials and rebuild the wall. All that concrete was expensive. Oh, my God!

Two carpenters and Mark stared at me, looking for direction.

With trembling hands, I showed them the note. "But don't worry, we're still going to build the window bucks and we're still going to have the wall raising," I said with a confidence that I didn't feel. "I just need to put in a call to the inspector and straighten this out. I'm sure he just didn't understand that this is a straw bale house and he was supposed to inspect the top of the stemwall."

Borrowing Mark's cell phone, I had the inspector paged and attached the cell phone to my jacket.

Then I tried to put my mind on the task at hand. One carpenter, Billy, was a definite free spirit with long hair and a big grin—referred from Kathy and Denny. The other carpenter, Randy, was very clean-cut, visiting from Iowa. He was renting a guest house from a friend of Matts and had told him that he wanted to learn straw bale building. The message had filtered down to me and so here he was. He turned out to be organized, skilled, pleasant—and had a chopsaw, a power saw that sat on the worktable and made quick, precise cuts in the lumber.

Following Jon Ruez's instructions, I measured the bucks to be the height of the window, plus whatever more would take it to within an inch or two of the top of the adjacent bale. That way, the successive courses of bales would lay across the top of the buck evenly. An extra inch or two would allow for the settling of the bales.

In the doorways, I allowed several extra inches for a doorjamb. I showed Billy and Randy the list I had made of the window and door sizes, plus a diagram of the construction for each buck.

I began to feel very weak and needed to be alone. The inspector still had not called back. Wandering into the open desert of my other acre, tears welled up in my eyes and a lump formed in my throat. I would have liked to just sit down and cry, but that would not get this dilemma solved.

I appealed to All The Forces That Be with every fiber of my being. Physically and emotionally, I teetered on the edge of collapse. After whatever time it took me to regain my composure, I strolled back toward the carpenters.

The inspector still had not called and normally he returned pages right away. I phoned his office again and found that the only time to get hold of him was between 7:00 and 7:30 A.M. the following morning. That would be too late. I had to know TODAY! The problem was probably the long distance code on Mark's mobile phone.

Calling Kathy on her mobile phone, I asked if I could go over to her trailer and call the inspector, waiting there for his return call. "Sure," she agreed. "The door is open."

With more prayers and trepidation, I paged the inspector again, then sat nervously by the phone. After what seemed like forever, but was probably about ten minutes, the phone rang. It was him.

"Hi, I'm the one with the straw bale house and the stemwall you inspected this morning. I'm the one who poured the concrete before the inspection," I explained.

"Yes," he replied coldly.

"The reason I poured the concrete into the stemwall," I explained, "was because I understood that the inspection was for the top of the stemwall where the rebar and J-bolts go into the straw bales."

"No," he replied, "I wanted to see the rebar inside the wall."

"Oh, gees," I moaned. "I guess I blew it. I've got twenty people coming this weekend to put up the walls, so what do we do from here?"

"Well," his voice softened. "You could file an appeal, but that wouldn't be settled until next week. Do you have any photos of the inside of the stemwall, before you poured the concrete?"

I thought frantically for a few moments on what photos we had taken. My brain files weren't in very tidy order, but suddenly a light flashed. I remembered snapping some photos while Mark was working. I could get them developed at the one-hour photo lab. "Yes! Yes, I'm sure I do!"

"Okay, then rephone the inspection for tomorrow and leave me the photos by the plans. I'll pass it. It's such a small structure, I'm not that concerned."

"Oh! Thank you!" I could barely speak. "Yes, I misunderstood on this one, but I took photos. Thank you very much!" I wanted to keep explaining.

"And I couldn't find the plans," he continued. "Put them somewhere in the middle of the job site, where I can see them."

"Oh, sure, of course. Yes, I will. Thank you!"

After hanging up, with shaking fingers, I phoned the inspection voice mail system and reentered the inspection for the following day. Then, flying out of Kathy's trailer, I let loose a big whooping "Yahoo!" The wall raising was still on.

Driving back to the job site, I climbed out of Mark's truck with a huge smile on my face. The guys were sitting glumly on the stemwall, taking a break. I probably should have composed myself enough to tease them for a while, but we were all too worried for jokes.

Mark stared at me. "Success?"

"Success! He just wants to see the photos. He said to rephone it in, which I did, and he'll pass it tomorrow."

"Whoa, did you dodge a big bullet, there!" he exclaimed with a grin.

"Yeah," added Billy. "If it had been a guy who called the inspector, he'd probably have said, 'Meet you out there tomorrow with a sledgehammer.'"

We laughed and I tried to breathe deeply throughout the afternoon. I carefully placed the tube with the plans in the center of the foundation.

The progress on the window bucks was slower than I expected—as usual. But nothing would faze me now. We had three days to complete them.

That evening the long-range weather report called for rain with a chance of snow overnight on Friday into Saturday morning. I called Matts and we decided to postpone the wall raising until Sunday. There was no way we could untarp the bales or ask everyone to show up with even a possibility of rain. I had to call all twenty people on my list. Several couldn't make it on Sunday or could only make it for half a day. But we'd have enough, I hoped, to get the job done.

On Thursday, I had to return to work at StarNet. Billy and Mark worked in the chilly north wind to finish a few more window frames and the huge buck that would surround the sunroom opening. They took the time to phone me, however, and let me know that the inspector had accepted the photos and passed the stemwall inspection. The wall raising would become a reality.

Saturday, the day that had been forecast for early snow, brought a typical Arizona morning—dry, sunny, and definitely no snow. We could have had the wall raising with no trouble, but we were also happy for an extra day to prepare.

As the morning wore on, I scurried around attaching all-thread to the existing J-bolts and placing cups of nails near each window buck. About

1 P.M., I looked up to see Matts climbing out of his white Subaru to help us lay the first course of bales. Between Matts's "Straw Boss" baseball hat and Rip Van Winkle beard shone eyes that twinkled with wit, wisdom, and a rare gentleness. He gave me a quick hug, I introduced him to Mark, and we went to work.

My introduction to straw bale building had been so rushed that I hadn't taken the time to inquire about Matts's history. I knew that several straw bale builders, including Denny and Jon Ruez, had begun their trade by attending workshops that Matts and his wife, Judy, had given more than ten years prior.

The wall raising wasn't the time to ask such questions, but later I learned that, indeed, Matts and Judy were largely responsible for the resurgence of straw bale building in the Southwest. In the late 1980s, Matts had followed a trail of articles about bale buildings that led him to photograph the hay bale houses in Nebraska. He and Judy then began showing their slides to "any group, no group too small, that would sit for forty-five minutes in a darkened room."

In 1989, they held their first workshop on the Steens' property at Canelo, building the very cottage where I had spent a restless night the previous summer as I decided to reduce the size of my house. And now my house, too, was ready for Matts's expert touch.

Matts immediately began scrutinizing bales for their straightness and uniformity, then selected a few for the wall. We started with the bales left-over from Kathy's house, since the bales from the farmer were still stacked sky high. Matts showed us how to jump on the center of a misshapen bale to get out any curvature. Then, laying the first bale in one corner of the stemwall, we measured exactly the point where the all-thread would poke into the bottom of it and marked it with a stick.

With all three of us lifting the bale, we rotated it down over the all-thread in just the right place, holding the threaded rod perpendicular. After sliding the bale down into place and pushing it down over the rebar stub, Matts critically surveyed whether the bale was lining up directly with the interior stemwall. The bales were about twenty-two inches wide, but the stemwall was twenty-four inches. I needed a couple of inches for the thickness of the earthen plasters on the exterior walls.

Since the bale was fairly close to the outer stemwall, Matts turned his back to the bale and gave it a couple of "mule kicks" from behind. That did the job. I handed Mark my camera and got a photo of myself beaming with joy, standing next to the very first bale we had put in place.

After laying bales up to the first doorway, we needed a custom bale, about half the size of a regular bale or about two feet long. Matts showed us how to thread a three-foot needle with nylon baling twine, wrap the twine around the bale, repeat that action with two more strings, and make slip knots to secure the ends.

With a little muscle and determination, we soon had the bale retied into two smaller, but secure sections. Carefully cutting the original strings, we separated the "mother" bale into two "baby" bales. I think I was grinning the entire time, because Mark warned me that I was going to get straw in my teeth if I wasn't careful!

What a joy to be me and be right here, right now, I thought, working with straw instead of concrete and having survived everything that was behind me. I wouldn't have traded places with anyone on the planet. We worked until about five o'clock and got most of the first course laid in place. Agreeing to meet at eight the next morning, we thanked Matts and began packing up.

As we were folding up the ladders, an antique Chevy truck pulled into the driveway and a friendly couple stepped out. Both of them looked like desert people—tan and casual in weathered jeans. They had seen the stack of bales, were interested in straw bale houses, and wanted to help. We told them the wall raising was the next day and Marilee, the wife, said she'd come help all day. She lived only a couple of blocks down the road and was a metal artist. She seemed like exactly the sort of person I would enjoy getting to know.

Mark and I spent the evening picking up sodas, juice, water, cups, bagels, cream cheese, and then ordering pizza for the following day. We crashed early, then rose by five to cook eggs and hash browns for breakfast. We roused the boys by six. The big day had finally arrived.

Not only would walls be constructed, but I would also meet the many people who were willing to volunteer their time to raise my walls, for the experience, the education, and to help me. May I never forget to return the favor, for one day all these people may be building their own homes.

Matts was there before we arrived, as was a carpenter named Jerry who had worked on my friend Mary's straw bale houses. I had already hired him to build the top plate after the wall raising. I posted wall maps and diagrams of the window and door placement at each corner, and by 9 A.M. sharp, Matts began his speech on how the walls should be built. Since I had learned much the previous day, I scurried around greeting people, getting the food ready, and placing supplies, such as pounding mallets, at each wall. One person from my office arrived, my good friend

Christina, but generally the people who came were the ones from the straw bale world who really wanted to learn. One friend from my meditation group, Lisa, came to take photos.

My neighbor Marilee showed up, as did Randy the carpenter; two architecture students from the University of Arizona; several people I had met from the listserve and workshops; Frank, the former landowner; and a friend of his from Colorado, whom Matts recognized immediately as being straw bale savvy. There was an artist from downtown Tucson who saw my notice on the listserve; and a wonderful software engineer from the University, Dyer, who found that raising straw bale walls on weekends was a good way to balance all his brain and desk work during the week. I couldn't agree more. Zej and J.J. were also there, of course.

After Matts finished talking, about six people lined up behind the huge buck that would surround the sunroom opening. With a "1-2-3 Up!" it rose into the air with great ease and fit perfectly into place. Mark and I screwed it onto the J-bolts in the stemwall.

Now we had to get the bales down from the fifteen-foot-high stacks that the bale squeeze had created. Matts let us know that throwing them down was not an option, because we would damage the bales and get straw all over the ground. So we created a slide for the bales with the scaffolding and OSB. I stood back and let Matts run the show; my house was in good hands.

Matts organized everyone into about four wall teams, each with an experienced captain in charge. He watched over their work while I continued to float around and answer questions, such as why I had placed the dining windows at different levels on the wall maps. Oops! At least we discovered that error while it could still be corrected. I tied a few custom bales, but mostly thanked people for working and helped them locate tools and nails, the temporary restroom I had set up in the trailer, and anything else they needed. It truly was a joyous, festive day, and I glided through it in pure exuberance.

Everyone worked diligently and carefully, toting bales around the site, "fine-tuning" them into the proper shape, tying custom bales, and checking everything with the level. Frank was nursing a hernia, so he became the loose-straw stuffer, looking for holes between bales and filling the top of the window frames with loose straw for insulation. While densely packed bales don't burn easily, loose straw will, and if it is piled right next to the walls it can ignite the whole house. So, a few other people spent their time raking up loose straw, which fell from every bale, and stuffing it into thick plastic garbage bags.

Pizza arrived via Andrzej at about one o'clock. We all paused briefly to enjoy the warm meal and sip on some much-needed liquid. However, the pause made a few people bid farewell, as they had other things to do, especially with Christmas approaching. Our afternoon crew whittled down to about twelve diligent people. Zej had to leave for work, but J.J. stayed.

As the afternoon progressed, so did the size of the walls, but it soon became evident that we could not finish by dark, especially with the short December days. I briefly considered trying to finish the walls with Mark over the following days, but quickly tossed out that idea. I was exhausted, as was Mark. The two of us could not lift many of the eighty-pound bales up six feet and properly into place.

I decided to simply continue the following Saturday. No rain was forecast for the week. So, reschedule I did, crossing my fingers that I could regather a good group of people and we could stay focused on the task even though Matts wouldn't be there.

*My glorious wall raising. I'll never forget the many volunteers who took so much care to build the walls straight and strong.*

As dusk fell over the western desert, we had about half the walls in place. We packed up our tools and bade everyone, including Matts, heartfelt farewells for their incredible work.

I was giddy with pleasure and fatigue. Before me stood the shape of a real house made of straw bales, with walls and openings for doors and windows. I walked around the inside, imagining where the rooms would be and looking out each window at the view. I think Mark was as proud as I was, and he had every right to be. A part of him was plastered into the stemwall and dusted between the layers of straw. What a tremendous help and support he had been!

J.J. helped us pack up, but he was coughing terribly. He was recovering from a cold and later that night I discovered that the dust from the straw had given him a full-blown asthma attack; he could barely walk across the room. I felt sorry I had made him work so hard. Even his inhaler didn't help. I vowed that I wouldn't ask him to help on any of the other wall-raising days.

Finally, in an elated, exhausted stupor, I realized I had an entire week ahead of me with no supplies to purchase, no trips to the building supply store, no invisible hundreds of dollars to spend, and two vacation days to sleep late. Pure heaven.

## Chapter Eleven

# TRAILER AND TRUSSES

*Let tears flow of their own accord: their flowing is not inconsistent with inward peace and harmony.*

—SENECA

FOR the next two days, I slept late, breathed deeply, moved slowly, and showed Mark some of the sights and alternative homes around Tucson. We drove into the pine forests of the nearby mountains, an ecosystem that Mark enjoyed far more than the dry desert. I was just happy to make no decisions.

Most fascinating for him was a compound of small straw bale houses at the base of the Santa Rita Mountains, owned by my good friend Mary. A kindred spirit, she was building these largely by herself, though much of the initial construction was the result of workshops. Each little house was a room with a verandah, connected by walkways and gardens, like something out of Swiss Family Robinson or an artistic hippie's dream. Mark examined her creative variety of gypsum- and earth-plastered walls with little niches cut into the straw.

We sat on straw bale benches, or bancos, outside one of her houses, sipping Mexican liqueur and nibbling crackers while the sunset spread rays of fire across the valley below. As the brilliant colors faded, sparkling stars lit the ebony sky.

I didn't know whether to cry or laugh at what my life had become in a few short months—the stress, the mistakes, the triumphs, the friends, the loneliness, the joys, the tears—the satisfaction of coming this far despite all odds. I felt alive and at peace, even though I had many miles to go before I could sleep in my new home.

As the sun rose the next morning, I said good-bye to Mark with a big thank-you hug. He had become a great friend and companion in a very short time, just as he had been for months on e-mail. His enthusiastic assistance and quick wit had carried me through this difficult week. I looked forward to returning the favor when his house was under construction. I could only hope that he had gained enough from his visit to make it worthwhile for him. Honestly, if I had assisted someone with their foundation and wall raising before I started my own home, I'm not sure I would have begun this house.

With a heavy heart, I headed back down the crowded freeway to work. Mark drove through the same rush hour traffic to join his family for the holidays and prepare for Y2K. He was convinced it was going to get ugly. I was too tired to think of preparing for anything, including Christmas, which was two weeks away.

It was probably best at that point that I didn't know Mark's future held major changes. He would soon find out that Y2K brought nothing more than champagne and a new dawn, and he would take a job as a traveling salesman, working fourteen-hour days. His evenings on e-mail would be gone and our friendship more distant.

Perhaps the only thing harder than building a house by oneself is to have someone arrive to share the burden and then have that companion leave. I prepared for the second day of wall raising by myself, feeling hollow, but soon I found myself back in the flow of the work with the four people who returned. Jerry and Randy showed up in the early morning; then Dyer, the software engineer; and Marilee. Andrzej and J.J. also joined the crew for a while.

Lifting bales up to the seventh and eighth courses was slow going with only one team, but the day flew by with jovial conversation and hard work. By sunset we had reached eight courses on about half the house. The other half we left at five bales high.

Since the next two Saturdays were holidays, Christmas and New Year's respectively, we decided to reschedule the completion of the walls for Saturday, January 8. I felt embarrassed asking people to return for a third day, but lifting heavy bales to the upper courses was something the boys and I could not do alone.

On Sunday, I bought a hundred-foot roll of painters' plastic and did my best to run the long sheets along the top of the walls as the wind picked up. A storm was due in the following day and telltale dark clouds were already gathering around the mountain peaks. Bales can get wet on the sides and dry out easily in the low humidity of the desert, but I couldn't let water soak down into the top of them: they would mildew and rot. No way was I going to take these bales down after putting them up.

Taking some of the little leftover pieces of OSB, I drilled half-inch holes in their center and placed them over the rods of all-thread where they poked through the plastic. The OSB would help hold the plastic down and keep it from ripping. Leftover concrete blocks and rocks also kept the top of the plastic in place, but nothing kept the flaps weighted down on the sides of the walls. Long staples made of wire and stuck through the plastic did nothing. The wind quickly ripped them out of the straw and flung them across the ground, laughing at my efforts. As the day progressed, the wind continued to increase until I was perched ten feet high on the sway-ing walls with a big plastic sail quite capable of blowing me off the wall. I decided my life wasn't worth the risk and climbed down. I covered as much of the remaining walls as I could with leftover pieces of roofing paper weighted with rocks.

I sure could have used some help, but there was no sense thinking about that. Tears of frustration rimmed my eyes as I struggled to dismantle the scaffolding myself and fit the heavy poles into our small Nissan pickup. My shoulders were sore and my body was numb.

For the rest of the week, I let my body collapse in fatigue and tears. On any given day, at any given moment, the tears could flow for no real reason; most likely a release of stress and exhaustion. I had made it to the wall raising, the money had held out, friends had come and gone, and now it was back to work, work, work as usual.

That I was now relying on my parents' kindness to complete the house weighed on my shoulders as well. I have always been proud and inde-pendent, preferring to give gifts rather than to receive them. But then again, receiving graciously was probably something I needed to learn.

My father let me know that he could only give me $10,000 over the course of the year, $1,000 each month. Anybody giving a gift larger than this amount had to pay the taxes on the sum, so the taxes would be his, not mine. Whatever happened, I promised him, I would not need or request any more than that amount. I was very grateful for the gift.

However, there really was no way I could determine exactly what the rest of the construction would cost. I was sure there would be lots of hundred-dollar trips to the building supply store that I couldn't foresee, and I certainly couldn't estimate how many carpenter hours I needed to put on the roof or frame the interior. Nor could I determine what an electrician would charge to finish the house. It was all a big blur of dollar signs.

I searched for ways to reduce costs further, and I determined not to do any construction, such as the porch, that wasn't necessary for the occupancy permit until after I was in the house. Once I had the final permit, I could get a mortgage to cover the land payments to finish up the remaining details of the house. The more I visualized the *lanai*, the more I wanted to build something rustic with rough beams and vigas. That would cost a little more, but it would be the most visible part of the house. The inner core of straw and earth plasters deserved an earthy, rugged surrounding.

I tried to count my blessings and feel relieved, but I just kept crying. As I drove to work each day, tears rolled down my cheeks. Sitting at my desk, I did my best to absorb myself in the business of the day so I wouldn't burst into tears. I had never been much of a crier in my life despite all I had been through, so perhaps I was making up for lost time.

At the recommendation of a friend, I spent several evenings steaming in a hot bath and letting the tears flow. Another friend, who is a therapist, told me that tears release toxins and how very healthy it is for the body to cry. Okay, so I was getting really, really healthy. Perhaps it was postpartum depression. I had just given birth to a house.

On Christmas Eve, I took a whole day off from both work and construction to cook a big dinner and a special birthday cake for Andrzej, who was turning eighteen on Christmas Day. My friend Lisa from my meditation group and her date, Carl, came over for the evening. We actually sat down at the dining table for dinner—tablecloth, china, and all. I hadn't done that in months. It was also the last organized meal for that teak table, which had traveled from Hawaii to New York to Tucson. As with many other items, it would not fit into the straw bale house or the trailer. I would put it up for sale after the holidays and use a smaller oak table that I had stored in the garage.

Doing domestic things around the house with good friends and my boys helped revitalize me. We had no tree at our house, barely any decorations, and no gifts. All Andrzej wanted for Christmas was some money to help buy a stage-worthy guitar amp, and J.J. was saving for a new computer. I gave them what money I could squeeze out of my strained checking account that night, with big hugs and thanks for being such great help and support through this very busy period.

They hugged me back and gave me a lovely card with a note saying how much they appreciated my sacrifices to build us a home. Inside was a gift certificate for a massage.

Through all the obstacles and challenges of my life, my children have been a pure joy and delight, companions through thick and thin. I could try to take credit for this, but I know they were both born with big hearts and an innate sense of joy at being alive. They can turn any task into a game. I know I have learned as much from them as I hope they have gleaned from me.

Toward the end of the evening, I brought out a box that I had hidden in my room, decorated with a big red bow. Out jumped a playful orange tabby kitten. He instantly began attacking the ribbons on his box and anything else we dangled in front of him until our evening was consumed in laughter. Toonses, our older cat, wasn't nearly as happy to see him as we were, but we made sure we cuddled her, too.

And that was our Christmas—one of the simplest and most joyous I had experienced. I wanted nothing for I lacked nothing—well, except a partner or best friend. I told myself that I had a house to build; companionship would come in its own time.

On Christmas morning, after sleeping late and cooking breakfast, I was back at the straw bale house. Now I could call it that, for it was more than just a foundation. I still felt somewhat weak and tired, but when I arrived at the site and saw my plastic sheeting ripped from a wild wind that had arrived during the week, my adrenaline began pumping. I made another attempt to hold the sides down with washers, long nails, and larger staples into the straw.

Matts happened to stop by and gave me a wonderful, low-tech solution: double-bag some plastic grocery bags and fill them with rocks. Then, tie a piece of leftover baling twine between the handles of the bags and drape them over the wall. This method worked perfectly. The plastic stayed down that day and through several storms in the two months before the walls were waterproofed with the top plate.

My body was still recovering, however, and out of carelessness, I fell off the top of the ladder, skinning and bruising my right hand. Then I hammered the little finger of my left hand into a big bruise and blood blister. I spent a little longer raking loose straw away from the house to minimize any fire hazard and called it a day. The next day would be spent digging out the trench for the underground electric wires, which J.J. and I had begun with a ditch-digging machine a month or more ago.

In mid-January we completed the walls. Many of the same people who had shown up for the first two wall-raising days returned for a third. I felt so grateful to them and wondered if I would do the same for someone; I hoped so. Even my boss from work came for half the day. With elation we placed the last bale into the top of the west wall by midafternoon and covered the walls with plastic again. This time I had help.

By now I needed to get the trailer livable, complete with utilities. When I had finally seen the mobile home, just before the wall raising, I was relieved to see that it was a full two-bedroom home, 40 x 12 -feet, with pipes and wires sticking out for water, electric, and gas. I had been told it was thirty years old, built in 1968, so I expected the chipped paint on the outside, but I wasn't prepared for the filth on the inside.

The plywood floors were piled high with old wooden pallets—probably thirty of them—and mounds of dirt and dust. The smell was reminiscent of old cockroach traps that I used to pull out of my kitchen corners in Hawaii. Doors were missing, the screens were filthy and ripped, and the walls were covered with crayon scribblings. But the basic space was fine. With a little work (okay, a lot of work) it could be habitable.

I removed the old wood and corroded pipes from the mobile home and was left with a mess of cockroach stains and general disrepair. What I couldn't scrub away, I painted over. After deciding not to go to the expense of installing a propane tank, I removed the gas stove and brought in the small construction table from the work site for my microwave/convection oven and two hot plates. That saved quite a bit of precious space and began to shape up the kitchen.

Measuring all our furniture and the trailer rooms, I determined how I could fit both the boys' beds into the larger bedroom and fit my desk and dresser into the smaller bedroom, plus a foldout futon for sleeping. With some leftover carpet runners from a friend, the area rugs I owned, and squares of inexpensive linoleum, the floors became lighter and brighter. Inexpensive venetian blinds dressed up the windows. A new toilet made all the difference in the bathroom, as did some turquoise paint.

Slowly but surely, the trailer became a place we could call home. I latticed in a catyard around the clothesline for Toonses and the new kitty, now named Matts after Mr. Myhrman. An electrician installed the electric panel outside both the straw bale house and the trailer. I roughed in the trailer plumbing and then called both state and county inspectors. At the same time as I passed the trailer inspections, I also passed several electric and plumbing inspections for the straw bale house.

In early February, one week past schedule, the trailer was ready for us and I had our worldly belongings packed into boxes once again. About one-third of the boxes contained things we actually used in our day-to-day lives. The remaining boxes and furniture would be piled high under tarps on the west side of the trailer to help insulate our temporary home from the afternoon heat. I wondered how many of those boxes I would decide to unpack when we moved into the straw bale house and how many I would donate to a thrift shop, realizing I hadn't missed the stuff at all.

I bought us each a nice set of colored dishes and packed away all my other dishes. We would each be responsible for washing our own color-coded dish before the next meal and I would just store them in the dish rack. I made sure that the items I carried into the trailer were attractive—including a couple of houseplants—so that it would be cozy, not depressing.

Randy, the carpenter, spent the entire Saturday, February 5, helping us move in a rented U-Haul truck. Over and over, I am reminded that one of the main joys of straw bale building is the people I meet. Randy was one of those special people filled with gentleness, yet great strength, from being at peace with himself. He was in Tucson for a few months, escaping the Iowa winter and learning what he could about alternative construction.

Once in the trailer, there was still much to do to make it feel like home and figure out how to fit our daily routines into this small space. I felt another wave of relief as this deadline to move passed and I realized my next move (hopefully my last) would be only about fifty yards away. The tears still flowed, but they came less frequently. I decided it was time to slow down the pace of my work, get my legs back under me, and reconnect with that joyful meditative center that I used to possess.

Many evenings found me perched ten feet high on the west wall of the straw bale house, watching the desert turn from gold to purple and then black, as green saguaros transformed into towering shadows against the night sky. The chirping of the birds stilled as the sun sank and coyotes howled in the distance. I alternated between deep-breathing exercises, meditation, and just sitting and staring into space if that was all my mind could handle—as was often the case. Slowly, I felt myself coming back to life.

Other than car problems and Kathy—yes, my first friend on my new land—threatening to sue me if I weren't out of the trailer by midsummer, life did slow down, relatively speaking. By the end of February I was ready to begin work on the top plate with Randy and Jerry.

I placed several phone calls to Jon Ruez, with whom I had barely spoken since the plumbing inspection, to get all the specifics on how this should be done. If I had learned anything, it was to ask every question I could think of *before* I began the work or bought the materials and not feel silly if the questions felt obvious. With the stemwall, it was the questions I had neglected to ask that got me in trouble.

Stuffed with straw for insulation, the long hollow box known as the top plate or roof-bearing assembly would fit on top of the bales, like a mirror image of the stemwall, capping the four walls and secured by the all-thread from the foundation. The trusses, shaped in an upside-down V, would rest on top of the plate and support the roof, so the top plate had to fit both the straw walls and the trusses.

As with every phase of this project, constructing this box wasn't as simple as it seemed. It would be heavy to lift if built on the ground and awkward to build on top of the walls. We decided to construct the wood frame and lower OSB portion on the ground in pieces, lift the sections onto the walls, stuff them with straw, and then place the OSB lid on top. A better idea would have been to construct the lower half of the plate before the wall-raising party and use all those people to hoist the heavy sections onto the walls. It was a little too late for that, however.

I still had the twenty-inch-wide strips of OSB that I had used to make my ill-fated foundation forms last fall. Some of them were very dirty, but some of them were in great shape because they had never touched concrete. I later learned that the glue holding the particles of wood together in OSB is made of phenol-formaldehyde resin: the board off-gases formaldehyde into the air around it. If I had known this at the time, I would have used OSB for the foundation forms, but plywood for the top plate and window bucks.

I was amazed at what the wind had done to the walls during the last two months. The east wall was blown almost concave. Often, it took five of us on the scaffold to push the wall out straight, sometimes bashing the individual bales with a brick to get them back in a straight line.

As we assembled the top plate piece by piece over a couple of weekends, the wind-blown, shaky walls slowly became strong and straight. Once the plate was in place, we couldn't budge them at all. I studied the carpenters' movements, watching how they drew or visualized exactly what they were going to do before they began, carefully measured everything to one-sixteenth of an inch, marked the wood precisely, and then cut. At every joint, they braced and double-braced.

As we were completing the last corner of the plate, Randy discovered that we had built a rhomboid, rather than a rectangle. Unlike the foundation, we hadn't taken the time to measure the diagonals of the house at the top of the walls to make sure we had a perfect rectangle before we began top plate construction. We had followed the straw rather than cutting the wood to fit the measurements of the house and then making the bales line up under the roof assembly. One corner was about five inches short.

Honestly, I didn't care. The house was standing and wouldn't blow over. That's what mattered the most to me. As long as the trusses would fit on the top plate, I was okay. But Randy assured me that unless the house was very close to square at its corners, we would have a difficult time applying the roofing. While the walls could be lumpy from the straw, the ridge of the roof needed to be perfectly straight.

That made sense. So, the following weekend, Randy sawed open one corner of the top plate, inserted some more 2 x 6s, and turned the house into something close to a rectangle. At least the long sides of the house were the same length. Next, we took the tape measure and measured across the width of the house to check the fit for the trusses.

The wooden trusses measured sixteen feet four inches across. Most of our measurements across the house were within a couple of inches of that, so we decided it was "perfect enough." Randy, being a trained carpenter, would have liked to see every measure within a quarter of an inch, but this was not a realm for perfectionists.

Now it was time to raise the trusses, but Randy was heading off on a long backpacking trip in California. At Jerry's suggestion, I hired a crew of four carpenters from a company called Straw Dogs. I had often wondered how the large wooden trusses, purchased months ago and stacked near the sunroom, would make the transition from ground to roof. They looked heavy and the walls looked high. Now, I would find out.

At 8 A.M. the following Saturday, I roused the boys from bed, even though they had been at a dance the night before. (Andrzej's band had provided the music, which I found very exciting. I couldn't imagine anything that would make for better high school memories than being lead singer/guitar player in a rock band. After buying two large stage amps with his birthday/Christmas money, his long-hidden guitar talent had an outlet.) As the sun warmed the clear March sky, the sleepy boys and I balanced the large, heavy, angled V's on our shoulders and marched them into the center of the house, trying not to damage any walls or vehicles on the way. Once there, the carpenters kept them inverted and handed the end tips up to workers standing on the north and south walls. They rested the ends on the top plate and left the trusses hanging upside-down inside the house.

Then, with the crew leader using a huge fork made from 2 x 4s, he pushed up the point of the truss until the men on the walls could pull it upright and nail it in place. After placing two trusses, they discovered that the roof plate was a little crooked. I could have told them that.

They agreed that whatever else went on beneath it, the ridgeline of the roof needed to be straight; that would be the most visible and important line for the roofing. So they braced a truss on either end of the house and ran a string to connect the apices. Then they began nailing the other trusses to the top plate, making sure each apex lined up with the string.

The top plate was more crooked than I had realized. While the distance between the sides of the house just about matched the length of the trusses, the corners didn't end up at exactly ninety-degree angles, so the trusses were not aligning perfectly on the top plate. At one point it became an unacceptable amount of difference, so we tied a towing strap to the bumper of the foreman's truck with the other end around the large sunroom buck. While the truck held the wall at the required distance, the carpenters nailed the other trusses into the top plate every two feet and one carpenter balanced on the peaks, nailing boards down the length of the ridge.

My shoulder felt bruised and sore after hoisting twenty-three trusses into place—and these were small trusses. Boy, was I thankful once again for shrinking the size of my house. Standing inside the living room area, I watched the ceiling appear. I could see how the height would expand the

*We tied a tow-line to a truck to pull the wall into place while we nailed in the trusses.*

space of the kitchen and living area and how the mezzanine would have enough height for standing. The interior glowed with golden light—a reflection off the wood, I supposed. I radiated along with it.

By noon, the trusses were secure and the carpenters loosened the towing strap from the south wall. I thanked them for a job well done and for sacrificing half of their Saturday. Then, I packed up and headed out to assist a friend from my very first Canelo workshop, Michelle Campbell, with her wall raising.

The Campbells' walls were largely completed by the time I arrived. Their house was larger than mine, but they also had about fifty people helping for a good part of the day. Jon Ruez was overseeing the wall raising, and he had a much more casual style than Matts. Jon didn't allow levels, and alignment was estimated, not measured. "Fine-tuning" could be done later. As always, the raising was a joyful event. The last bale was in place before sunset. I placed my leftover plastic inside their walls—happy to be rid of it!

Randy was back in Tucson the following weekend, and it was time to cover my trusses with sheets of OSB to strengthen and support the roof. Jon had recommended another carpenter to help Randy with this sheathing, so I figured it was all set. I'd supervise and hand the sheets of particleboard up to them. But midweek, the other carpenter called and said that he couldn't come; he had to work at another job. This would be Randy's last weekend in Tucson, so we had to either do the sheathing now or I'd have to find a new work crew.

The roof was very steep—not quite a forty-five-degree angle, but somewhere close; it was a 9:12 pitch, which meant that for every twelve inches across, it rose nine inches. Though I had pushed myself past many limits in this house construction, I had no desire to challenge my fear of heights. I had taught myself to jump out of an airplane when I was younger and more foolish, but leaping into the open air with a parachute and nothing solid in sight was very different from balancing high above the protruding rebar stubs of the sunroom stemwall.

Staring up at the steeply angled trusses, I tried to imagine realistically how much work it would be to stand on them while balancing and nailing heavy sheets of OSB. My brain went all fuzzy. I really had nothing to compare it to.

"Well," I thought, "how hard could it be? Roofs are sheathed all over the world every day without anybody getting hurt. Okay, I'll offer to help."

Randy agreed to work with me. The boys could hand up the sheets and I'd climb up on the trusses to help nail them down.

Saturday, April 1, was cloudy and cold—very unusual for Tucson. High winds buffeted the trailer overnight, waking me with visions of tumbling off the roof chasing flying sheets of wood. When I stepped out of the trailer into the pale dawn, the air was still and cold. I took a few deep breaths of the crisp air, trying to leave my fears behind.

The first course of OSB, near the eaves on the south side, was fairly easy to apply. We built a scaffold out of extra bales so Zej could slide the sheets from the back of Randy's truck onto the top of the bales, then push them up toward the eaves. From there, Randy grabbed the sheet and swung it sideways up toward me. Standing firmly on the top plate, with trusses to brace myself, it was easy for me to grab the other end of the sheet as it swayed in my direction. Then we slid it over the trusses into place and nailed it at the corners. Later we would have to go back and apply nails every six inches around the edges and every ten inches in the center area to pass the roof-nail inspection.

The second course was a little harder. Randy nailed several 2 x 4s on top of the OSB, near the bottom of the roof, both for him to stand on and so that when he swung the OSB, he could catch it on the 2 x 4—in case I missed. I stayed balanced in the trusses, catching the sheets as they swung my way, then trying not to trip over the hammer that hung from my tool belt as I stepped across the roof, truss to truss. It was cumbersome, but I was fine as long as I didn't look down. Randy was doing by far the most work. He seemed much more sure-footed than I as he stepped across the sheer boards.

The third course was harder for Randy, because he had to swing the OSB really high for me to reach it, but it was easier for me, because the trusses had horizontal braces near the ridge. I stuck my hammer upside-down in the pocket of my tool belt and maneuvered between trusses with relative ease. Then Randy finished off the highest part of the roof with smaller strips of OSB, which he managed all by himself. Since I wasn't really needed, I climbed back down the end gable and ladder, glad to be down on terra firma in one piece.

There were still several hours of daylight after we finished the south half of the roof, so we laid the first row of OSB on the north side before the light became too flat to work. With tired legs and a sense of accomplishment, I crawled into a hot bath of Epsom salts and ordered out for our usual Saturday night pizza. Since Randy was essentially on his way out of town, he just slept in his truck on the job site.

The next morning, we were both sore and moving slowly: Randy's arms, from swinging up the OSB; and my entire body, from gripping and balancing on the trusses all day. But we needed to cover the rest of the roof before sundown. After a late breakfast, we were back up on the north side of the house. Zej handed up the OSB again, reading his computer programming books between sheets. The day was warmer, sunny, and clear. Birds cheered us on from surrounding saguaro and treetops. This time, I enjoyed being high up in the crystal blue sky, eye to eye with the saguaros.

My legs were shakier—probably from a combination of fatigue and fear—as I maneuvered around the trusses that day. We repeated our routine with Randy swinging the sheets up to me, then both of us walking the OSB into place and nailing our ends, until the entire roof was covered, minus a three-inch gap on either side of the ridge for a heat vent and a small square for us to climb down through.

Since we had a couple of hours left in the day, we decided to go ahead and nail down the OSB. Every place that the wooden sheets met a truss, we needed lots of nails. Randy skillfully maneuvered around the very steep roof, gripping with his toes and nailing as he went. I balanced on 2 x 4s that Randy had nailed to the OSB and moved as little as possible, nailing everything I could reach from where I was perched and making sure I didn't look down because it would make me instantly dizzy. When I finished a section, Randy would help me move onto the next set of 2 x 4s, where I would plant myself as firmly as possible and resume nailing. Between thumps of my hammer, I was saying prayers and reminding the Universe that I didn't have medical insurance.

I heaved a huge sigh of relief as Randy declared that we had done all we could do without a really tall ladder to reach the lower edges of the OSB. I would do that myself later. After I crawled down from the roof through the little hole we had left in the trusses, Randy nailed it shut and climbed over the end of the gable down to the roof plate.

We paused inside the house, which now had a ceiling, noticing how much larger it felt with the high overhead vault. Stepping outside, we both reached for our cameras to capture the house with almost-a-roof in the golden rays before sunset.

As I reached the end of my roll of film, I realized very sadly that I had to say good-bye to another good friend. Randy would be driving to Palm Springs for a week-long camping trip with his brother and then northward to Colorado for the summer. Not only had we worked together for the last few months, but we had shared three sunset/moonrise hikes around the desert, comparing life experiences. I'd been around enough years to treasure such rare friends. But let go I must, and so I did, with a thank-you, a big hug, and hopes that our paths would cross again.

Chapter Twelve

# ROOF AND ROMANCE

*After a while you learn*
*the subtle difference between*
*holding a hand and chaining a soul*
*and you learn that love doesn't mean leaning . . .*
*And you learn that you really can endure*
*That you really are strong*
*And you really do have worth*
*And you learn, and you learn . . .*

—Virginia Shopstall, *"Comes the Dawn"*

SUMMER arrived early in Tucson. The winter had brought barely a handful of rainy days, so that only the hardiest wildflowers dared to open their petals into the hot sun. Brilliant orange poppies that usually carpeted the desert floor in the spring stayed securely beneath the ground, waiting for another year. I couldn't blame them. The driest winter in recorded history had merged into potentially one of the hottest summers.

By mid-April, thermometers were reaching the upper nineties, flirting with one hundred degrees, reminiscent of those sweltering days building the foundation. I pulled a new white overshirt out of my closet, since the one from last fall was largely in rags. Only the monsoon rains could rescue us and they might not arrive for three more months.

Though there was much work to be done beneath the baking sun, each evening as I climbed the west wall of the house to bask in the golden glow of the sunset, I glanced up at the roof sheathing. This summer I could work in the shade, refinishing and hanging the doors, framing the interior walls, plumbing, and wiring.

As the palo verde trees and creosote bushes burst forth into vibrant yellow blossoms, a new strength dawned in me. I was strong and tan now, probably in better shape than I'd been in the fifty years prior. I no longer craved leisurely weekends with friends, for building this house had become a way of life and a part of me. I looked forward to each weekend, finding fulfillment in the fresh air and anticipating the challenges. As darkness spread over the job site each Sunday evening, I regretted that there weren't more hours to keep going and see even more progress.

I especially loved the mornings when the air was cool and filled with birds flitting and chirping among the tree branches and saguaro tops. Quail cooed and scurried about their business among the shrubs, geckos darted across the sand, and occasionally a rabbit paused at the edge of the driveway to view the house's progress.

As soon as I pulled out my tools each weekend, Matts the cat would dart from his hiding place to assist with any project I began, especially if it involved wires, strings, or straw bouncing to and fro. If there was no fun in it for him, he would perch himself atop a bale or wide windowsill and majestically survey my progress.

People stopped by often now, and I did not feel alone. Some people were just curious to find out how one builds a house out of straw. Others came to help for a day, so they could experience construction before they began their own homes. I was usually willing to pause and chat, happy that no bank held a time frame for completion over my head.

After the top plate was completed in mid-March, I took a break from my own house to help Matts (the man, not the cat) and Judy with a wall raising. The day was a thoroughly festive event filled with familiar friendly faces. I remet many people from my own wall raising and from former workshops. My friend Mary with the straw bale compound was there, along with the draftsman Dan and my consultant Jon.

We chatted more than worked and had a delicious Mexican buffet lunch while entertained by Matts's washboard band. I felt honored to be included in the event. This was the first opportunity I had to talk to Jon, other than over the phone with a list of work-related questions. He was just as kind in person as on the phone, and offered to give me information on traveling to Rocky Point with the boys for spring break.

Rocky Point is the American name for Puerto Penasco in Mexico, at the tip of the Gulf of California. It's about a four-hour drive from Tucson and a favorite ocean escape for many Arizonans. I hadn't had anything like a vacation in a long time and I didn't want the boys to spend the entire spring break cooped up in our trailer, so I figured I'd take a weekend off construction and visit the ocean.

A week later, over a casual dinner, Jon drew me a map of Rocky Point, noting locations of an inexpensive hotel to spend the night, the best place to get tacos, a great restaurant on the hill for an elegant sunset dinner, and the various beaches. He also showed me where, in the town, he was finishing up a house that belonged to his ex-wife.

As the conversation turned to our lives, he casually made a comment about his metaphysical interests. Instantly, I perked up. The workings of the Universe have always been a passion of mine and rarely do I meet people who share this fascination. I wanted to learn more about this man, but at the same time this was more frightening for me than building the house. I was completely in awe of him for all his self-taught building knowledge and dependent on him to get my house finished. I was also well aware that romantic relationships can mess up good business relationships.

We were so free and easy together, however, laughing often and talking like old friends about our many interests in common, that I couldn't deny the attraction—and he had these delightfully deep, dark, brown eyes. I gathered enough from our conversations to know he was divorced, but I couldn't tell whether he had mended enough to be interested in a new relationship—or whether he already had one.

I should keep this as a friendship, I thought, at least until the house is completed. By then, we would really know each other, and there simply is no way on earth I should jump too fast into anymore relationships!

I worked pretty hard on talking myself out of pursuing anything but official consultation. Let's see: I was working full time, raising two boys, and building a house every spare minute. When, exactly, did I envision fitting in a relationship, anyway? I was doing very well on my own—well, sort of okay.

But love and logic have never played on the same team, and rightly so, or this would be a very dull world. One way or another, I had all sorts of questions to ask Jon, so the conversations continued. So did the laughter, along with my desire to sit down next to him over dinner again.

He didn't invite me, but since I was far less shy than in my high school years, I decided simply to be honest; I told him how much I enjoyed metaphysics and that a couple of things he said had sounded interesting. Could we have dinner and talk some more? He agreed, and so we met a week later for a quick dinner before an alternative construction slide show.

It was all very friendly, but I got a hug out of him and gleaned enough information to gather that he had no significant female in his life. I still wasn't sure whether he wanted one and had mixed feelings myself . . . okay, friends it would be. I had enough strain in my life without adding romance to the list.

About a month after our first dinner, in one of our phone conversations, I mentioned that I was going to Rocky Point the following Sunday and Monday with the boys.

"I'm going on Saturday and Sunday to work on the house," he added.

"Really? If you'll still be there on Sunday afternoon, we'll stop by and see the house."

"I'm not sure I'll still be there. I like to get home by sundown, which means leaving in the midafternoon."

"Oh, gee, then maybe we should come on Saturday and Sunday."

I think his voice perked up. "If you do, I'll take an hour or so to show you around Rocky Point."

"That would be great."

"And you could stay at the house. We have lots of mattresses."

"Really? Well, let me talk to the boys. I don't see why not. And I have this map that says there's a great restaurant on a hill to watch the sunset. I'll buy dinner."

And so it was that one weekend in mid-April we found ourselves in Mexico. Jon took much more than an hour out of his work to drive us around the town and drop us at a wharf for lunch and beach cruising. He even picked us up and drove us to another beach, where he poked around the tide pools in the reef with us until the sun lowered over the hazy blue ocean.

Taking deep breaths of the humid, salty air, listening to the lapping of waves on the sand and gulls squawking over their prey, reminded me of my leisurely childhood summers on the shores of Massachusetts and relaxed afternoons on the beaches of Kauai. But now, beside me, were my two sons who had grown taller than I—and Jon, this new friend who felt like an old friend. Our energies melded together as we joked and chatted through the afternoon.

After showers, we headed up the hill to a restaurant you would find only in Mexico, painted a bright blend of orange and purple. The balcony already churned with happy noises from crowded tables of beachgoers who had foregone the showers to come straight up for margaritas. Judging from the decibel level, they were way past their first round. A mariachi band circled through the tables, dodging waiters and playing requests, as the sun sank toward the orange horizon. I didn't care what it all cost as I soaked in the joyful atmosphere.

As the sun's last rays disappeared beneath the sea, the crowd burst into applause and the music resumed in full force. It was festive, just what I had imagined Mexico should be like. After dinner, I felt Jon's arm circle my waist as we walked toward the car. I wanted to continue the merriment by setting off a few fireworks on the beach, so Jon drove us to a spot next to a small hotel.

A full moon bathed the sand in pastel light and shadows, while faint music echoed across the beach. A brisk breeze sweeping in from the cool ocean nudged us into each other's arms for warmth, while the boys entertained us with a mini-fireworks display reminiscent of New Year's Eves around Hanalei Bay. Jon's embrace, which felt like a memory from my distant past and spoke to me even more deeply than his words, told me that he felt the attraction, too.

We talked and we hugged, dissolving emotional barriers as we bared our fears and dreams. Construction was far from our minds; we were simply a woman and a man, entwined in some mysterious bond.

While Jon worked the following day, the boys swam in the surf and chased each other up and down the beach with handfuls of seaweed. I sat on the beach reviewing my life and letting go of residue from my past relationships, determining that life was moving to new dimensions. All that I had been through had given me the strength to be who I was today. I thanked my turbulent past, blessed it, recalled the lessons, and bid the rest farewell. It was time to move forward in joy and hope.

That afternoon, I followed Jon's car down the open road between Rocky Point and the Mexican border, then across more open highway to the last gas station before the roads to our houses split in different directions. There, we paused for ice cream. We both knew that we weren't really saying good-bye; this wasn't an end, but a beginning, and we no longer needed excuses to get together. Though not even a kiss had passed between us, our souls had connected. The future was ours to create. Nothing could have amazed or delighted me more, when I had just about given up on relationships.

Our friendship and romance grew with a natural ease and joy. We could talk for hours over dinner about anything, and when Jon showed up at the job site, work became fun.

Jon, of course, was an expert with eleven years' experience building straw bale houses and a truckload of tools—actually, a truckload and a storage locker. However, this did not mean that he was going to build my house. Jon admired my determination to do as much as I could myself and wanted to see me live up to my goal.

It reminded me of my first childbirth, when I went into labor with the idea of doing everything naturally, without pain medication. When I was about halfway through the delivery, delirious from pain, ready to toss all natural ideas out the window and plead for whatever medication anybody would give me, my husband stood there and refused help, saying, "She's going to do this on her own."

Now Jon stood by me, saying he would guide me through each phase, answer questions, lend tools if he wasn't using them, and assist on extremely difficult tasks, but this house was mine to build. For a good part of the next year, he would be living and working on houses outside of Tucson anyway, finding only an evening here or there to come visit.

Surprisingly, there wasn't too much of me that wanted him to build the house, though I loved working alongside him whenever we got the chance. I had come to appreciate the joy of creation as I moved through each weekend's work and the confidence I gained by learning, learning, learning . . .

I respected Jon even more for not wanting to take over and simply impress me with his skills. He was able to put himself aside enough to see who I was and what I was about. Amazing. Working under his gentle, knowledgeable guidance became pure pleasure. I no longer felt that I was treading along the edge of a cliff that might crumble each time an inspector arrived.

The boys began to volunteer with the construction more enthusiastically, also. With the straw bale house right next to our trailer, they could work for an hour, then go back to their computer for an hour. Maybe they felt guilty, sitting in the cool house while their mother slaved away in the heat, but perhaps they were likewise discovering the joy of creating and accomplishment, watching the house take shape.

As May approached, the palo verde trees dropped their yellow blossoms, as the mesquite and ironwood trees burst into cascades of pale purple. Though the prickly pear pads were parched and wrinkled from lack of rain, they produced large waxy yellow blossoms. The tips of the saguaro stalks and arms gave birth to green knobs, which in turn transformed into lovely white lilylike flowers. They looked ridiculous, of course, like cumbersome, frozen giants with a handful of dainty daisies, or like lumberjacks sporting an outcropping of spiked hair on the tops of their otherwise shaven heads. But then, desert foliage originated from God's sense of humor, I'm quite sure. It wasn't meant to be taken seriously.

Andrzej volunteered to help me finish nailing down the sheathing after we returned from Rocky Point. The 2 x 4s that Randy had nailed over the OSB were still in place, so I gathered my courage and ventured onto the roof one more time. Zej walked lightly over the boards with a cup of nails in one hand and a hammer in the other. Barely daring to breathe, but with Zej as inspiration, I inched away from my 2 x 4 perches to reach new areas of the roof. Crouching low and pressing the toes of my shoes into the rough particleboard, I hammered very, very carefully. There was nothing to hang on to, so I didn't want to disturb my balance by missing the nail head.

The thuds of our hammers echoed through the open air for about three hours before we had nailed down the entire roof. Inching downward off the roof was worse than climbing up, but we both made it with great relief.

Phoning the county voice mail system, I scheduled the exterior sheathing and roof nail inspection for Tuesday then left the house plans and inspection sheet on the worktable. I determined to wait for another month's $1,000 payment from my parents and hire a full set of roofers to put on the metal sheets. I didn't want to set foot on that roof again!

Tuesday evening, after hurrying home from work to check the inspection sheet, I found a note from the inspector on my clipboard: "Rejected, see highlighted area on plans." Unable to imagine what could be wrong, I unrolled the plans. Highlighted in yellow were the words, "Engineered truss diagrams to be provided when requesting roof inspection. Truss calcs must be signed, dated, and wet sealed by an Engineer who is registered in Arizona. Truss calcs to be cross-referenced to floor plans."

Ack! Did I have to get the trusses engineered for a straw bale house? That could cost thousands of dollars! My trusses had been calculated by a computer program. I phoned Jon.

With his usual unruffled, soothing voice, he explained that when the trusses were delivered, the lumberyard should have given me a computer print-out with an engineer's seal on it and the engineering codes for the trusses. He assured me that this was perfectly sufficient for the inspectors. Every computer program had an engineer behind it.

The following day I phoned the lumberyard to find they had forgotten to give me that piece of paper. But no problem, they had me on file and would print one out. I rephoned the inspection for Thursday, April 21, got the paper, attached it to the inspection sheet on the worktable, and passed the inspection on the second try. Ten down, fourteen to go.

About a week later, as Jon and I were driving back from dinner, I said, "Now that Randy is gone, I'll need to find new carpenters to do my roof. Do you know anyone?"

He pointed to himself.

"You? Do you have time? You'd need someone to help, wouldn't you?"

"Yes, yes, and yes."

"It's really steep," I warned.

"I know; it's ridiculous."

And so, on a very hot weekend in mid-May, I found myself back up on the roof. I had phoned around town to see if I could rent rock-climbing equipment, but found none available. This time, Jon figured out a system of ropes attached to a piece of bent rebar that hooked into the heat vent opening at the ridge, then fastened to a strong belt at his waist.

The first task was to cover the entire roof surface with roofing tar paper. We weren't sure if the three-foot-wide rolls would slip off the roof, so Jon and I began cutting twenty-foot strips of paper, each holding an end and walking it up separate ladders, then stapling the strip into place with hammer tackers, heavy-duty staplers that spit out staples when they were hammered against the wood. I felt a little more sure-footed on the OSB now, but not much. As we covered the higher parts of the roof, I balanced on the ridge, moving Jon's ropes back and forth and sliding staples down to him.

The next step was to cover the tar paper with the metal roofing sheets that I had ordered before the wall raising. The two-foot-wide sheets of thin galvanized steel had raised ridges every few inches. They were large and cumbersome, but they weren't heavy. After a respite in the cool of the trailer, I took the easy task of lifting the long sheets and balancing them against the eave. Since Jon and Zej were more nimble on the roof than I, they climbed the ladder to screw the sheets into place with galvanized screws and rubber washers that sealed the hole where the screw penetrated the metal.

Zej perched himself on the ridge to screw in the upper corners of the metal while Jon tied himself into ropes and secured the lower edge. When thermometers hover around one hundred degrees, it's hard to say how hot black tar paper becomes, or silver metal, but my one trip up to assist them felt like visiting a pizza oven.

Slowly but steadily, metal covered the black paper in neat vertical rows. Zej courageously learned the art of balancing on the ridge while leaning his body weight behind the power screwdriver, pushing the screws through the metal. Jon smoothly lifted the sheets into place, helped Zej line them perfectly, and screwed his end down with ease. He had obviously done this before.

After eleven sheets, we were halfway done with the south side and both guys desperately needed a water break. We took refuge in the trailer again, seeking liquid and coolness. We all agreed there was no rush on this job, and the roof could be completed at a later date. Enough was enough.

Popsicles helped for a few minutes. Jon and I lay on the floor directly beneath the evaporative cooler, letting the moist, frigid air blast over us. In our dry desert climate, I use a cooler instead of an air conditioner, since it requires much less electricity. My evaporative cooler, a large fan and water pump inside a cage with fibrous pads on the sides, perched on the roof of the trailer. The pump dampened the pads while the fan blew the humid air though a duct in the ceiling. We left the bedroom louvers cracked open, so the air spread through the rooms, cooling us as it evaporated.

Early the next morning as I sat at my office desk, Jon called on his cell phone. "Good morning, how are you?" he asked.

"My legs are really stiff and sore," I remarked.

"Mine too, but I'm working it out," he said. "I decided to finish the side."

"You're on the roof?" I asked incredulously.

"Yes, before the heat sets in."

"Are the boys helping?"

"I think they're asleep. I didn't bother them. But I'm not being very quiet. I'm sure they can hear me and they'll come out if they want to help."

"Well, let them know that you're there. I'm sure they'll help. Thank you!" I wished I could hug him.

"No problem. We'll get you up here to screw all this down later. You'll need screws every three feet. I'm just doing the edges."

I received one more phone call looking for the bit to my screwdriver, which sounded as if the boys had joined him. As I drove up the driveway at the end of the day, I beamed with delight to see the south side of the roof covered with silver metal.

Completing the other side of the roof was more difficult than I had imagined, mostly because of the heat. We waited a few more weekends to see if the mercury would drop, but it stayed at about 105 every day. I spent my time on some other tasks.

In mid-June, while the boys were on Kauai visiting their father, Jon and I took a weekend trip to Rocky Point to escape the unrelenting heat and finish up some work on Jon's former house. When we returned on Sunday night, the sky above Tucson was filled with towering black thunderheads. Streaks of lightning darted across the mountaintops. Rolling down the windows, we let the musty smell of wet desert fill the car. Monsoons had arrived! We hadn't had rain since March and now my driveway showed signs of puddles!

The straw bale house had taken some water on the side where the roof wasn't completed. I hadn't thought to prepare for rain when we left, since the forecast was for more dry, baking weather. Tools on my bench were soaked and little cardboard boxes of nails were unraveling at the corners, but that didn't daunt the joy of desert rain.

We spent a few hours moving the worktable into the house, draining water out of the bottom of buckets, and replacing wet cardboard with dry containers. It was a good excuse to go through some of the mess on my tool bench, but it was also time to give the roof some priority.

However, despite all the work and excitement from the rain, in the pit of my stomach sat a tight little knot. Kitty Matts had failed to run out to greet us. He had been missing for a few days before we left, and now I knew he had fallen prey to the hungry desert coyotes. It was a risk I had taken. I had installed a cat door in the trailer, which led into a latticed laundry area. I covered the top with screening, but each morning, I'd find him proudly perched on the top of the trailer. Where he had found an escape hole, I never knew. He just loved the outdoors. I could empathize with that.

Seeing him chasing around the desert, attacking every little leaf that blew by, and joyfully being a part of the construction, the boys and I had decided to give up trying to cage him. I had hoped that somehow he'd be the one cat to survive the desert. He seemed so much a part of it. I bid him a silent good-bye, thanking him for the joy of his company.

We had only been here for a few months and had now lost two cats. Toonses had disappeared within a couple of days of our move into the trailer. She had darted out the front door, never to return. It was sad for us, but perhaps a blessing. Her seizures had become frequent and very extreme. I don't think she really knew us most of the time.

No more cats, I resolved firmly. Nailing a board across the cat door on the straw bale house, I vowed to become a bird person—feeding the wild birds and quail and enjoying the uncaged creatures of the open Sonoran Desert.

The following week, on June 22, as the boys returned from Hawaii, the perfect day arrived to finish the roof. Puffy white layers of glorious clouds—a rare sight in the desert—shaded the baking sun. While I went to the airport to get the boys, Jon lay the roofing paper by himself. Don't ask me how.

The boys had taken an overnight flight from Hawaii, gathering two hours of sleep at the most, so they were in no shape to be balancing on a 9:12-pitch roof. It was my turn. With my screw gun tied to my tool belt and my pouch filled with roofing screws, I climbed the ladder trying not to let fear overcome me. By now, I was learning how to focus on the roof and not look down at all.

Jon balanced down by the north eave, supported by his harness, rope and rebar hooked into the ridge vent. Grabbing the end of the rope, I pulled myself to the upper apex of the roof and straddled the ridge. J.J. rested the roofing sheets against the side of the house, and Jon slid them up to me. While he aligned the bottom, I laid the top in place. When we both agreed it was straight, we let our screw guns whir, placing screws into the shallower ridges at each end. Then the next sheet was slid up, aligned, and secured. We had our system down, now. By late afternoon, the whole side was covered with waterproof silver-hued steel and we could both rest our very weary legs.

Jon had a rash at his waist from the rope and a couple of slices on his leg where the edge of the metal sheets had brushed past. But that phase was completed and we were moving closer and closer to the day where we would never have to go on the roof again! The ridge still needed to be attached, and screws needed to be applied every three feet along the lengths of the metal. That would be another day.

That day arrived the following Saturday, July 1. It was a typical morning, hitting 85 degrees by eight in the morning and probably 100 by eleven. We sat inside the cool shade of the straw bale house, in our "thinking chairs," an old log chair that I found at Gerson's and a rocking chair that wouldn't fit under the tarp with the other excess belongings. We set these two chairs in the west end of the house with a fan blowing behind them and a small table in front, where we could contemplate the day's work and draw diagrams, if necessary.

At the ridge, we had to cover the gap between the two sides of the roofing, the heat vent, with window screen to block all bugs from entering through the vent. We then had to figure out how we could get up to the roof ridge—and how I could later screw down the roof—once the heat vent was covered and we had nowhere to attach the ropes.

I tried to figure out how we could fasten a rope all the way over the roof and then another rope through loops on our belts, the way rock climbers do. Then Jon suggested tying a ladder up on the roof. That seemed better, but one step further was to take my folding ladder and just bend the last section over the top of the roof and have the other three sections to climb up and down!

With that great inspiration, we donned our tool belts and ventured into the desert heat. The monsoon's humidity made it feel like a steam bath. Jon raised the ladder onto the roof and folded it over the ridge. I climbed hesitantly after him with a roll of screening. I tried to walk along the ridge with my heels in and toes out, as Jon showed me, but my leg muscles couldn't take it. I sat back down and shimmied along like a monkey. The metal roofing was very slippery.

As Jon stepped freely ahead of me down the ridgeline, his shoe must have caught on an uneven piece of metal, because all of a sudden he tripped. I saw his body stumble and fall onto the sloped roof. He lurched back to his feet, but slipped again on the slick surface. This time, as he slid down the roof, his hand instinctively reached up and gripped the ridge, ignoring the rough metal edge that cut his fingers. In another split second, he had stopped his fall and was climbing back up to the apex.

My heart was pounding and my hands were trembling, but Jon brushed it off as no big deal; he was thankful for his speedy reflexes. We examined the cuts on his hand, determining that he was fine to continue working. He cut himself all the time, he claimed.

I shimmied along the ridge, placing a row of screening over the vent, while Jon followed, securing the screening with screws. After we had placed two pieces of the ridge cap over the screening, we saw black clouds forming over the mountains. Thunder rolled through the hills. As a bolt of lightning crackled in the distance, we scurried down to safety, happily calling it a day. We left the ladder up on the roof so I could finish screwing down the metal sheets later.

On Sunday, I boldly climbed up onto the apex, moved the ladder directly over a roofing seam, slid a tape measure down the length of the roof, and marked the ladder every three feet where the screws should be placed. With both feet firmly on the rungs of the ladder, I could balance enough to press the screws with all my weight until they whirred through the metal sheets. Jon had taught me how to back off the screws just a little so I didn't stress and eventually crack the rubber washers beneath the screw heads.

When I had secured everything within reach of the ladder, I climbed back up to the ridge, sat down with a foot on either side of the roof, raised the ladder to a balanced position, moved it over a few feet, and climbed back down, setting screws every three feet. After an hour or so, I was sweating, puffing, and my legs ached from the strain. I climbed down to this wonderful, solid, secure planet Earth and vowed to continue just a little every day.

It took me three weeks, doing a little each day, to screw down the entire roof. Toward the end, the work seemed almost easy. I must have been growing muscles. With great thanksgiving, I finally climbed off the roof, vowing never to return.

In Hawaii, the completion of the roof is celebrated with a topping-off feast—often a luau or potluck for everyone who has worked on the house so far. That is not a tradition in Arizona as far as I had observed, and I didn't have much spare time or money for parties, anyway. Jon and I found a pint of Belgian chocolate pudding in my refrigerator. After the sun slipped behind the mountains and the desert cooled down, we climbed the scaffolding on the west end of the house, ate the pudding right out of the container, and watched a summer lightning storm streak through the black valley. It was a thoroughly enchanting celebration.

## Chapter Thirteen

# WINDOWS
# AND DOORS

*We find greatest joy, not in getting, but expressing what we are. Men*
*do not really live for honors or for pay; their gladness is not in the tak-*
*ing and holding, but in the doing, the striving, the building, the living.*
*It is . . . fun to have things, but more to make them.*

—R. J. Baughan

Once the roof was on, it seemed as if the house should be almost completed, but quite the opposite. Counting the myriad steps ahead of me, I
faced a stairway leading into the clouds and beyond—windows to be
mounted, doors to be hung, gable ends to be framed, eaves to be covered,
ceiling to be insulated, subfloors and floors to be laid, loft to be built, 1,280
square feet of exterior wall to be plastered, slightly less interior wall to be
finished, spiral staircase to be constructed, electric wiring and its fixtures to
be wound through the trusses, plumbing and its fixtures to be run through
the walls, kitchen counters and cabinets to be built, shower tile to be
applied, fire sprinkler system to be installed, and probably plenty more I
wasn't even thinking of.

And once that was completed, the entire porch area awaited construction while the barren, scraped desert cried out for a garden . . .

All I could do was begin and keep working, propelled by the vision of
a real bed in a cozy, friendly home that was the product of my sweat and
dreams, and hopefully a legend for my grandchildren. This house already
felt like a mansion after living in the trailer for six months.

Trailer life was fairly functional and almost comfortable. My room
became a den during the day, with my computer as the factotum, to balance

my very active checking account, scan in photos for my Web page, and serve as a word processor for my writing. If my construction journal was to be accurate, I needed to write it as I went along, even if that meant staying up a little later at night or getting up at dawn. I would never remember all these details and experiences at a later time. When I wasn't home, my computer was also a receptacle for games networked over to the boys' computer.

We stored Andrzej's stage amps in front of my futon during the day. They were on wheels, so when night came, I turned off the computer, rolled the amps over to that side of the room and unfolded my futon. Likewise, I moved the room fan around on its extension cord so that it faced the computer during the day and the futon at night.

The evaporative cooler, which would later be moved over to the new house, kept the trailer livable all summer. When the humidity soared during the monsoon season of July and August, the mobile home felt almost tropical, reminiscent of summer nights in Hawaii. The ceiling grew a little saggy and soggy, but the plants loved it and so did my parched skin. This was the first time I had gone through a summer without an air conditioner and I was actually quite surprised how comfortable it was. Judging by my utility bills, the cooler's electricity consumption was about half that of an air conditioner.

At night, I used a regular fan to stay cool and opened one of the louvered windows in my bedroom for a cross breeze. The only drawback of this was unannounced visits from Alien Kitty in the middle of the night. Raised in the desert after losing his mother to coyotes, Alien was a wandering rogue with no use for cat doors; a cracked louver was an invitation to visit. He'd climb onto the trash can outside, or a few spare bales, then make a flying leap for the window.

Inside, I would bolt awake to hear something crashing and scratching at the wall. Eventually, the clawing would lessen as he forced open the louvers with his nose and front paws. I'd feel his furry body straddling my neck and hear his motorlike purrs through my leftover dreams. I had to cover myself completely with my blankets or he would likewise decide that an uncovered hand was an invitation for kitty play.

Usually, I would wake up enough to push him into the main room where I kept bowls of dry food and water, then close the door behind him. By morning he would be ready to leave, allowing me to open the front door for him, perplexed by my vain attempts to push him through the small swinging panel in the back door.

I had admired his soft markings since he was a tiny kitten who showed up at the wall raising with some brothers and sisters that had long since vanished, along with Matts. But somehow, this cat survived. He wasn't as orange as the others, more of a soft peach color with a white face and large white paws. His light, oval face with large, dark eyes had inspired his name.

And while he had mastered the art of dodging coyotes, he was a typical snuggle-kitty around humans. He charged through our windows as soon as we arrived home in the evenings, not for food, but for cuddling. Except for the day that he knocked over the rack of drying dishes as he tried to exit the kitchen window, he was a pretty fun kitty.

The main room of the mobile home contained not only the boys' computer, but our stereo and TV, couch, dining table, chairs, bird cage, and lots of formerly outdoor plants that had been falling prey to the rabbits. I had to bring them inside and fit them in any available nook—on the refrigerator and under the bird cage—so they wouldn't be munched bare.

The trailer sloped considerably to the northwest; I had hired the least expensive movers to set it up and I got what I paid for. The evaporative cooler runoff and the gutters all drained into the downhill side. Consequently, the more it rained, the more the blocks supporting the northwest corner of the trailer sank into the moist ground.

But it was temporary, we told ourselves: motivation to get the straw bale house built. Someone once told me to select an old, beat-up construction trailer for just that reason. If it's too comfortable, the construction period will take twice as long.

Besides, a little slope has its advantages. We knew which side of the house to search for the rubber-band ball and other lost kitty toys. Also, it was easy to know which side of the dinner plate should hold the ketchup or the salad dressing. I used shims to keep the hot plates level and we all got to the point where we barely noticed the slant.

We gave up a few luxuries, such as the newspaper, after we found there really was no room to open and read it. J.J. discovered school projects to be a real challenge when large poster boards were involved, and we didn't even consider unrolling the house plans with more than one person at home. But the trailer became home sweet home for the short hours each day that we occupied it. Since I was either at the office or the straw bale house, Zej was busy with his music, and J.J. spent most of his time at his girlfriend's house, we rarely got in each others' way.

Installing windows and doors was my next step, along with framing in the gable ends of the house—the triangles above the top plate and below the trusses at each end of the house. Even though I had my home improvement books for reference, the questions for Jon were still endless. What kind of paper do I use for water-proofing the edges of the windows?

What kind of screws should I use to fasten the window frames? How do I fit the window into the buck? How do I frame in an old, recycled door? How do I fasten the doorjamb to the concrete stemwall?

He drew me more diagrams and answered every question patiently. Since I had to complete the house on the remaining approximately $5,000 from my parents' gift, which was getting eaten up faster than I predicted (of course), Jon suggested I not even build the sunroom and just focus on the interior. As with the porch, that could be built later with mortgage money.

It seemed like a good idea, except that I was anxious to get the aviary built for my cockatiels. Once in their new home, they could experience the joy of flight with full wings, have a water fountain to splash in, and room to avoid each other when they weren't getting along. Most of the day, Merlin and Arthur were the trailer's only occupants, as we all scurried in various directions. I varied radio stations to keep them company while we were gone. To keep them from feeling too cooped on some evenings, we shut all the windows against Alien Kitty, and opened their cage door.

Soon, as Arthur became brave enough to try his wings and fly around the limited space of the trailer, one of his favorite perches became the top of Jon's sparsely follicled head. Merlin's wings were not well trained. He lost altitude or flew into walls. We would inevitably have to catch him and endure his bites to get him back into the cage. Once he discovered the joy of spreading his wings, we discovered ways to get him back in the cage without getting bitten. An aviary would be wonderful, but it wasn't a necessity, so I decided to postpone the porch construction.

Jon accompanied me to the building department to request permission not to build the porch or the sunroom. With diagrams of how we would attach it later, the building inspector agreed, and made a note to that effect on the plans. I would need to resubmit the plans when I decided to build it. That was fine with me.

So, in late May, while I was waiting for the roof to cool down, I proceeded with the window installation. To keep myself from getting heat exhaustion, I bought a plastic blow-up pool that I put underneath our trampoline, in the shade, using leftover pieces of OSB as a platform. It was my little oasis from the heat. Amazingly, the water stayed quite cool under there, and I found that a midafternoon dip lowered my body temperature enough that I could work all day in the ovenlike conditions.

The bucks for each window had been constructed to fit the bale height, not the window height, so each one needed a wooden frame built either on the top or the bottom. When we had built the roof plate, I studied how the carpenters drew diagrams of exactly what they were going to build before beginning, measured to the sixteenth of an inch, made a double "V" mark and cut very precisely. Now, as I installed the windows, it was my turn to do the same. Like a true professional, I found myself making notes on leftover scraps of wood and sticking them in my pocket as I headed to the lumber store.

For the dining area windows, which I had mounted too high, I added a box above the windows that I stuffed with straw. For the other windows, I framed in a narrower box at the bottom of the window, which I likewise insulated. They often came out less than precise and perfect, as my carpentry skills took a little time to blossom.

On the outside of each buck, I first stapled black stucco paper over the wooden frame. Then, with the boys to help lift and hold, I fit the windows in place and fastened their metal flanges with rust-proof exterior screws. After caulking the upper edge of the window and covering the flange with another layer of paper, the window was in. It all was fairly easy—compared to roughing-in the plumbing, that is.

As I headed out to work one Saturday, I noticed a rancid smell coming from the saguaro by the sunroom. Walking around to its south side, I spotted a sticky liquid oozing out of some holes and cracks in its surface. Examining further, I spotted a rotten ring around its middle, about five or six feet above the ground, that was the source of the ooze.

One of its arms was leaning sideways, ready to fall off. My heart sank. This was my guardian saguaro, from which the first measurements for the house had been made. I wondered if we had dug too close to its roots and if so, if we could save it. Towering over the ridge of my roof, it must have stood in this spot for a hundred years or more. I wanted to be a part of preserving the desert, not destroying it.

I called a horticulture expert at the Tohono Chul Park to ask for his advice. He agreed to come view the cactus the following Monday evening. When he arrived, he took one look at the saguaro and said it was a good thing I hadn't waited any longer—this one was dead on its feet. It was old and dying a natural death, he said, but I was sure that all our digging had hastened its demise.

He estimated that it weighed about eight tons! Fortunately, it was leaning away from the house. We needed to cut it down and this was extremely dangerous. Since saguaros are not made of solid wood, but have only a single circle of ribs supporting them, they can snap off erratically.

Retrieving his chain saw from his van, he asked us all to stand back and watch the arms of the saguaro carefully. The arms could fall as the tall cactus trembled from the chain saw, of course crushing him as they did so. We were supposed to yell at him over the noise of the saw if we saw anything breaking.

We all backed off and watched with bated breath. First, he went beneath the large arms on the south side of the cactus, away from the house. Revving the saw, he cut a wide notch at the base. The arms jiggled and sagged, but they stayed in place.

Then he went around to the north side and swiftly cut through the stem toward the notch. As he completed his cut, the gentle giant gave up its stance and collapsed into the desert, away from the house, with an earth-shaking thud. I watched sadly, but thankfully. I couldn't imagine what would have happened had it fallen onto the straw bale walls.

We measured its length at about thirty feet and bid it farewell. I would leave it in place to rot, replenishing the desert soil that tractors had scraped bare. If I didn't disturb the corpse, its rib structure would remain and hopefully I could use the ribs to line the semicircular wall around the spiral staircase or build cabinet doors.

During the weekday evenings, I had been refinishing the doors, removing the old finish, then roughing up the wood with a wire brush to give them a rustic look. I worked in the quiet of the half-built house, with the creatures of the desert buzzing and chirping in the darkening twilight beyond its open doors. The only human noise was the gentle brush of my scraper against the wood. Becoming intimate with every little grain and knot in the wood, cleaning out the tiny corners, and chipping away at the old paint to make way for the new finish became a peaceful joy in itself. Perhaps I'd take up whittling when this house was completed. I could almost imagine myself in a rocking chair on the front porch, carving away at an old piece of wood, while the desert sang to me . . .

In mid-June, Jon informed me that I really should let him help me hang the doors; this was not as simple as it seemed. I had no problem with that, whatsoever. We went to the building supply store together and Jon pointed out the best kind of jamb with rubber weather-stripping to seal out the rain. We also bought three dead-bolt locks with matching keys for all three doors so I could have the same key for all three doors—nothing like thinking ahead!

The door bucks were eighteen inches wide and, while I had mounted the windows on the outer side of their bucks, I decided to put the doors on the inner side to make a little entryway and save weathering of the doors. The bucks had been framed about three inches wider than the door, so we had plenty of room for the doorjamb.

Using a four-foot level and checking carefully for the most vertically plumb side of the door buck, Jon screwed the first side of the jamb into place. It only required a very small shim to make it perfect. Then, laying the bottom sill in place on top of the concrete stemwall, he leveled it with tiny pebbles, because even with all our care on the foundation, the stemwall wasn't perfectly level. Jon filled the gap under the sill with Heavy Duty Liquid Nails caulking, which dried into rock-hard glue. Then we lined up the second vertical jamb. This side would hold the hinges and bear the entire weight of the door.

I held the "leg" carefully in place, checking the vertical both front-to-back and side-to-side several times with a long level while Jon worked his way up the plank. Sliding pairs of shims in and out until the perfect level was reached, he screwed the jamb securely in place. The top piece of the jamb needed to be cut slightly to fit the rectangle and screwed very carefully into place so the wood didn't crack. Then we mounted the hinges from the doorjamb onto the side of the door and Jon cut the door to allow for a half-inch sweep on the bottom. Voilà, the house had its first door!

Since Jon was becoming increasingly busy with other houses and various jobs to ground hi-tech buildings for lightning, I decided to hang the back door myself. After placing one vertical "leg" and the sill, I showed Jon how perfectly level it all was. He agreed that it was all very straight, but there was this one small problem—I hadn't left enough room on the other side of the threshold for the other vertical jamb. We were about a quarter-inch short of the space needed.

Somewhat chagrined, I suggested that I should chisel out the threshold that I had glued in with Liquid Nails and unscrew the jamb, but Jon insisted that it would be much easier just to bash the base of the buck to create the needed space. Bashing—the supreme delight of working with straw.

We didn't have a big pounding mallet, so he just took one of the heavy CMU blocks with both hands, backed up to the jamb, and rammed it between his legs. The buck moved almost enough to give us the needed room; now we were only about an eighth of an inch short. One more whack and the job was done.

Now I had room to install the other leg of the jamb. Once again, Jon was busy and it was up to me. Even though I tried to be careful, without anyone to hold the leg while I screwed it in place, the side of the jamb ended up about an eighth of an inch out of plumb. I rescrewed it a couple of times, then decided this had to be within the range of "acceptable."

When I began construction of the house, I thought I wouldn't mind things being crooked as long as they held together, but I was changing my mind. Crooked construction, as in my foundation form and roof plate experience, often made for extra hours of figuring, redoing, and added costs to make the next phase fit. It was far easier just to do it right the first time. Straw was the exception, somewhat. It could be bashed, sculpted, and weed-whacked into shape as long as the house corners weren't involved. Those couldn't budge.

Jon arrived the following weekend to do the final tuning on the jamb, attach the top piece, the bottom sweep, and hang the door. It fit absolutely perfectly—swung open evenly, closed with a smooth glide, and latched with only the slightest push. What a joy!

With the main doors in place, I was ready to lath. Metal lath is aluminum mesh that is cupped to catch stucco on one side and precision-tooled to slice any human flesh that comes near it. I could simply walk by a stack of metal lath on the ground, then look down and see blood running from my ankles. After a few hours of applying lath, no matter whether I wore gloves or how cautious I was, my hands would be covered with small cuts and crusted blood. It was just part of the process.

There is much discussion in the natural building world on how metal lath does not mix with straw and earth plasters because metal expands and contracts at rates different from clay and straw, so may later cause cracks in the plaster. It also can rust. Burlap is considered preferable for covering smooth surfaces that need to be plastered.

In my case, the lath wouldn't be taking much water, so I wasn't worried about the rust. The lath, as I understood it, would strengthen the joint where straw might slip against the wooden bucks, so the plasters wouldn't crack in that area. Putting burlap over the bucks wouldn't help that issue, but I didn't really have to decide, because I had codes to pass and those codes required metal lath at all windows and doors, extending six inches into the straw. Period.

Jon recommended that the lath should form a relatively straight line from the wood to the straw, in order to strengthen the connection. Also, if the straw stuck out from the window more on one side than on the other, which it usually did, the window would look crooked. He said that I'd want to trim the ends off the straw walls before I covered the bales with earthen plasters.

Wielding a weed whacker at shoulder height, he skimmed over the bulge of one bale, sending straw flying in all directions, trimming it back to the level of the window buck. When the cloud of golden dust settled, the bale was sculpted straight across, leaving tightly packed straw where loose ends had previously protruded.

"It depends on the look you want, also. How much funk do you want in the outer walls? You can make them perfectly straight with this, or just use it to take the loose ends off the straw and leave the walls a little lumpy."

From my experience using earth plasters, I knew that it was much easier to get the mud to stick to a firm bale than to uneven, loose straw ends. So the next weekend, I strengthened my upper arms further by learning the fine art of vertical straw whacking. It wasn't too difficult as long as I climbed up the A-frame ladder, so that I was whacking at chest height or lower and not right in front of my eyes.

The swirling piece of fishing line cut a narrow groove into the bales, sending bits of straw and often bits of rock and sticks in all directions. My shins often got blasted, and I needed a face mask to breathe through the flying swirl of straw dust.

As I learned to skim the weed whacker lightly over the surface of the straw, I watched clean angles form around the windows and major bumps in the wall smooth into gentle curves. I didn't mind a few lumps in my walls—after all, this was a straw bale house—but I could see that the plasters would be much stronger when the wall was essentially a flat surface.

While the side of the metal lath near the windows could be nailed or screwed into the wooden bucks, the other side needed to be fastened into the straw with long staples made of heavy fencing wire. With two pairs of pliers, Jon showed me how to bend the corner of a piece of wire neatly into a right angle to form a staple. However, when the next lath-day came, I strained and groaned with my pliers, trying to manipulate this wire into a sharp right angle. Apparently I hadn't developed the muscles necessary for thick wire bending yet.

Each window needed at least thirty staples, and as I was in no mind to spend half a day straining over the staples for each window, I figured there had to be an easier way. Centering the two-foot piece of wire over the end of a sawhorse, I bent it into a large upside-down "U." To make the corners into nice ninety-degree angles, I hammered the center of the staple onto the sawhorse until it was flat. Using this method, I could make thirty staples in about ten minutes.

I worked my way around the house with wire staples and short nails, lathing every window and door buck into place. When I reached the cat door, I sighed. Decisions. I had nailed a board over the flap, vowing to allow no more cats into my life after Matts kitty's death. But Alien Kitty was becoming quite domesticated. Not only was he spending most of his days curled on our sofa, enjoying the coolness of the house, but he was learning how to enter through that funny little flap in the back door. We had yet to discuss what to do about neutering him if he intended to make himself at home . . . but in a spurt of optimism, I pried the board off the cat door and lathed around it.

## Chapter Fourteen

# GABLES AND EAVES

*Formulate and stamp indelibly on your mind a mental picture of*
*yourself succeeding. Hold this picture tenaciously. Never permit it to*
*fade. Your mind will seek to develop the picture.*

—NORMAN VINCENT PEALE

BY midsummer, I took my awakening carpentry skills to the gable ends—the open triangles above the top plate and beneath the roof on each end of the house. Since the straw bales stood only as high as the top plate, the gable ends were completely open. The east end would contain the loft and a 4 x 4-foot window in the center, which would need a frame. Since the east end was in the shade for the hottest part of the day, I could frame and insulate the gable wall, rather than stuff it with bales, and leave much of the top plate exposed as a long shelf in the loft, or mezzanine as we called it on the floor plan.

A baking Saturday in July was spent constructing the window frame on the ground, trying to make it fit the gable opening exactly. This proved extremely difficult, not only because a family of hornets had settled into a gap in the wall beneath the top plate and disliked my pounding over their heads, but also because the top plate was convex, pushed down on each end by the weight of the trusses and up in the center by an oversized bale.

I tried to cut the 2 x 4s at odd angles and nail them together to fit the slope, with an exact square to fit the window in the center. With one end of a rope tied to the window frame and the other end slung over the end truss, I pulled the heavy window frame into place on the ten-foot-high roof plate. J.J. supported it from beneath while he climbed a ladder—only to find it didn't quite fit.

Fortunately, the frame was too small, so I could still get it into its space. But from then on, I found it much easier to construct things bit by bit on the ground and assemble them in place. The top plate was simply too uneven for premeasuring large areas. I framed in the rest of the east end with 2 x 6s standing sixteen inches apart. There was a certain creative joy to making a perfect cut, sinking the nails, and watching the wall appear.

The west gable would take some real thought, for I wanted to place a small stained-glass window in the very center of the triangular area. This west end took too much afternoon heat for a large window, but it would be the most visible part of the house from the driveway. On the outside, I wanted the stained glass to be the center of a symbol that I planned to etch into the stucco. On the inside, the gable would be the top of a niched area where I could rest some plants or baskets above the top plate. The rest of the gable wall would be as thick as the roof plate, filled with half bales for insulation.

Jon again patiently drew me diagrams of how I could construct all this. He built a frame for the stained glass sandwiched between a piece of safety glass and regular glass. I did the rest, again working with the odd angles of the roof plate and trusses. Framing in the exterior side of the gable wasn't too hard, since I could stand on the roof plate. Then, when a friend was visiting, he hoisted half bales onto the roof plate for me.

Framing the interior wall of the gable was more awkward. Straw bales poked me in the ribs and face and blocked the swing of my hammer on one side. A truss three inches away from my hammer stifled my movements on the other side, and there was no place to stand except the upper rungs of the ladder. Every few minutes, I had to climb down and move the ladder another foot, then climb back up.

My patience was definitely tested. Four-letter words crept toward my lips—a rare occurrence! With growing respect, I thought of carpenters who frame walls every day for a living. At least I knew that once the task was completed, I would never have to do it again—ever.

At the end of the day, my body ached and groaned as I climbed down from the ladder rungs. A few nails were protruding in places where I could not reach the hammer to drive them the last half inch. But the boards were in place and the bales would not fall.

Later, when Jon surveyed my work, he mentioned that I could have done it all much more easily using a cordless power screw gun and screws instead of trying to swing a hammer. Live and learn. Well, that's why I hired a consultant.

The next day, I sent my sore body back up the ladder on the outside of the gable to cover the framing with OSB sheets. Here I was again, just as in the foundation days, with heavy boards of compressed wood and glue that took advanced strategy to move all by myself.

Now, the top plate was ten feet above the stemwall and the apex of the roof was about twenty feet high, so when I was balanced on the upper rungs of my sixteen-foot ladder to reach these areas, I was teetering pretty darn far above the ground, by my calculations.

I measured the first piece four feet horizontally along the top plate from the corner, dropped a plumb line at the four-foot mark, and then measured the height of the plumb line. I also measured the height to the roof at the corner. With all those numbers in my head, I climbed back down the ladder and sawed a large rhomboid to fit the space.

However, as I headed back toward the ladder with the four-foot sheet under my arms, I realized I couldn't possibly climb the rungs while holding it. And I certainly couldn't keep it in place vertically while I nailed. I wondered how carpenters did this.

I tied a towrope around the sheet, climbed to the top of the ladder, and slung the end of the rope over a truss. Tugging on the rope, the piece of OSB slowly rose into place. But I had to nail the OSB onto the truss, from which the rope hung, so I had to untie it before nailing.

Bracing the sheet with both my hands and all my strength, it was all I could do not to fall off the ladder or drop the sheet. How in heaven's name would I be able to take a nail out of my pouch and hammer it into place? I would need at least four hands, by my calculations, and I only had two.

If I dropped the sheet, I would probably destroy it and possibly the window below me. OSB is not only very heavy, but it can splinter and break quite easily. As I balanced on the top rung, I remembered Jon telling me sometime back that this would be difficult and I should cut small pieces that fit the various sections of the truss, so I could manage them. I'd remember that for the next piece, but for now, I was up here and I needed help!

"Andrzej! Help! J.J.!" I hollered toward the trailer, hoping to rouse the boys, who had been up late the night before.

"What?" I heard their voices echo across the barren desert.

"I'm stuck up here on this ladder. I need help!"

Andrzej came running out of the mobile home. At my direction, he retrieved Jon's extension ladder from inside the straw bale house and propped it against the wall next to me. Scaling to the upper rungs, he reached over and held the board in place while I quickly and eagerly pounded a few nails into place.

"Thank you!" I exclaimed when we were safely on terra firma. "I may need your help again, but from here on out, I'm cutting smaller pieces. That was too scary!"

From then on I cut only two-foot pieces of OSB and lifted them into place with relative ease. I learned that if I started a few nails near the edges before I left the sawhorses, I could use the protruding nails as handles, holding the wood in place with one hand and pounding the nail with the other.

Still feeling like a contortionist, my foot movement limited by the rungs of the ladder, I leaned as far as my hammer would reach to cover the gable ends slowly but surely with particleboard. As I made my final descent from the top of the ladder that afternoon to dip in the wading pool and cool off, my entire body ached. My feet felt like they had ridges on the bottom from standing on ladder rungs for two days, my arms and shoulders were stiff and sore from holding and pounding, and even my stomach hurt from the twisting and lifting.

My five air-conditioned days in an office would be a godsend after just two days of working in the desert heat. The people in my office were by now quite accustomed to my Monday morning bruises, sore muscles, or sunburn. Many of them would stop by my desk to see if I'd made it through the weekend in one piece.

Before I tackled the east gable the following weekend, I decided to cover the eaves—the gap along the north and south walls, between the roof and top plate.

Fortunately, this work was a mere ten feet above ground, so I worked easily from the extension ladder. With a special holster for my screw gun on my tool belt, I mounted my ladder with hammer, nails, screws, and screw gun so I could screw in the areas under the roof where it was too hard to swing a hammer. It was fun to see myself learning the tricks of the trade and increasing my efficiency. My cuts were becoming more and more precise—well, most of the time. Nevertheless, it took two full days to fill in the eaves. My legs still ached from spending sixteen hours on the top of a ladder, and my arms hurt from constant hammering and screwing. I even had "screw gun burn" on my right thumb. I kept staring at the gable ends, dreading the day I had to climb a twenty-foot ladder to cover them with metal lath.

Jon sympathized completely. One Friday in early July, he called me at the office. He had found some used scaffolding in two six-foot segments, which would reach twelve feet high, for seventy dollars. Would I like him to pick it up for me?

"YES!" I exploded into the quiet StarNet lobby.

While I could still say "I" was building this house, it struck me that this project was too vast for any one person, no matter how large and strong the person was, and regardless of whether she worked in an office full time or had years of construction experience. Sometimes it simply took another pair of hands to hold the other end of a plank or lift a bale. Often, it took two minds tossing ideas back and forth to come up with a solution.

I thought back on the many people who had toted bales for the wall raising, the Steens' floor plan, Kathy's bargain shopping, Lonny's crew who had rescued the foundation, my parents' money, my sons' help, Mark's assistance to prepare for the wall raising, Randy and Jerry's carpentry, and now Jon.

My workbench was stacked with his tools—hammer tackers, table saw, jigsaw, sanders, wire wheel on an electric drill, router, sawsall, weed whacker, and a five-hundred-watt light so I could work in the evenings. I needed every one of the tools and had no idea what it would have cost me to buy or rent them all.

In my wildest dreams, I never imagined meeting someone who would be so much help with the house and such a great companion. Not only did he assist me with construction, but he also understood the frustrations, the aches, the pains, and the triumphs. Sometimes, the workings of the Universe amaze me. Jon knew what would be necessary before I did, and my path was paved with tools and instructions before I arrived at the threshold. It became clear that I wasn't building this house alone, any more than we ever do anything alone.

In all honesty, I was a pretty good match for Jon, too, for how many women will happily spend their Saturday evenings at Home Depot, drooling over the latest power tools? And as much as he sympathized with my sore muscles, I could empathize with his.

My costs on the house were now at about $27,000 and there was much, much to go. For calculation purposes, I called my house a thousand-square-foot house with the loft, so that was $27 per square foot at this point. Not bad. I had about $4,000 yet to come from my parents and then I was on my own.

It was easy to slip back into fear about the project, wondering if I would find myself stranded with no more money and no occupancy permit. But it was also getting easier to guide my mind out of old, bad habits of worrying. If this project were destined to be cut short, it could have happened many times already. This house was blessed, and the best thing I could do was acknowledge that and work with the consciousness that the money would arrive as it was needed.

One day in July, while driving to work on the open roads of the Saguaro National Monument, I received an inspirational flash to sell my nice, cushy Honda Accord with the cruise control, CD player, and power everything. It was worth somewhere around $7,000. My commute was only a few blocks on a bumpy dirt road, but that was enough to beat up the car anyway. I had replaced four motor mounts, an axle, and a cracked radiator since moving onto the property.

The car would be much happier in some paved neighborhood. All I really needed was a truck like Andrzej's 1988 Nissan pickup. I traded cars with him anyway on most weekends and Fridays so I could haul materials.

I offered to buy his truck from him for $3,000, which was what we had paid for it. With that, he could buy himself a car. The only reason he had purchased a truck was because of my insistence that we needed one for the house construction. He enthusiastically agreed.

Andrzej had graduated from high school in May and immediately took a job posting the *Arizona Daily Star* onto the Internet in the wee hours of the morning. He had already saved a few thousand dollars that he could use to buy a respectable car.

I would, of course, remove the large flame decals from the sides of the truck and the homemade "End Our Pain" high school bumper sticker. The extra $4,000 should get me through to the final permit—and no vision could possibly be more exciting.

Some days, I felt such a wonderful connection with the Universe on the entire project that energy surged through my Being. Since Jon's slip on the roof, I began each day and each ladder climb with a prayer, asking for strength, safety, and guidance. When I felt the first signs of fear begin to quaver inside me, I switched my brain chatter to affirmations of the guidance that was flowing through me and took deep breaths to calm myself. My meditations expanded from quiet evening moments to calm, concentrated activity.

But then again, on many days I was exhausted; my muscles ached, my head throbbed, and I didn't have the mental strength to lift my own spirits. Building was just plain hot, grungy work with the summer plodding along with temperatures ranging between 103 and 110. On the hottest days, I scheduled simpler tasks and worked fewer hours, knowing these were the times when I was at the greatest risk of injuring myself. At these times, I was very thankful to be in the trailer and that I had no time limits for this construction.

As for Kathy's threats to sue me, well, whatever would happen, would happen. Last February she had insisted that six months was long enough for me to finish the house and she regretted giving me the trailer. She indicated that her situation had changed, but she really didn't explain the reasons behind her big shift in attitude. She just thought that since she had loaned the mobile home to me, I should return it when she asked for it. I let her know this was impossible, since I was building on $1,000 per month and my best estimates were that I would be done by the end of the year. There was no way I would be able to move into the straw bale house by the summer. That just made her more angry.

I received a letter from her attorney in June threatening to sue me for fraud if I didn't return the trailer's title and the trailer to her immediately. Her attorney had a post office box for a return address, instead of a law firm, so I didn't take him too seriously. Kathy was beyond reasoning with and I couldn't move out of the trailer until the house was done, so there really wasn't much I could do but worry. I decided not to do that.

With the scaffolding securely mounted by the east gable, I happily ascended the metal bars in mid-July to apply black stucco paper to the gable ends. That was fairly simple. I could cut strips with a utility knife, hold the paper in place with one hand and secure it with a hammer tacker from the other hand.

Then, wearing gloves, I laid twenty-eight inch by eight foot strips of metal lath horizontally over the paper, balanced it in place with my forehead while I hammered the first roofing nail to hold it, and then cut it at the roofline with tin snips.

I didn't think much of the work until Rudy, my neighbor with the horses, wandered over as I was about halfway through the lath. He had an electric staple gun in his hand.

"I seen you up there pounding those nails and I figured you're gonna be up there all day. So, I brought you this." He held out an electric staple gun. "You got power?"

"I sure do, thanks."

"The guys at work just staple on the lath with this. It takes a little push, but it will be much faster than pounding them nails."

"Wow, thanks!" I scaled down the scaffolding, happy for a break.

"I've been watching you up here," he said. "You're really something. People drive by wondering what you are doing. I just tell them you're crazy." He grinned.

I laughed. "You're probably right. I'll be really glad when this upper structural stuff is completed and I can work at ground level."

"Yeah. You got more energy than anybody I ever seen, working in this heat and everything."

"I don't have much choice. I soak my shirt in water and then use the evaporative cooling. I also work on whatever side of the house is in the shade."

"Like the Mexicans, huh? Work in the morning, then siesta in the hot afternoon, and work again in the evening."

"Yes, something like that."

We called Jon, who said that the electric staple gun wouldn't be strong enough to penetrate the OSB. But Rudy also had a compressor, and Jon had a power stapler that would fit the compressor, so I still had hope for easier work ahead of me on the west gable.

We chatted until the sky turned fluorescent orange, silhouetting the tall saguaros. I needed to secure the piece of lath I had left flopping at the edge of the gable. I thanked him again and scaled the scaffolding. My right wrist and forearm felt strained and sore, so I just cut the metal to fit with tin snips, tacked it with a few nails, and called it a weekend.

The compressor and power stapler were, indeed, everything I hoped for. I lathed the east gable in one evening. All I had to do was hold the lath in place with one hand, cock the trigger of the gun, and press it against the metal. Instantly a staple shot into place and the lath was fastened to the OSB. No longer did I have to use my forehead to hold it in place while I held the hammer and nail in my hands. Instead of requiring several pounds on each nail and the danger of pounding my thumb, all I needed was to push the stapler against the wall and the job was done. No wonder guys got all excited over power tools!

Somewhere along the line, here, I had slipped from mild passion about building my house to extreme obsession. House construction was about the only topic of conversation that interested me, even with my computer-oriented coworkers. My eyes instinctively wandered to the rafters and corners of every building I entered, examining the finer details of its construction, and the tool belt Lisa gave me for my birthday fascinated me. I knew right away which tool would fit in the various pouches.

Dinners at our house went from simple meals to refrigerator-scrounging free-for-alls as each daylight hour meant I could get a step closer to the plasters and interior work and a step further from working ten to twenty feet above the ground. Fortunately, the boys each had jobs and their own cars now, so they barely noticed my absence— but then again, they weren't around to help much, either.

While Andrzej enjoyed his work with the *Daily Star*, J.J. had taken the perfunctory first job at Burger King. With his newfound wheels, in the form of a 1988 Mercury Sable, he was becoming a scarce commodity around the homesite. Not only could he escape the confines of the trailer, but he could save gas by driving from Burger King directly to his friends' houses, using his backseat as a suitcase.

My drive to completion also stemmed from impatience, since this was all taking much longer than I had anticipated and the hours of labor still stretched endlessly before me. It had been six months since the wall raising and I hadn't even begun on the interior.

Then again, Jon told me of a 5,000-square-foot straw bale house in central Tucson whose main roof ended right over the bales. It was then supposed to be flashed down to a lower roof, but before that happened the summer rains had pelted the main roof and drained right on top of the bales. The cement stucco on the walls held the water in nicely, so the bales became slimy sponges. The owners concluded that their only choice was to bulldoze down their walls and rebuild them. All in all, I had been extremely fortunate and kept a good schedule.

Nevertheless, for my peace of mind, I needed to get to a point where I could see the final permit shining before me and calculate its coinciding with the last payment from my parents in November. They were due to visit from Hawaii in four months, and I not only wanted a stunning house to show them, but space to cook and eat a momentous Thanksgiving dinner. It would be my way of saying thank you for their support.

Likewise, I felt a pressure from my friends to act as if I had a plan and knew what I was doing. Without exception, every person who came by the house asked me, "So, when's the move-in date?"

I brushed that question off as lightly as I could, telling them I would move in when the house was ready. I was working as hard and as fast as I possibly could. The main reason I was building without a loan was so I wouldn't have deadline pressures. That sounded good, anyway. In actuality, I was pushing myself very hard, working every spare minute all weekend and every evening from the minute I got home from work to the time I crashed into bed.

Before I could consider the gables completed, I wanted to surround the small stained-glass window on the west end of the house with a symbol. I carefully formed a shape out of foamboard, nailed it onto the gable, then covered it with lath and stucco. At first, I wanted to pick a design that meant good things, such as joy, serenity, prosperity, and wisdom. However, not being much for symbols or rituals, I found myself just looking for something pleasing and then I could decide its significance for me. I saw no reason to defer such meaning to the Ancients.

I decided on a version of the symbol on the New Mexico flag—a circle with four sets of protruding lines. I had heard that this was an Indian symbol called a *zia*, representing the sun or the four corners of the earth. To me, it looked like the earth as well as a shining sun. It was simple but dramatic, combining the rectangle of the stained glass, the circle and straight lines of the *zia* itself, and the triangle of the gable—the basic shapes. So, for me, it would mean a combination of the elements of the earth in the house, the warmth of the sun in the passive solar design, and simple living in its basic shapes. Of course, it would also mean the joy, serenity, prosperity, and wisdom that result from simple living in harmony with Nature.

The design filled the gable perfectly, and suddenly the house had personality. I stepped back to survey my work with a big grin on my face.

## Chapter Fifteen

# INTERIOR FRAMING

*The best lightning rod for your protection is your own spine.*

—Ralph Waldo Emerson

I SAT comfortably in my air-conditioned office on Tuesday, August 15, while Jon and another carpenter, Larry, built the loft. For me, this was the height of luxury. All I had to do was write out a check for about $1,000 for the lumber and wait for it to be delivered, like a normal person. Jon picked up all the metal bolts and connectors for me, to be sure that we got the right sizes.

The mezzanine, which is the loft's official name on the plans, rested on two huge beams, six inches by fourteen inches and sixteen feet long, that ran along the north and south walls. The corners of the beams sat on six-inch-by-six-inch vertical posts that were bolted to the stemwall. I wondered how two people were going to get those massive beams in place, but I couldn't be there to watch them go up.

Jon later told me that he stood a ladder against the east wall, next to one of the loft's supporting posts. He then nailed a plank across the roof trusses, directly above the beam's final resting place. With one end of a thick rope tied around the end of the beam that was away from the ladder, he slung the other end of the rope over the plank and back down to the ground. With J.J. and Larry tugging on the rope, they raised one end of the beam several feet. Then Jon lifted the other end until it reached the rungs of the ladder. "See-sawing" their way up, the beam eventually arrived at its destination on the top of the posts.

By the time I arrived home after work on Wednesday, the beams were nestled proudly in place, bolted securely in metal brackets, with long TJIs fastened between them to support the loft floor. TJI stands for Truss Joist

Incorporated. These joists are comprised of seven-inch strips of OSB standing vertically supported by thicker boards along each edge. They are strong, inexpensive, and kill fewer trees than regular joists. Most of the plywood floor was also in place, except for the area near the center of the house where a large curve would need to be cut to fit one half of the spiral staircase.

Jon and I played on the upper floor, admiring the view of Diamond Head, as black thunderheads formed over the mountains. If we'd had just a little more room, or perhaps a railing, we could have danced. We delighted in the seven-foot height in the center for standing and all the room at the edges, under the trusses, for beds, desks, shelves, and low closets.

According to the code, a mezzanine is supposed to be open to the room below, but it can have dividing walls of up to forty-four inches. We measured that height and figured it would be perfect to give the boys' beds some privacy from the main room and be the backdrop for a low closet for each of them.

As the evening storm grew closer, gusts of wind blasted through the desert. The saguaros around us swayed, palo verde trees bent low, but the straw bale house stood solid. There was not a tremor or a shudder to be felt, except from Larry's hammer securing the last nails into the TJIs. This would be a wonderfully solid house, especially compared to the rattly old trailer.

That Saturday, Jon and I were ready to begin building the walls between the bedroom, bathroom, and spiral stairway. However, since the subfloor in most of the house was gravel and I was going to cover that with an earthen floor, we had to pour concrete footers for the interior walls. They needed a firm foundation and termite-resistant footing.

We spent most of the day staking strings where the walls would go and leveling them. For the semicircular wall around the spiral staircase, we used garden edging supported by cement stakes pounded into the gravel. It was a pretty lumpy circle, but it would largely be covered by the earthen floor. With leftover pieces of lumber, I made four-inch-wide forms and filled them with shovelsful rather than a truckload of concrete—child's play after the foundation.

We needed a few supplies for the next day, so we scheduled our usual Saturday night date at Home Depot and a quick dinner at the taco restaurant next door. As we stood outside the store, an enormous and brilliant double-rainbow formed over the city, with lightning flashing through the dark clouds behind it. It was truly awe inspiring.

However, it was also worrisome. At the restaurant, I selected a table next to the window so I could pay attention to the lightning, which was passing by us as the sky grew darker and darker. Lightning is magnificent from a distance, but it felt terrifying so close.

Munching on my black bean taco, I watched the lightning transform into huge veins as it continued west across the mountains, heading toward the area of my straw bale house. These were not little flashes any longer; they were huge, glowing tentacles darting from menacing black clouds. They viciously clung to their prey, injecting it with gazillions of deadly volts before retracting into the dark sky.

"Does lightning always hit something?" I asked Jon, apprehensively. I was well aware that my house was the tallest structure within many miles and covered with a metal roof.

"Sometimes it just hits the open desert," he assured me. "Sometimes, if you know where lightning has struck, you can go see the sand fused together."

I felt a little better, though I silently visualized protective light around the house and the trailer. Telling myself not to slip into worry mode, I drove with Jon to a movie and returned home after dark. The storm had dissipated by then, though the wet desert had a wonderful musty aroma that told me rain had passed through the area. We needed it. Despite all the summer lightning, August had been a very dry month.

The straw bale house was standing majestically and securely on its foundation. Checking for messages, I noticed the dial tone was gone on one phone. After checking each connection in the lines, I found that the surge suppressor, which sat between the phone line and my computer modem, had blown. Lightning must have hit. The suppressor had done its job.

Jon had placed a stronger surge suppressor on our electric panel and it had probably blocked the lightning from blowing out anything else. The suppressor wasn't attached to the phone lines. After rerouting the phone lines and making sure the computer still worked, I fell soundly asleep.

The following morning, with a mug of green tea, I strolled over to the house to admire the latest progress. I loved starting the day that way, and with a few stretches in the fresh morning air. Today was exciting because now I could really visualize the rooms. The curved wall around the stairway would be a wonderful touch.

Returning toward the trailer, my steps froze. Before me, barely ten feet from the west end of the straw bale house, the arms of the sole remaining guardian saguaro lay scattered at its feet. I had walked right by it on my way to the house, without even noticing! Rushing over to the arms, which must weigh hundreds of pounds each, I also noticed a large gash in the base of the saguaro.

I couldn't imagine what might have happened. Some disease might have attacked it, weakening the arm joints, or some vandal might have slashed it with a machete. In complete shock, my mind froze and my jaw dropped.

"This looks like a lightning strike," Jon surmised, walking up behind me. "Look at the top. It's black and the spines are burnt off." We examined the core of one arm, which was also burnt.

"Oh! . . .Oh! . . . Oh!" was all I could exclaim, over and over. My intuitions had been accurate; that lightning had my name on it and the house had been protected. Like a true guardian, this desert giant had taken the hit for us; it had saved the house. Visions of rebuilding and redoing all the work on my house flooded through my mind, making me weak.

"Wow!" I heard Rudy's voice behind us. "I saw that last night! It was like a bomb went off. It shook my house and it was so bright, like the sun came out. I thought it was closer, because it was so loud. Good thing you weren't home; it probably would have knocked your eardrums out. I looked over here and saw flames and smoke coming out of that saguaro. I told my kids, but they didn't believe me. It really got hit! Whoa!"

"Can we save it?" Jon asked. "Why don't you call your saguaro man and ask him if we can cover the holes from the arms with something and somehow keep it alive."

"No way," Rudy said. "That's dead. You're just lucky it didn't fall over onto the house last night."

"It does lean toward the house a little," I added. "That man who cut down the other saguaro told me to look out for this one. If it dies, we'll have to pull it away from the house."

I phoned over to Tohono Chul Park, but the man who cut down my other saguaro would not be in for two days. That might be too long. On closer examination of the saguaro, I could see the top bending to the south, rot forming along the burn lines, and ooze coming from the gash at its base.

No, there was no way this saguaro would survive any explosion that blew its arms off. It was probably charred at its core. Poor thing. From deep in my heart, I silently saluted and thanked this beautiful creature for protecting us. My second guardian would have to come down.

Still stunned and saddened, I got out a long tow rope and the A-frame ladder. Jon didn't want us to rest any extension ladder against the saguaro, because its balance was probably very tenuous from the loss of its arms. A push in the wrong direction might topple it.

Climbing the rungs, I wrapped the rope around the trunk about eight feet up, then triangulated it out to two stakes, to the northwest and the southwest. We estimated that the top of the cactus wasn't more than five feet above the ridge of the roof—about twenty-five feet in height. The distance from the saguaro to the straw bale house was only about ten feet, but the distance to the west, from the cactus's trunk to the trailer, was thirty-seven feet, so we could safely let it fall to the west.

Jon didn't have his chain saw with him, so we left the cactus staked. We would take it down another day. I felt relatively assured that if it hadn't fallen on the house so far, it wasn't going to do that now. However, my nerves were frayed; I was in no mood to work.

*My noble guardian saguaro stands armless after being struck by lightning. The skeleton still stands by the house.*

Since Jon needed to do some plumbing at a beautiful straw bale house in the foothills south of Tucson, I took the day off and went for a drive with him. He had built the house about five years ago and was anxious to show it to me. Not only was the house an elegant example of straw bale construction, but the artistic women who owned the house had boldly painted their walls with deep reds, purples, and blues. I was trying to decide whether to be that brave.

On Monday, Jon installed a lightning grounding system on my house, consisting of a copper rod on the roof and large copper lines that ran down each corner of the house into thirty-foot trenches pointing away from the walls. He had enough leftover materials from his other jobs to do it at a minimal cost. Zej helped him dig the trenches, but the copper rod installation was still hot, grungy work in the desert heat—back up on the steep roof, again. I would be so glad to be in the solid, grounded house by the following summer. My nerves still felt raw.

Jon couldn't find his chain saw. He figured he must have lent it to someone, but he wasn't sure to whom. That was actually fine with me, because I hated to see the second house guardian go down. Even dying, she looked majestic next to the house and I could say "thank you" every time I passed by.

On Wednesday, August 23, I arrived home from work with a truckload of cement mix for the subfloors and a group of University of Arizona lightning researchers behind me. One of Jon's conversations had reached the ears of a member, who immediately asked us not to cut down the saguaro and let them come study it.

Eagerly, the three researchers climbed out of their white sedans, marveling at the wonderful specimen of a cactus. My life's limited experience with university professors had led me to presume ignorantly that behind their gray hair and pale skin was a regimented outlook on life. But this evening, their excitement was contagious; I couldn't help admiring how much they enjoyed their work as they bustled around the base of the tall cactus, examining every inch, taking notes, snapping photos, and huddling to share their discoveries. Apparently it was rare that they reached a saguaro right after a strike, were able to document exactly when the lightning had hit, and had a witness to tell them what happened.

I interrupted Rudy's dinner to ask him to come over and give a full report to the scientists, which he did, describing the brilliant flash of light, the shaking of the ground several acres away, and then the flames running up and down the trunk, while smoke (which he was told was actually steam) exploded from the top of the cactus. He verified that it was about

7:30 in the evening that the strike took place—just about exactly as I was eating my taco!

The top five feet of the saguaro had fallen off that day and now lay on the ground amid the broken arms. To my amazement, one of the researchers showed me photos of the last strike they had documented. The top had fallen off the cactus after five days (we were at four days now) and on the sixth day, the remaining stalk had dropped its skin in a matter of hours, like a molting snake. Left standing, was the graceful wooden skeleton of ribs.

I surveyed the growing gash at the eastern base of the saguaro, which was still causing it to lean toward the straw bale house. Then, I double-checked my stakes and lines that supported the massive, but dying trunk toward the west. Inside me, I really didn't want to cut down the saguaro and hoped this was a message that I didn't have to.

"Sure," I agreed. "I'll wait a few days and see what happens. I'd love to have a standing skeleton here, to remember the saguaro by."

"Great! And please don't touch any of the metal objects around the base of the saguaro, here," added Leo, the researcher who knew Jon. "Tomorrow we'd like to bring out another member of our group who can run a magnetic detector over the bits of rebar and nails to tell us exactly how the lightning traveled."

"Sure, that would be interesting."

"We think that the gash at the base of the saguaro was from the lightning traveling over to this large piece of rebar and then bouncing back to the saguaro. It may have saved your power lines."

"I hadn't thought of that. I won't touch a thing."

Rudy told me that my neighbors to the north had lost their power and their computer had been blown out when the lightning hit. It was amazing that this force had passed within thirty feet of our electric box and only a couple of breakers had been thrown. The little black box that Jon had put on our electric panel had definitely done its job.

The skin didn't drop for two weeks. We worked in the shadow of this dying monument, watching ooze pour from its gashes as its skin became brittle and black. On the second Sunday after the strike, it dropped another section of its top and now was no threat to the house. The lightning experts, who by now were familiar faces at the job site, told me that my staking rope was keeping the skin from falling.

Deciding that the house was no longer in danger, I removed the rope carefully from the cactus's tenuous sides. There was still something majestic and peaceful about this creature, though it was merely a stiff carcass by now. Within minutes, I heard the skin cracking and falling in pieces, and by the end of the day at least half of the skeleton was exposed. The wood shone radiantly in the setting sunlight.

This would be our Christmas tree each year, I decided. We would decorate it with lights and make it a monument of joy. Now, it held no danger of poking us with its thorns, nor of falling on the house. It would still be our guardian in its new form.

On Saturday, we poured concrete into the kitchen and bathroom floors. The county didn't allow earthen floors in any area with running water, so I had decided to lay lovely rust-colored Saltillo tile floors over a concrete subfloor. This was hot, heavy work reminiscent of the stemwall construction, but the big difference was that we had a roof over our heads for shade and electricity for cooling fans.

When the concrete was dry on Sunday, Jon and I had great fun marking exactly where everything would fit in both the bathroom and the kitchen.

In the bathroom, by code, the toilet had to be sixteen inches away from the tub and the vanity, and twelve inches from the wall. Measuring in all directions, my plumbing pipes protruding from the concrete were in exactly the right place. Jon probably didn't appreciate how very amazing that was, but I did.

In the kitchen we drew an outline for the refrigerator, stove, and my butcher-block table and then figured out the exact size of the kitchen cabinets. It was very exciting. Along with the coolness in the air and a new season approaching, I felt we were moving into the final phase of the house. The list of things I still needed was pretty long, but it was becoming finite, to the point where I almost dared to write it down on a piece of paper and make an estimate. The most immediate task was to frame in the walls, then fill them with plumbing lines and electric wires. How to do this was a big blur in my brain.

As we had been pouring the concrete beneath the future wall between the bathroom and bedroom, I kept asking Jon if we shouldn't be pushing J-bolts into the concrete, as we had done in the stemwall. We would need something to bolt the wall to. He kept telling me not to worry, we could "shoot" the boards down into the concrete later. I didn't get a clear picture of what he meant, until the time came to do it.

After laying baseboards for the wall in place, from out of one of his magic toolboxes Jon pulled another gray power tool. This one was cordless and looked like a gun. He inserted a silver nail with a plastic washer into the front of the tool and a row of little brass circles that were imbedded into a yellow plastic strip into the handle.

Standing firmly on the board to hold it in place, he explained to me how to aim the nail right where you want it, then lean on the gun with your body weight and pull the trigger.

"Boom!" The nail exploded into the board and concrete beneath it. The air smelled like fireworks.

"It's a gun!" I exclaimed. "I've never shot a gun, but that's the smell of gun powder, isn't it?"

"Yes, it's a gun," he agreed with a smile, as he loaded another nail and handed it to me. "Your turn. Just don't do it too close to the edge or you'll crack the concrete."

I cringed, but I knew Jon was serious. He liked to stay in the consultant role and encouraged me to learn every phase of construction. So, while Jon held the board in place, I pressed the nozzle into the board with all my weight, closed my eyes, and squeezed the trigger.

"Boom!"

Cautiously opening my eyes and raising the gun, I spotted the nail imbedded perfectly into the board. Nothing to it! I cocked the gun, reloaded, and blasted about six more nails before Jon decided to share in the fun and "shoot" a few more nails himself. In a short time, we had lumber lining the curved stairway wall as well as the bedroom/bathroom wall. In the few sections that were too small to shoot, we glued the boards down with Heavy Duty Liquid Nails.

Jon helped me frame in the wall between the bedroom and bathroom. At this phase, I was really seeing the advantage of building small. I am eternally grateful that I only had one bathroom to plumb and two short walls to frame.

Jon examined the thirty studs that I had purchased to frame in the wall, selected about five, and put the others in a big pile.

"We'll need to return those," he stated firmly, "they are too twisted. I'll show you how to select lumber."

I looked at him in astonishment, but he was serious. Sure enough, at the end of the day, we loaded twenty of them into the truck and took them back to the store.

I had always looked for clean wood with straight sides and without too many knots. According to Jon, however, the most important criterion is that a board shouldn't be twisted. Lifting one end of the lumber to eye-level and scoping down its length, he examined it for a straight line from top to bottom.

Returning to the house, Jon wrote "straight" on one of the boards and used it for a ruler. We measured every sixteen inches around the various plumbing pipes on the north side of the wall and alternate sixteen inches on the south side. Using the ruler board with a four-foot level beside it, he then marked exactly where each board should line up on the ceiling. I figured the wall would hide them, so why would it matter if they were perfectly straight? But it did matter. The sheets of drywall, the final wall covering, needed to end right down the middle of a stud, just like the sheets of OSB had ended on the trusses. If the studs were crooked, we'd end up with drywall hanging in midair with nothing to fasten to.

During the course of construction, I had wondered how rigid, straight interior walls would contrast with the softness of the straw walls. Earth plasters could be applied to drywall, but I decided that for immediate purposes, I would cover the rigid walls with burlap soaked in a clay slip. That would blend with the clay coating I intended to spread over the earthen plasters. The burlap would also provide a rough surface if I later decided that I wanted to coat these walls with the same plasters as the straw bale walls.

Since the interior wall coverings weren't necessary for the final inspection, I could plaster them at my leisure. Well, if I had any memory of what leisure was.

Jon then got out his measuring tape and figured the exact length of each board from the bottom mark to the top mark, called them out to me to the sixteenth of an inch, and I cut them on the table saw. It was fun for me to do something so precise. We cut the wood about an eighth of an inch longer than needed so it would stand wedged firmly into place while we screwed it.

I was used to nails, but I had to agree with Jon that each blow of the hammer tended to knock the lumber out of place. With screws, the biggest challenge was pushing hard enough to drive them through the wood. Normally, as I began to drive a screw, it would wobble around for a while, then go flying into the air. If I were perched on a ladder as I did this, I needed to have one hand bracing myself, so I didn't similarly go soaring. But now Jon gave me a wonderful gadget: some highly intelligent carpenter came up with a screw gun bit that pulls down over the length of the screw, so it can't spin out sideways while being driven into the wood!

Using that tip, and with the help of my ever-growing biceps and triceps, I was able to drive the long screws diagonally from the ends of the studs into their supports. I was learning and loving it as I laughingly replaced my screw gun in its holster at the end of the day, blowing imaginary smoke from its tip.

The spiral staircase arrived in late September, in pieces, in a large cardboard box weighing 350 pounds. It reminded me a little of a jungle gym I put together when the boys were small, so I had a semivision of being able to assemble it. However, when Jon's job in Tubac was delayed another week and Larry had free time also, I did not object in the least to them finishing up the loft and installing the stairway. Time was becoming my greatest limitation.

Once again, I drove home from the office to see this lovely, spiraling structure reaching into a horizontal arch in the mezzanine floor. The stairway would be a focal point of the entire house. I walked around and around it, admiring its graceful shape.

And now, as the framing was underway, in the times when Jon was busy, I completed all the lathing around the doors and windows. It took me until mid-September, almost exactly a year from when I had begun the foundation, to bid a relieved farewell to my tin snips and call for the stucco mesh inspection. I figured this one would be a breeze. I had done everything perfectly.

Arriving home on Thursday, I saw one of those dreaded notes from the inspector, meaning I had failed. His largest objection was that we didn't have roofing tar paper wrapped over the lower course of bales. This was drawn on my plans and it was the code, to prevent soaking the lower bales when rain splashes back up against the house. Since I had a foot-high stemwall and would someday have a porch, my previous inspector had said this wouldn't be necessary. But now I had a new inspector and he wanted the paper put on the lower bales.

For me, this was not just another task that seemed unnecessary, but a real hindrance to earthen plasters. I could easily spread mud onto a rough bale, but I couldn't make it stick to tar paper.

Since I had to work, Jon kindly spent four hours at the building department the next morning, talking to the senior inspector and filing an appeal over the moisture barrier on the lower bales. He phoned me once, from the desk at the building department, wondering just exactly where on my plans it specified earth plasters, because all he could find was a vague referral to stucco being attached to the bales with wire mesh. For earthen plasters, we wouldn't be using the mesh.

At that point, I panicked, but fortunately I wasn't the one at the building department.

"It doesn't say earth plasters on my plans? Well, we have to get approval for them then, because I've intended to do those all along."

"Yes, I'll work on that," Jon replied officially, as if the inspector were sitting next to him.

Finally at about 11 A.M., I got a call from Jon that he had talked to the chief plans examiner and received permission to use earth plasters. If we built the porch, we wouldn't have to put any stabilizer, such as lime or asphalt emulsion, in with the plasters.

"Perfect!" I exclaimed.

"They will have the results of the appeal about the moisture barrier on Monday afternoon," he continued. "But they don't think we'll have any trouble passing."

"Great. Thank you, thank you! It's so impossible for me to do these things when I have to be at work." I took a couple of much-needed deep breaths.

On Monday, I spoke with the senior plans examiner, Mr. Overhill, who was very kind and soft-spoken. The appeal had been approved, pending the inspector's verification of the stemwall and my signing a "hold harmless" letter. When I asked him if he had a form for the letter, he said I just had to write out something about how I would take full responsibility for removing the moisture barrier and any water damage that might result to the bales.

"No problem," I replied. "I had no plans to sue the county in my future, anyway."

"Well, you'd be surprised," he answered. "There's a rash of lawsuits going around the country. Right now there are quite a few in California. It's as if they follow each other. If anything goes wrong with a house, people will hire someone to research the plans and permits. If they find any reason to believe we didn't follow the code in our inspections, they will sue us. Several times we've had to settle for several thousands of dollars."

I was only partially amazed; lawsuits have become such common fare these days over anything and everything. We insult lawyers but happily use them if we perceive money in our pockets.

"It's not really the builders that we worry about. It's the buyers down the road," he explained.

I assured him I would happily write such a letter and felt a new understanding for the pressure put on inspectors to follow every little detail on the plans and codes. We do it to ourselves, I thought, without realizing the cycle.

Through the strain of appeals had emerged something beyond my expectations, however—I had been given permission to use earthen plasters with no stabilizer, as long as I built the porch. My brain started churning—there must be a way.

I already had the porch roofing; I had ordered it way back before the wall raising. But the lumber to support the roof would cost several thousand dollars, by my estimates. Without the porch, I was already coming up short when I projected my expenses to the final permit. I had used up the money from my car sale and only had $2,000 more coming from my parents. Yet I needed to hire people to install the fire sprinklers, insulate and drywall the high ceiling, and I still had a $1,500 impact fee to pay.

I would need to borrow the money somehow. Ten thousand dollars should get the porch built and fund the remainder of the construction. Jon knew a loan officer in town, Maggi, who had approved several construction loans with him as the builder, even though he wasn't a contractor. I gave Maggi a call. She was very helpful, but after a couple of days called me back to say that all her sources for construction loans refused to make a loan partway through a project; I would have had to set this up from the beginning. She had another source that would loan me the money, but wanted $3,000 in fees. That seemed ridiculous.

Then she asked where I banked, which is the credit union at Tucson's Newspapers. She suggested I try for a signature loan from them. So, I walked over there and filled out the papers. Lo and behold, three days later they approved a loan for $10,000 at 10 percent interest. They would take the payments out of my paychecks and there would be no prepayment penalty if I turned it into a mortgage in a few months.

Suddenly I had visions of not only building the porch, but buying real light fixtures and maybe kitchen cupboards! On top of that excitement, Randy was returning in a few weeks and said he would have time to work on the porch.

Layers of nagging fear lifted from my shoulders as I realized this house was going to make it to completion. I called Jon and made us a celebratory dinner reservation at one of the elegant resorts in Tucson.

There, as we gazed out over the waterfalls and lush gardens, the sun joined us in celebration. More dramatic than any stage, a strip of glowing orange sky radiated between the distant dark mountains and a bank of gray cumulus above them. Hanging like a curtain in front of the brilliant sunset, mists of rain vaporized before they reached the ground.

I thought perhaps the sun had set, for it was nowhere visible, but as I wondered, it slid elegantly beneath the clouds, a reddish orange ball glowing through the black spray. We were both speechless; it was beyond beautiful into the realms of spiritual awe, reminding me of a Japanese haiku painting come to life.

Nature is amazing, not only for its beauty, but its incredible variety. Every sunset is different, 365 days, year after year. We had a delicious, romantic dinner, as I was brimming with thankfulness not only for Jon, but also for the beautiful medium of straw, and especially for the means to finish this house.

*Chapter Sixteen*

# THE PORCH

*The ornament of a house is the friends who frequent it.*

—RALPH WALDO EMERSON

BY the weekend, with a glorious $10,000 in my checking account, it was back to work to lay the foundation for the porch. My plans called for 6 x 6-inch vertical posts every fourteen feet all the way around the house, supporting larger beams and rafters. The sunroom area, of course, would be framed with 2 x 6s, then covered with conventional siding on the outside. I decided that I'd really like the rustic look of vigas or round log posts with rough-cut beams. That seemed only fitting for a house with straw bale walls and mud plasters.

I asked several companies if they had ever made vigas from trees that had died of natural causes. They had no idea what I was talking about, so I gave up. From that answer, I realized that ecologically correct posts would be more expensive than I could afford. I ordered freshly cut, hand-peeled vigas and twenty-foot, 6 x 8-inch beams. As I paid my $1,500 impact fee, $1,000 for fire sprinkler installation, last year's property taxes, and $3,500 in materials for the porch, my checking account balance dipped very quickly.

I was bold enough to get an estimate on real kitchen cupboards, which came to about $5,000. If I used pressboard instead of real wood and cut all the trimmings, I could get it down to $3,500, but I decided it wasn't important. For a few hundred dollars, I could purchase the skeleton of the cupboards from Home Depot and let Jon teach me how to make saguaro-rib doors—later.

I went back to the county building department to get permission to change from 6 x 6 posts to vigas, hoping to be treated kindly by Mr. Over-hill again, but he didn't remember me. He insisted on knowing the species, grade, and fiberstress statistics on all the vigas before he would approve them. The logs had to be stamped with the grade for the inspector to see, and I'd probably need a letter from the viga supplier verifying their grade, as well.

My patience was wearing thin with all these inspection requirements, but the viga distributor told me that someone had sued the county a few years ago for using ungraded lumber in the house. That was why every bit of lumber had to have a grade on it. Okay, one more detail.

In October, at the same time that I was dealing with all these inspections, I received a summons from small claims court and Kathy, asking for $2,400 damages from my failure to return the trailer. At least she wasn't suing me for fraud in a superior court.

I still didn't think she had a case, because she had given me the title with no written or verbal agreement about the date of the trailer's return, but now it would be up to a court to decide. I e-mailed Dan, our draftsman who had sold Kathy the trailer. He said that he would be happy to come and verify that Kathy had told him she was loaning the trailer to me indefinitely or selling it to me. One way or another, I hoped to settle the matter. I was quite sure nobody could evict me.

In the courtroom on November 11, I listened in astonishment to Kathy's stories as she emphasized the favor she had done by loaning me the mobile home, saying we had a six-month agreement, then claiming I had "stolen" the title and the trailer from her by installing it onto my land. She moaned about her inconvenience at having no storage for her extra belongings, no place for her son to live, an inability to apply for a loan when she needed the trailer for collateral, and so forth.

It was very difficult for me to sort out what I could legally be responsible for in all that, but I knew it certainly was no favor to let me pay a couple thousand dollars to move and fix up the trailer and then try to kick me out. I presented documentation on how much work I had done, how much money I had spent, and noted the lack of any written agreement. Nonetheless, I could feel the judge sympathizing with Kathy's story. She barely looked at my documentation and cut off Dan's testimony before he uttered three sentences.

Perhaps I should have counterattacked, accusing Kathy of trying to profit from my labor when I was in a desperate situation, but there was not a cell of my being that could endure behaving like a victim, not even for a few minutes in a courtroom. I had given up looking at life as a big Monopoly game where the object is to die clutching the most money. Thanks to my straw bale house, each day had become a creative experience.

My friends and I (including Jon) believe our lives are a series of choices, even if we aren't always conscious of having made the choice. We often wonder why certain events happen in our lives and what we are supposed to learn from them. If any of us fall into the blaming mode, we try to joke each other out of it.

Of course, this meant that the conflict with Kathy was my choice, so I wondered why I had brought this into my life. This lawsuit happened at a time when I was wrestling with county permits to get permission to avoid the moisture barrier on the lower bales, use vigas instead of square posts, and use earthen plasters instead of cement stucco. The strictness of the inspection process stemmed from the county's fear of lawsuits by home-owners. Maybe I needed to understand that this lawsuit business is a major problem in our society and I need to be very cautious in all dealings, even with supposed friends. Lesson learned.

The hearing officer made it clear that this was small claims court and she could not order the return of the trailer; all she could do was order a payment. I figured the money I spent fixing up the trailer was equal to Kathy's "inconvenience," but I still sensed the court's hostility.

Sure enough, I later received a judgment in the mail that I owed Kathy $1,000 with 10 percent interest from the date of the judgment, but no deadline for payment. I would chalk it up to rent and experience. I would borrow an extra thousand with my mortgage and barely notice as I paid her off.

The hearing officer wanted to know when I planned to move out and return the mobile home. I told her the end of February, about four months from the date of the hearing. I tried to pick a realistic date so that Kathy would have no cause to pursue this matter any further and whatever judgment the court handed down would cover the entire period I lived in the trailer. I wasn't happy, but I felt relieved that this whole issue was settled. I sent Kathy an e-mail telling her that I didn't want to slow down my construction by paying the money now, so I would pay her with interest when I got my mortgage.

Kathy replied that she would excuse the $1,000 if I returned the trailer immediately, but if I kept it, she wanted $325 in rent for every month, beginning November 11. If I didn't agree to that, her attorney would file suit in a superior court.

Lawyers again! Pushing all fear of them aside, I sat down with my receipts for repairing the mobile home and came up with about $1,100 in property taxes and repairs that would remain with the trailer when it was returned and another $900 in my time to plumb, paint, and clean it.

If Kathy wanted to be my landlord, I knew the courts had rules on what she should pay.

Early on a Saturday morning in mid-November, before beginning the day's construction work, I sent her another e-mail letting her know that I had added up the expenses she should pay as a landlord, if she wanted to be one. I had calculated that my repairs had been worth seven months rent at $325 per month, as she was asking. She could reimburse me some of my expenses, if she'd like the trailer returned sooner than that.

I didn't hear back from her and I wasn't sure whether that was good or bad. I could almost sympathize with Kathy because she seemed desperate to get the trailer. But no matter how I felt, there was nothing I could do but keep working as hard and fast as I could and be thankful we hadn't been evicted.

Life in the trailer was growing tiresome and claustrophobic. I wanted to do my best to return it by the end of February, for everyone's sake, so I set that as a goal. At least now I had a move-in date, so I could answer that unending question.

I was still going through the motions of the house construction, spending every weekend, every evening, and every lunch hour working on, shopping for, or sorting through details on the house, but my mind and body were becoming weary. I felt like the parent of a wayward teenager; deep inside me I still loved it and admired its growth, but I also wondered how many more tribulations I had to go through before it would stand on its own foundation, without my perpetual support.

However, Randy was due to return in a couple of weeks, so weary or not, I needed to keep up the pace and prepare the porch foundation. On a Sunday in early October, Jon and I had set up batter boards and run strings to level the post bases. We first tried this with a little bubble level hung on a long string between the footers. The results kept coming out uneven, so we pulled out the weathered water level. Jon had never used one but was quite impressed with its accuracy. We ran level strings all around the house and ended up at the exact height we had begun.

Then I took out the pickax, just as I had done a year prior, and dug holes in the earth for the post foundations. I almost felt nostalgic. Mostly, I was amazed at how much more confident I was now than a year ago. I felt knowledgeable about concrete as we poured the lumpy mixture into the footers to form level bases for the vigas.

Randy's truck drove up the driveway on October 25, returning from the northern climes to soak up the winter desert sunshine. He looked just the same, smiling and handsome, radiating a healthy glow from his natural foods and outdoor exercise. It was great to see him, get a big hug, and catch up on the months that had passed since sheathing the roof.

He admired the progress on the house and told great stories of attending the Nebraska Straw Bale Conference to learn the latest building methods. He had attended lectures about building with no all-thread pinning and simply letting a thick layer of cement stucco hold the walls together. Another engineer had compression tests to show that two-string bales are stronger than three-string bales. Someone else lectured on building with bamboo.

I agreed with him that this was all very interesting, but I also thought it was very confusing. We are still in the pioneer stages of straw bale construction. At times, I'm thankful for the building codes that make some of these decisions for me. At times I'm not, for I wish I had more freedom to use new methods.

Jon kindly drove up from Tubac to meet Randy and go over the details of building a straight porch roof with irregular logs for posts. The post ends would need to be trimmed, but the vigas didn't fit into Randy's table saw and a chain saw would be too imprecise. We decided to even them with a handsaw, being careful not to cut off the grade stamp that the inspector would require.

By now, the house was sort of livable—sealed from the elements, anyway, with a solid loft for sleeping. Randy unrolled his sleeping bag in the loft and unfolded his backpacking supplies. His stay would be a little like camping, but also a little like a real home while he built the porch. We inserted a hose through the wall for water supply and hooked up a flush toilet for him, at least. I was delighted to have his help once again.

By the weekend, Randy had the sunroom walls constructed and the vigas cut to the same length. I helped him stand the wall frames upright, then raise the four corner vigas and brace them with 2 x 6 rafters. We ran strings around their top to make sure they were level.

When Jon arrived on Sunday, he assisted Randy in raising more than half of the upper beams. While I busied myself with other jobs, I admired the precision with which Randy leveled the posts, measured the beams, cut them and sanded their ends into exacting, smooth ninety- or forty-five-degree cuts. He worked with them patiently until they formed a perfect joint atop each post. I sprayed the metal connectors with copper rustoleum paint, so they would blend with the wood, and treated the viga logs with waterproofing sealer.

Randy spent the next few days laying rafters across the beams, but he needed another pair of hands to finish raising the beams, so I took a welcome day off from office work. I guess I was a little help, anyway, but the beams were very heavy. Propping A-frame ladders by two posts, I held one end of a beam while Randy raised the other end onto the top of one ladder. Then we switched places. While I steadied my end, he raised the other end up onto the post, about nine feet high. It took us all day to cut, lift, and fasten the remaining eight beams into place, attaching them with heavy metal ties and large lag bolts.

As Randy trimmed the beams, the musty aroma of fresh-cut pine transported me to forested mountaintops and Christmas wreaths. Standing under the growing protection of the verandah, I silently thanked the trees who gave their lives for these magnificent huge beams and log vigas. While the beams were rugged, rough, and splintery, the freshly peeled vigas were silky and sensual. Every log was different with swirling knots and graceful grains. I loved running my fingertips over their smooth, strong surface. I don't know if I had realized how much wood the porch would need, and I had meant to build a house with very little lumber, but nevertheless, I was grateful for every inch of it. It was sturdy and magnificent.

As if to compensate for the wood I had used, my neighbor to the north, who runs a landscaping company, came over the next weekend. He had twelve sweet acacia trees that had outgrown their pots, so that their roots were growing into the ground. He was afraid they would die when he dug them up, so he couldn't sell them. But if I would like to try my luck at transplanting them, I could have them.

Of course I wanted to see if I could keep them alive, so I took all twelve of the tall, spindly trees and planted a couple at the end of the day. We were about three days before the full moon and the nights were crisp, but not yet too cold. I spent the next few evenings transplanting trees around the house under the light of the waxing moon, staking them against the north winds and supplying them with plenty of water.

The following weekend, in mid-November, I helped Randy attach rafters every two feet around the top of the beams. It was a cool, cloudy day, the sort that normally arrived only in the dead of winter in this part of the country. We had suddenly gone from the hottest, driest summer, to the wettest, coldest conditions, reminiscent of New York. The jet stream was dipping way down to the border of Mexico and bringing a new cold front every few days. I knew I shouldn't complain—the desert would celebrate with spring wildflowers, the new trees I had transplanted would rejoice, and the water table under Tucson sorely needed replenishing.

The nights were generally staying in the forties, but a couple of them dropped below freezing. Randy was camping in the loft with no heater and no insulation in the ceiling, so he was our first test of the straw walls and passive solar design. Happily, he reported that he was just fine in his sleeping bag. In the morning he was a little cold, but not bad. I could be pretty sure that once we had insulated the ceiling, a few electric baseboard heaters would keep the house cozy. Already, as the sun shone through the large glass windows and the French doors on the south, the house warmed up quickly. I eagerly looked forward to living in this wonderful dwelling as we continued to blast electric room heaters in the thin-walled trailer.

We were ready to place rafters over the sunroom, so I needed to calculate how much overhang the roof should have to optimize the passive solar design. With graph paper in hand, I calculated the angle of the sun at the solstices in midsummer and winter. In Tucson, I had to be sure the sun didn't hit the large windows in the summer. From about April to October, shade was more desirable than sunshine.

After drawing various angles, I decided on a two-foot overhang of the rafters in the sunroom area. This should keep the sun completely away from the large windows in the summer months but allow its warming rays to enter through the windows from November to March.

Bundling up, we kept working between rain showers. When Alien Kitty saw me up on the top of an A-frame ladder, he scampered up the other side of the ladder, hopped onto the porch beam, and scurried around the new playground we were building. Cats have absolutely no fear of heights. While we hammered, he circled the house, jumping over the rafters and pausing majestically to survey the terrain below.

By late afternoon, the porch rafters were all completed, so we began to install the fascia board and the roof. The fascia, a wide board nailed along the end of the rafters to protect them, would later give me a place to attach a gutter to harvest many gallons of rainwater from every storm. This house contained about 2,000-square-feet of roofing. My biggest problem would most likely be trying not to overflow my water tank in a big storm.

We completed the fascia and about a quarter of the porch roof by the end of the weekend, placing translucent panels above the house windows to allow the maximum amount of light inside. Given one more day, we could have finished the roof, but Jon was in a jam with his house in Tubac. The wall raising was scheduled to begin on Thursday and one of the carpenters had hurt his back. He asked if Randy could work down there on Sunday to finish the window and door bucks. I, of course, could now sympathize with anyone on a deadline for a wall raising, so I let the porch roof go as Jon and Randy headed down to Tubac.

Randy had decided to drive back to Nebraska to visit his girlfriend and family for the holidays as soon as he was finished in Tubac. I'd have to complete the roof with Jon some other weekend. But that was okay. I was grateful for Randy's skilled labor once again and for having completed 95 percent of all the porch work.

As the day drew to a close, I retired to the trailer. From the kitchen window, I could see the west end of the straw bale house. Its transformation from a narrow barn to a graceful home with verandah was miraculous; I barely recognized it. Its uncovered sunroom area reminded me of New England front porches from my childhood, where a swinging bench beckoned passersby to slow their pace and sit for an evening, sharing stories and watching the world go by. Where the porch had roofing, I envisioned the old plantation homes on Kauai, surrounded by *lanais*.

The porch would most likely be my favorite part of the house, I predicted. I began formulating ideas to use every inch of it, both for practical and artistic purposes. I had already created areas for the hot water heater, tool shed, and laundry facilities behind some lattice, an outside dining area, and a meditation space outside the bedroom. Now I could also imagine a welcoming entryway with lots of plants and an artistic niche in the wall, maybe two. My dream was almost a reality.

## Chapter Seventeen

# WIRING
# AND PLUMBING

*Our houses are such unwieldy property that we are often imprisoned
rather than housed in them.*

—Henry David Thoreau, *Walden*


I HAD a hard time learning the electric wiring. Jon tried his best to
explain to me how wiring is like plumbing, how an amp is like the volume
of water, a volt is like the water pressure, and a watt is volts times amps
and therefore tells you how much "water" (electricity) you are getting. The
size of the wire is the same as the size of a plumbing pipe. I drew pictures
and kind of got it, but not really.

Finally, he told me that I didn't have to understand electricity to wire
a house; I could just buy the boxes and wires in the sizes that he told me,
follow the diagram he drew, and I'd be okay. He'd put in the circuit breakers. That worked better for me, and I was again very thankful for his presence. I couldn't even imagine trying to figure out all this from a book.
Without Jon's help, I would definitely have hired an electrician. The house
costs were now up to about $40,000—way over what I had imagined.
Even though I found it all bewildering, I was very thankful to be able to
learn this much about wiring and do much of the work myself.

My parents were arriving from Honolulu for Thanksgiving, which was
about a month from when we began the wiring. The house would be far
from complete, but I needed an overhead light. The stove could run off
an extension cord if need be. We'd set up the table on the cement slab in
the kitchen and one way or another, there would be a very elegant dinner with as much gratitude as gravy.

Referring to the wiring diagram that Jon had drawn on the back of the house plans, I spent a weekend installing boxes to hold the switches and outlets all over the house, screwing them to wooden stakes that were pounded into the straw. The following Saturday, Jon had time to help me run wires to the boxes. We spent the day perched on the tops of ladders and scaffolding with one of us feeding wire from large spools while the other one guided the plastic-sheathed copper into the rafters and stapled it along the trusses.

Most important, we numbered each wire on both ends with a permanent marker. Then, with any luck, when we connected all the wires to the circuit breakers, we'd know which wire went to which fixture.

Sunday brought our first winter storm with pelting rain and temperatures in the sixties—perfect for wiring a house. We let the rain pitter-patter on the roof while we tuned the radio to *A Prairie Home Companion* and some classic folk tunes, pulled wires down the top plate and through the trusses, stuffed them into the straw, and occasionally snuck in a hug, a kiss, or a slow dance. It was a delightful way to spend a Sunday. House building can definitely be more fun with two people.

Sure enough, all these wires did their job. Between rain showers, Jon showed me how to attach a light fixture and an outlet to the wall boxes. When he installed a couple of breakers in the panel, they worked. What a luxury to have real outlets instead of extension cords!

My small, simple house had thirty circuits in it, partly because I had no gas lines and didn't want to go to the expense of installing a large propane tank. I would use a five-gallon propane tank to fuel my stove only. I decided on an electric water heater, which I eventually hoped to replace with a solar system. Instead of using central heating and air-conditioning, I installed an evaporative cooler and electric baseboard heaters. From my estimates, I really shouldn't need much heating in this well-insulated house, anyway.

As weekends flew by, the wires that needed to be run across the house seemed endless, but I became pretty accomplished at pulling wires. I could feel the difference between the stiff 12-2 gauge wire and more pliable 14-2. I moved around the walls, securing each connection, my tool belt stocked with the wire cutter, crimper, stripper, Jon's special wire pusher tool, tiny copper tubes, and yellow wire caps.

I wasn't allowed to install the switches or outlets in more than a couple of boxes, however, until the inspector came and we passed our intermediate electric inspection. Instead, I "dressed" each box by capping the wire that would come from the breaker box and contain the electricity, then curling all the wires snugly into their little square home in the wall.

It was actually fun, except where I had to come near the metal lath. As always, I'd walk away with scraped knuckles and cuts all over my hands. Just as I thought I was finished, Jon looked at the mass of wires running under the big buck between the main room and the sunroom.

"How do you intend to cover these?" he asked.

"I don't know, maybe with a bunch of cob," I replied, referring to the mixture of clay and chopped straw we would use on the wall.

"I don't think that will pass code," he reminded me. "The inspector will want to see that you are covering these with at least one and a half inches of wall."

I told him I'd think of something and the next evening, after work, I decided I had better frame a small subwall into the buck to shelter the wires. Chances are that nobody would ever try to hang a picture right there, poking the wires with a nail, but it's better to be safe with large amounts of electricity. This was a pretty huge mass of about ten wires.

In trying to shelter the wires, I entered the world of what Jon calls "wire stretching." These wires were big and strong and we had cut them to fit from the circuit breaker box to the outlet boxes in both the sunroom and the main room. Suddenly, I needed the wires to make a couple of extra turns and go just a little farther. So, I went back to the outlet box and found I could gain about an inch of wire if I pulled it out of the box a little more. Then at each turn, I moved the wire closer to the corner to try to gain that extra inch. It was a slow, painful process, repeated with ten wires, that took me an entire afternoon. But bit by bit the wires were "stretched" to fit their new channel and I had a more acceptable path for them than through a mass of cob.

We remembered a few more things we had forgotten, including a switch control for the cooler, a spotlight on the niche by the stained-glass window, and an overhead fan for the sunroom. But eventually we finished everything. All wires were tucked tightly one and a half inches into the straw and secured with wire staples. With sighs of relief and celebratory exclamations, the last wire was run and the last box was prepped for the inspector.

I heard it was best to phone for the intermediate wiring inspection at the same time as the intermediate plumbing and framing inspections. I also needed an above-ceiling inspection. From what I understood, that was for the wires that ran through the trusses.

Now I had to figure out the plumbing. The walls around the bathroom shower in the house were the only walls that had to be completely finished for the final inspection; I would need to waterproof them. I had already decided that colorful Mexican tiles would be my preferred method of waterproofing.

On my second trip to Mexico with Jon, in June, we stopped at a tile store to order a hand-painted sink for the bathroom. I wanted to do that before I ran out of money and tried to talk myself into buying something recycled, because I loved these sinks. All along, I had felt that I would be happy to live in a smaller house as long as I could put beautiful, cheerful touches into it, so it radiated joy. One of the wonderful compensations of building a smaller house, I also figured, is that one can add some quality tile, fixtures, or furniture without spending lots of money, because so little is needed.

I had seen several of these sculpted clay sinks and loved their earthy warmth and bright, hand-painted colors. I could visualize the sink as the focus of the bathroom, along with some Mexican tile over the tub.

So, with no color scheme in mind, I perused the myriad sinks lining the walls of the tile warehouse on the outskirts of Puerto Penasco. A grin crept across my face as I surveyed their playful designs—I could have happily taken almost any of them home with me.

The store walls were covered with rich tile in deep blues, greens, and reds. Some danced with bright, childlike etchings, while others radiated peaceful religious symbols. If a person could get fat from imbibing colors, I would have waddled out the front door.

In the end, I ordered a pale beige sink painted with a smiling dolphin in turquoise and cobalt blue. Perhaps it was the Hawaiian in me who wanted to bring a little ocean to the unending beach of the Sonoran Desert. It would take at least a month to have it made, which was fine. I was far from ready.

Actually, it wasn't until September that we made another trip to Rocky Point to pick up the sink and select tile for the tub/shower. So that I wouldn't fall in love with some tile that was not available, the owner led us directly to their warehouse. On the way, we passed a couple of Mexican workers quietly painting elaborate scenes on some large sections of tile. At least the Mexican artists have an outlet, I thought, even though they are probably not paid anything close to what we consider a living wage.

Jon and I had a wonderful time arranging tile in diagrams on the floor of the warehouse. We avoided bulky designs that would make the small bathroom feel cluttered. We both loved the rich cobalt blue. When I pulled out some tile graced by a blue dove with open wings holding a turquoise branch in its mouth, then lay the birds in a line inside a blue border, the effect was magical. I could hardly wait to get to the fun part of decorating the house with these bright colors.

Before we could purchase the tile, we had to calculate exactly how much we would need. Unlike the hardware store, I couldn't simply skip down to Mexico for more. Over a relaxing dinner at an open seaside restaurant, Jon and I pulled out my graph-paper sketches of the shower area and calculated the number of each color tile we would need. We purchased the tile the following day. I was far from ready to install it, but it made me glow with delight just to have the boxes of bright tile in my possession as we drove them home in the back of Jon's jeep.

Now, as we completed the electric wiring in early November, I needed some plumbing lines, so the sink and shower weren't all for show. Interior plumbing consists of two steps: venting the drainpipes and running the water supply into the house.

Every plumbing fixture has a U-shaped "trap" beneath it, which catches debris that might go down the drain. The other purpose of the trap is to keep septic gases from entering the house through the drainpipes. This is accomplished as the trap stays filled with water. A vent pipe rises from beyond the trap through the roof, providing air to the system, which not only keeps water in the trap by equalizing the air pressure, but also allows the system to drain. My plumbing book likened this to putting my thumb over the top of a straw that was full of water. The water won't drain from the straw until I remove my thumb, "venting" the straw.

Venting was done with the same large, black ABS pipe that I had used for the rough-in plumbing. This time I ran it at a slight upward angle through the bathroom wall and up to the roof. For the kitchen sink, we used a vent that stayed right under the sink.

For the water supply, both Dan and Jon recommended using the Pex plumbing system, a system of flexible plastic tubing that bends around corners, so there would be no joints inside the straw walls that might leak. Each fixture had its own tube for both hot and cold water, and all the tubes were fastened to a large manifold in the tool shed on the porch.

We mounted a large roll of blue tubing in the shed and pulled tubes around the house, much as we had done with electric wires. We ran lengths for the hot and cold water to the kitchen sink, then two more that reached through the far wall for the washing machine. After those long runs were completed, we ran five short runs into the bathroom—shower hot and cold, sink hot and cold, and toilet cold.

Presto! It was done in just a few hours. Finally, something took less time than I imagined! Jon secured the pipe every four feet to either the top plate or into niches in the walls. He also soldered the connections at the water heater. My mind was tiring and the fewer details I had to learn at this point, the better.

Thanksgiving was upon us now, so we opened the large cardboard box containing the new propane stove and moved it carefully onto a wooden pallet in the center of the house, using some of the cardboard to cover the spaces between the pallet boards.

The stove was white and pristine, straight from the factory, in contrast to the dusty tools, cluttered workbench, and gravel subfloor. Jon spent an hour or so fiddling in the back of the stove to connect a small propane tank. We plugged it into an outlet and voilà! I had a real, working stove, for the first time in more than a year.

Given my druthers, I would have dropped the construction for a day and baked oatmeal-chocolate chip cookies, but there was no time for such frivolity. I needed to retrieve my holiday decorations, china, silver, and the oak dining table from under the tarp. With a mixture of trepidation and curiosity, I removed the cement blocks at the corners of the tarp and pulled back the edges.

Many of the boxes near the surface had water stains, as did the lampshades. I figured I'd worry about the boxes when I got to them, but the shades went straight to the landfill. In the top layer of boxes, I was appalled at the rat droppings in every niche. I wasn't sure I wanted to see what the lower layers looked like. Even with two cats, the rats must have found the tarp territory a cool retreat from the summer heat. They could probably withdraw to corners that cat paws couldn't reach. As I removed layers and layers of boxes, I groaned to find my cozy backpacking sleeping bag, in which the rats had chewed gaping holes. I kept digging, thankful for all the labeling I had done as we had packed.

Several boxes of holiday decorations appeared. I set them aside. A box of china made itself visible. Digging through it, I saw my old china, a tablecloth, and some candlesticks. Perfect! Another box held some wineglasses and serving bowls.

The oak table, of course, was upside down on the bottom of the pile. So, we kept digging. The back of my other sofa became visible as we neared the oak table. It had some obvious holes chewed in the fabric. I groaned. This was the sofa I had hoped to use in the straw bale house, since the other one was too large. Maybe I could put a plant behind it. But as we pulled the boxes and plastic bags off the top, there was no hope. The rats had chewed large holes in all the cushions. With a sigh, I helped Jon load it into the truck and take it to the landfill. I'd find another one, or use chairs. It would be okay, I told myself, knowing that I didn't have a spare hundred dollars for a sofa. Something would work out.

Finally, we found the old oak table and its leaf. After carrying it to the straw bale house, we set it on the concrete slab of the kitchen–dining area. The boxes of china and tablecloths sat next to it, waiting for Thanksgiving.

The Sunday before my parents arrived from Hawaii, I tidied up the construction mess in the straw bale house as much as possible and centered the old oak dining table on the cement slab that would be the dining room and kitchen. After finding a vase in my box of china, I purchased some bright flowers and placed them on the table. Now the house almost looked like a home; it was ready to show to my parents.

With joyful nostalgia, on Sunday, November 19, I greeted my parents at their hotel in downtown Tucson. I hadn't seen them in more than three years and it seemed that every time they visited, I was in a different location, with a new job and new people in my life. This visit was no different.

Yet while we sat and chatted, catching up on the events of the years, we were simply family once again; all barriers of time and space melted away. Even the details of the house seemed transient compared to the bond

*My mother and I prepare for an elegant Thanksgiving dinner with family china, candlesticks, and fresh flowers—within my new straw bale walls.* Photo by John C. Roberts.

of the two people who had known me since my entrance onto the planet and loved me through so many years and so many experiences.

As Thanksgiving Day dawned, with cloudless, blue skies and crisp temperatures hovering in the upper sixties, the oak table was surrounded by six chairs and adorned with a freshly ironed white tablecloth, candlesticks, wineglasses, old family silver, and china. Cooking a sit-down dinner seemed like a foreign task. I don't think I'd done this since last Christmas, but slowly it all came back to me. Even using a real stove and oven rather than a microwave and hot plates seemed strange, but wonderful. I didn't have to worry about the big pots falling off the burners.

The path between the straw bale house and the trailer was well trodden that day, since the refrigerator and most of the food was in the trailer, but the oven and table were at the straw bale house. I smiled as I bustled about, not only at having my family present, but to see the house dressed up for a party. Fresh flowers and candlesticks look lovely against straw walls.

Jon and my parents arrived in the early afternoon, and I delegated a few tasks. The boys peeled potatoes while my mom made the green bean casserole and Jon took charge of the mashed potatoes. Unfortunately, in all my unpacking I had forgotten to find a mixer or a masher, so that all we had for mashing the potatoes was either a fork or a wire whisk. Both were clearly too flimsy for the large, multipotato job at hand.

We decided that there must be a power tool for the job. After tossing around a few possibilities, we settled on a power drill with the widest spade bit we could find. Spade bits flare out at the bottom to drill large holes and we'd been making quite a few lately for the electric wires and plumbing tubes. I'm sure Jon's hands felt right at home as they loaded up the one-and-a-half-inch spade bit and whizzed through the potatoes with ease. They came out as smooth and fluffy as any batch I'd ever made in my fancy Kitchenaid mixer.

We had a few moments before dinner to sit down and toast the reunion with sparkling apple juice. It was fun to feel leisurely and elegant, if only for a few minutes. The house smelled like a home as we piled the workbench with steaming, savory dishes and loaded up our plates. We sang an old hymn that I remember from my childhood, "Come Ye Thankful People Come," and then settled into silence as we enjoyed the results of our cooking.

Certainly, I felt grateful for everything around me—the house nearing completion, the family that had supported me through it, Jon's love and guidance, my children who had helped and shared the trailer with relatively few complaints, and simply the opportunity to live out a dream. I couldn't think of any period of my life when I had felt more fulfilled and alive since the birth of my children.

## Chapter Eighteen

# THE INSPECTOR

*Never despair, but if you do, work on in despair.*

—EDMUND BURKE

MY parents had a few more days in Tucson before they drove north to Sedona, and Dad wondered if he could somehow help with the house. Immediately, the earthen plasters popped into my mind. Jon and I had been so busy with the interior details of the house that I hadn't even taken time to test my formula for the plasters. I needed to determine the proper ratios of clay, sand, and straw before I had a big plaster party, as well as get an idea of how long this would take, so we decided to start on one wall.

I knew I shouldn't do testing right next to the front door where everyone would see it, but that was the area of the porch with a roof over it, so we did. For two mornings, Dad came out and mixed up batches of mud with me in the wheelbarrow, adjusting the ingredients until we got the right consistency, then smearing the mixture across the damp straw with our bare hands. There is no way to stay clean with this project, and we both ended up covered with mud by midday. My father is a wonderful sport about such things—the source of my do-it-yourself genes.

I had wanted to find him something that wasn't life threatening, but even this task required balancing on the top of a tall ladder to reach the upper bales. But Dad was in great shape and that didn't phase him. By the weekend, we had a rich, chocolate brown wall by the front door and the first layer of mud by the bedroom door. While it was still damp the following day, I smoothed the plaster further with a metal trowel but left the area by the window rough so I could sculpt a frame around it in the near future.

I could have had my parents sign the wall, but instead I asked them to press their palms into wet concrete stepping-stone. This would be the first stone for a walkway I had planned out the front door. At my next work-shop or whenever I was ready for a housewarming party, I wanted to have everyone who had contributed to the house make a stone for the walk-way—kind of like Hollywood Boulevard, only with far more significance for me.

With this wall as inspiration, I scheduled my next work party, the earthen plaster party, for January 27. It would be after the holidays this time, not right before Christmas as my wall raising had been. That date should give me enough time to complete all the other little details of the interior before the party and to build the earthen floor after the party before my completion deadline of March 1. I sent out an e-mail to everyone who had worked at the wall raising and many of the people who had stopped by in the past year, offering to help. I would hold to that date firmly, I said in the e-mail, rain or shine, since we had a porch for protection.

By mid-December, I was ready for four difficult inspections, known as "the intermediates," to examine everything inside the walls before we covered them. I would need to pass the final frame inspection that would study the construction of the interior walls, the intermediate plumbing inspection for the venting and supply pipes, the intermediate wiring inspec-tion for all those electrical wires and boxes, and the above-ceiling inspec-tion for any part of the wiring and plumbing that ran into the ceiling area. Another builder told me that passing these was like trudging over the crest of a mountain; it would all be downhill from there.

This time, I decided to take the inspection day off so I could meet the inspector, and celebrate Christmas with my boys before they left to visit their father on Kauai. I crossed my fingers and said a few prayers as I phoned in the inspections. The next morning, I was out at the house early so I wouldn't miss the inspector, busying myself with odd jobs and paint-ing the gable ends while I waited. By two o'clock, it was time to take the boys to the mall and out to dinner for Christmas and the inspector hadn't come. It wasn't a disaster if he rejected the inspections, but I would so much love to just pass one clean the first time, I thought. I really, really hoped I wouldn't come home to a white slip with notes on it.

As I entered the house in the dark at seven, there was a white paper with more notes on it than I'd ever seen before—a list of about ten things! I sighed out loud, then got out the cordless phone and called Jon. We ran through the list together and he clarified some of the items. Most of them were minor. We needed a fire break, or a strip of ceiling, in the center of the double wall between the bathroom and bedroom; anchor bolts were needed in the sunroom on either side of the door; and the inspector wanted me to cut little niches in the framing beneath the sunroom windows so he could see the anchor bolts that went into the concrete. Photos of J-bolts sticking out of the concrete were no good, he said.

But the biggest problems were again that we had made changes that weren't on the plans. I had changed from a propane water heater to an electric one when I discovered how expensive propane is. I needed to write that on the plans and get it approved by the building department. Also, I had moved the refrigerator and reduced the number of outlets in the sunroom. Outlets are required every twelve feet, and I may have reduced it down to less than that. Also, in the loft, the railing for the stairway was considered a wall, so I might need an outlet in one of the closets at the top of the stairs, or in the floor, to qualify for an outlet every twelve feet. The spiral staircase had changed much of the layout for the electric wiring routes and cooler ducting, also. The diagram of the cooler ducting, along with the routes for the propane pipes, was known as the "mechanicals." He wanted to see those changes, even though I hadn't phoned in the mechanical inspection yet.

"Nit-picking!" I exploded in frustration. Everything we were doing was to code, and I had been told many times that minor changes would be okay with the inspector as long as they were to code. This was the same inspector that had made us file appeals for the roofing paper over the bottom course of bales and get permission for earthen plasters on the last inspection. I wanted my old inspector back!

Maybe if I waited long enough, the inspectors would rotate. I called the building department to find out that inspectors were rotated annually, sometime in June. I sighed again. That would be too long to wait. This would be my inspector for the final permit, so I had better knuckle down and clarify everything.

Jon was in Tubac, fighting the flu and very busy, so I sat down the following evening with ruler and paper and attempted to redraw the electrical and mechanical diagrams. Actually, an evening in front of *National Geographic Explorer* on TV, inside the warm trailer, was a nice break from construction. It wasn't too hard to trace the floor plan and redraw the electric diagram. For the mechanical, I copied most of what was on the plans, moving the ducts around the staircase. I was surprised at how much I knew by now, a year and a half since I had first laid eyes on the blueprints at Dan's house.

Jon dropped by my office the following day to review the drawings. His cold had settled into laryngitis, but he agreed to take them to the building department for me. He seemed to have a rapport with Mr. Overhill, the senior plans examiner, that I did not possess. If I requested the changes on my own, most likely I would be told to leave the drawings at the front desk and they'd review them in a week or so.

Before framing the loft, Jon had drawn up a diagram for supporting the floor around the spiral staircase. There was no explanation of how to do this on my plans. When we took the diagram to the building department for approval, the building official at the front desk unrolled our plans and immediately referred us to Mr. Overhill. He looked over the plans and coldly told us we'd have to take them back to the draftsman, Dan.

Apparently, when the loft had been rejected, Dan had gotten into a bitter argument with Mr. Overhill over allowing the mezzanine when two-story straw bale homes weren't allowed in Pima County, and also about how and where to place the spiral staircase. Dan had gone to Mr. Overhill's superior and received an approval of the plans, but Mr. Overhill was not happy. He had wanted more details on the plans and since he didn't get them at the beginning, he would get them now.

Very calmly, Jon assured the senior examiner that he had taken over this project, and he would draw any necessary details from here on forward. I let the two men continue their discussion as Jon not only received confirmation that we could build the loft, but some great advice on how best to construct it.

When the discussion turned to supporting a spiral staircase with an earthen floor, I explained what was involved in building such a floor and Mr. Overhill warmed right up. He told me of a long-surviving earthen floor in a government building in Santa Fe and asked to see my floor when it was completed. I promised that I would let him know when that day arrived and silently vowed to do my very best job on the floor.

Now that we had more diagrams to be approved in order to pass our intermediate inspections, both Jon and I knew that Mr. Overhill was the only official who could approve the drawings. Jon went by the building department on Thursday, December 21, and was told that Mr. Overhill had gone home for the day. The official at the front desk confirmed that nobody else had permission to make changes on these particular plans. Mr. Overhill would be in the next day, the Friday before Christmas, and then would be on vacation the following week. Jon had work to do in Tubac on Friday, but he figured he could make it to the building department by three, since Mr. Overhill wasn't scheduled to leave until four. I crossed my fingers.

About now, I began to give up on keeping any sort of time schedule for the completion of the house. Everything simply took the amount of time that it took and there wasn't always much I could do about it. If we missed

Mr. Overhill and had to wait until after the holidays, then the insulating and interior finish wouldn't begin until sometime into January. Not only had I missed any hope of moving into the house for Christmas, but completion by the end of February, as I had promised the court, looked bleak with the many details still to go. I had never heard back from Kathy about rent, and I had no desire to call her and stir things up. So, sue me Kathy, I thought, there's only so much I can do.

Jon arrived on Friday evening and proudly handed me a set of all my drawings and changes, approved by Mr. Overhill. I let out a big sigh of relief and gleefully spent the weekend adding outlets to the sunroom and loft, wiring for phone and satellite cable, installing a ceiling strip in the bathroom wall, and all the other little details required by the inspector. The day after Christmas, I rephoned all the inspections for Wednesday, December 27.

I was napping on the afternoon that the inspector arrived. The laryngitis flu was working its way into my body, so I had taken the afternoon off work. When I woke from my nap, I saw the white government pickup parked by the straw bale house. I ventured forth in my slippers and finally greeted the inspector. This was the first time we had seen each other.

A short, stalky man with gray hair and a pleasant face, he greeted me with a big smile and handshake. With a fatherly concern, he walked me through the house, showing me more things we needed to fix. The light over the tub should be recessed for a waterproof fixture. The electrical wires leading to the main box were bunched too tightly, so they might overheat. The sunroom would need to be enclosed for the final frame approval. I would need outlets every four feet around the kitchen, and so on. I wondered silently if this inspector would ever be satisfied and why I couldn't have ended up with an easygoing inspector like my friends had, who glanced around the place and approved things.

The inspector complimented me on the stained-glass window in the gable, but had this curious smile on his face that made me wonder if he were laughing at the house, or just being friendly. I had a feeling this wasn't exactly the sort of house he would build himself. At any rate, he wasn't hostile and most of his concerns were valid; he was just a very thorough inspector. The main problem now was that he wouldn't pass the final frame inspection until we had installed the ducting for the cooler, passing the intermediate mechanical inspection. This meant I still couldn't begin insulating and covering the walls. I also had to get a specialist to come out and design the ducts to fit the openings. That would take time.

I watched bleakly as the inspector took out the proverbial white sheet of paper with the four inspections printed on them. Next to each one, he wrote "reject," and then listed the six things he wanted changed beneath. I took the paper, thanked him, and strolled back to the trailer. As I sat there, in a weak haze of menthol steam, surrounded by lozenges, tissues, and vitamins, I let the house go. I didn't have the energy to think about it, nor push toward any more deadlines.

My voice had vanished, so I couldn't even make phone calls to order supplies, and my body was screaming at me for rest. This flu felt like it was on its way toward bronchitis if I didn't slow down. I watched an old Shirley Temple movie on TV, then worked on my journal and Web pages until bedtime. It was time to let go and let things take the time that they needed.

For a few days, heading into the New Year, I fell into a delirium of exhaustion, TV shows, and dreams of Kathy towing away the trailer or hauling me into court if I missed my deadline at the end of February. The boys were on Kauai, frolicking in the surf with their father, and I once again wondered why I was building this house. I really couldn't remember. The joy I used to feel from completing each phase of construction had vanished into an endless stream of things yet to be done. Would they ever end?

I hadn't balanced my checking account in a few days, and I didn't know if I had any money left, either. I had used up the entire $10,000 from my parents and the cash from the sale of my car had gone into building the loft. The additional $10,000 credit union loan had vanished into the porch construction and other endless purchases. Now, I was borrowing money from Andrzej.

I still didn't know how much more money I would need. I had to purchase kitchen counters, the bathroom vanity, light fixtures, insulation, more clay soil for the plasters and floor, oils for the floor, reed matting for the ceiling, and probably more. I had no sense of money any longer; I didn't even know what I would be charged for the ducting and I didn't care.

If I were going to survive to the finish line, I needed to let go of this stress and rediscover my joy of working in the moment, enjoying the process, and not worrying about the future. The weather had been perfect lately; we were having consistently sunny days in the upper sixties and low seventies while the rest of the country was covered in an icy blizzard, but I hadn't noticed. Jon and my boys had been by my side whenever I needed them, but I hadn't told them how much I appreciated their love and support. I had barely noticed the little birds who flitted and chirped around me while I worked nor the way Alien Kitty devotedly climbed my ladder to meet me at the top.

I turned my thoughts within. Okay, God, I've made it this far and I thank you for that. But I'm staggering toward the finish line. Both of the guardian cactus have died and what happened in the courtroom back there with Kathy? I don't mind paying $1,000 if that seems fair, but I need this pressure to ease up. If Kathy's out there planning another lawsuit, would you handle it for me? Distract her until I'm done? Find her another trailer? I can't work any faster, and I can't spend money on attorneys. Okay? I need some rest on all levels—body, mind, and soul. Please? Thanks.

Prying myself off the sofa on Friday, December 29, I began the details for enclosing the sunroom and preparing for the mechanical inspection. I purchased a door, several sheets of siding, and black pipe for the propane connections. Jon arrived Saturday morning with a promise that the cooler ducts were under construction by a reliable sheet metal company. As I slipped into my paint-covered work clothes and wandered out to the straw bale house with my cup of tea, a peace fell over me. It would all be okay, somehow.

Still feeling fairly weak, I told Jon how very thankful I was for his presence and strength. With lozenges and tissues on the worktable, I made some of the minor additions the inspector requested, while Jon began enclosing the sunroom. We pushed the propane lines through the wall behind the stove and dug a trench to take the lines five feet away from the house. I was only going to use a small five- or ten-gallon propane tank to power the stove, but this was the code. The weather was gorgeous, once again, and a flicker of joy returned.

As I headed to work on January 2, 2001, the sunroom had windows, siding, and a door, and all the details for the inspector were completed except the ducting, which was due to be installed that day. We still had to frame in the closet around the ducting, which might delay the inspection another week, but I tried not to worry about that.

On Monday evening, the ducting was installed through the north wall branching into shiny silver tubes that spread through the ceiling over the bathroom and bedroom. Hiring people to do the work is so delightful! I immediately began framing the closet around the ducts, though I was still weak and the long, gold screws just wouldn't budge. My body wanted to be back on the couch in front of the TV, but I kept working.

On Friday, I felt good enough to phone six inspections for Monday: the intermediate mechanical, electric, and plumbing, along with the final framing, above ceiling, and gas pressure test on the propane lines. Jon came down that weekend and installed a pressure valve at the end of the propane lines, then pressurized the pipes with a bicycle tire pump. The pipes held the pressure and everything else looked in order, so we spent the majority of the weekend covering the porch roof with metal sheets. Randy had gone to help Jon in Tubac before the porch roof had been completed and with all the details of the plumbing and wiring, I had left the rafters uncovered for two months.

We were both tired. Jon's job in Tubac was at the same phase as my house—full of details and labor while he worked toward "the intermediates." But rain was due in the coming week, so I wanted to get as much of the roof on as possible. At the beginning of the day, I dropped my trusty screw gun off the roof one last time. This time, it landed on the tip and the whole mechanism wobbled. Its nine lives were used up, and I felt as if I'd lost a good friend.

This was the first tool I had bought when I began the house; it had driven screws from the foundation forms to the roof and now for much of the framing. Repairs would be more expensive than buying a new one, but I couldn't throw it away, so I put it in its case and tucked it under the worktable. Jon lent me his gun to complete the roofing that day.

Monday was a nervous day at my office job as I wondered if I were passing the inspections. I had already scheduled the insulation company to come on Thursday, because I simply couldn't wait any longer. Everything was set; I couldn't think of anything more the inspector might find and if I passed all the inspections, I only had the final inspections to go. Gee, I thought I had left this tension of passing exams behind me when I left school!

I almost called Andrzej halfway through the day to ask him if there was a white paper from the inspector, but I didn't want it to upset my day at work. I waited until I drove home, dashed out of the truck, and bolted into the main room of the straw bale house. There, in the darkness of the evening, I saw the shadow of a white paper on my clipboard. Not good. I flicked on the light to see what was written on the paper.

There were no words at the bottom. Glancing at the top, the six inspections were listed and "OK" was scrawled next to each one. I stared at them again, to be sure it was an "okay" and not a "reject," because usually the white paper meant rejections. Lifting up the paper, I saw the inspector's initials next to each one of the inspections on my main sheet.

Tears of relief welled at my eyes; I had made it over the mountain peak. Brushing away my tears and unclipping the paper, I dashed back toward the trailer to call Jon and tell him we had passed. It took a few hours for the realization to sink in that I had passed twenty out of twenty-four inspections and I was on my way home. The joy gushed forth as I called my parents, e-mailed my friends, and danced lightly on the gravel floor. I even e-mailed Kathy saying, "I just passed all my intermediate inspections, so I only have the finals left. It looks like I'm on schedule for the end of February. Thanks for being so patient!"

## Chapter Nineteen

# FRIENDS IN DEED

*In prosperity our friends know us; in adversity we know our friends.*

—JOHN CHURLTON COLLINS

IN choosing a house design, I hadn't really thought about the height of the ceiling. I had figured that a high ceiling would make the house look larger, but I hadn't considered what it would be like to build the ceiling, any more than I had considered the steep pitch of the roof. At that point, I hadn't even known what was involved in building a ceiling, anyway.

As the construction progressed, a wonderful, arched dome appeared over the main room, and indeed, it made the room look more expansive to have such a high space. The center of the ceiling was eighteen feet high and the edges were about eleven feet. As Jon was working on the steep roof the previous spring, he had insisted that I should be sure to hire a crew to insulate and drywall the ceiling, because he knew it would be a really difficult job; one that he surely didn't want to do.

The trusses above the ceiling would need to be insulated, then covered with drywall. Drywall sheets are large, heavy, and fragile. The 4 x 8-foot sheets are made of gypsum, or plaster of Paris, pressed into half-inch boards and then covered with heavy paper on both sides. The paper holds the boards together. If drywall gets wet, the paper turns to mush, as does the interior gypsum. If it is dropped, the board crumbles.

To drywall the ceiling, these cumbersome boards would have to be hoisted in place and aligned perfectly down the center of a truss while being screwed in place. I assured Jon I would do my best to hire out that work.

Now, it looked like we would be the ones drywalling the ceiling. As we passed the intermediate inspections, I gathered bids to drywall the house. The lowest was $3,000. I only had about $1,500 available to complete the house, no matter how I tried to adjust the figures and cut costs. I had nothing left to sell and I had used up my credit union loan, so I figured this meant I was supposed to drywall the ceiling myself—somehow.

First came the insulation of the ceiling, which had been underway since the summer. I had decided on two types of ceiling insulation, since the roof is where the sun really bakes on the house. With the boys living in the loft, the area directly beneath the roof needed to stay as cool as possible. Under the roofing, stapled to the upper board of the trusses, we would install a thin layer of double-sided foil called a radiant heat barrier. This would reflect the heat that came down through the roof up and out the vented ridge. It would also reflect the temperature that rose from the house back down into the living space. Beneath the radiant heat barrier, we would install thick fiberglass batts as further insulation.

Since Zej was home by himself in the afternoons, he was volunteered to install the radiant heat barrier while Jon and I worked on the plumbing and wiring. I bought Zej an electric stapler and set up all the supplies in the loft, along with a mark on the floor for the length at which he should cut the long rolls of foil into strips.

He did work on it, slowly but steadily, completing about one truss a week. When we moved the scaffold into the house to run electric wires through the ceiling, I helped him get the job done just a little faster. We spent a Saturday afternoon together with the scaffold placed in the center of the house. Crouching on long 2 x 10-inch boards that rested from the top plate to the upper scaffold rungs, we could reach the sides of the ceiling.

It was awkward, clumsy work, facilitated only by the fact that we were relatively small people, so we could curl up into the tiny spaces of the rafters and staple over our heads. With two people working, one stapling over the top plate and one in the center, we moved fairly quickly down the line of twenty-two trusses toward the west end of the house. By the time we passed all the intermediate inspections, the radiant heat barrier was in place.

Now, we needed to fill the trusses with R–30 fiberglass batts. ("R–30" is the R-value rating of the fiberglass. R-value, a standard way of rating the insulative capacity of building materials, equals the number of seconds it takes for one joule of heat to penetrate one square foot of the material for each degree of temperature difference between the two sides. Batts that fit into conventional house walls framed with 2 x 4s usually rate R–11; straw bales are about R–55, varying with the type of straw and the density of the bale.) Fiberglass is itchy, nasty stuff that emits tiny fibers that can cut the breathing passages and leave rashes on the skin. I had already tried insulating the walls of the tool shed, around the hot water heater, and learned quickly to wear long sleeves and a breathing mask. I happily paid a few hundred dollars to hire a company to insulate the ceiling.

By early January, after passing the intermediate inspections, we were ready to drywall the ceiling. For several weeks, Jon and I had been tossing around ideas on how to do this—along with trying to find a cheaper bid, so we wouldn't have to. But that was to no avail. Somehow, we had to lift the heavy drywall sheets from the ground below and hold them in place. Phoning several rental companies, I found that the only drywall lifts available reach eleven and a half feet at the most. They will hold a full sheet of drywall and tilt at an angle, but it simply wasn't high enough.

Jon recommended that we cut the sheets in half and slide them up the long, twenty-foot ladder to people on the scaffold. The only problem that I foresaw was trying to reach the outer edges of the ceiling that were beyond the scaffold. Jon figured the edges of the ceiling could be reached from a ladder propped against the wall, but then again, even half sheets are heavy for someone balancing on a ladder. After my work on the gable ends, hoisting and nailing heavy OSB board, I could imagine how difficult this would be.

As the weekend of January 13 approached for the drywalling to begin, the carpenter who was going to help us had other things to do and couldn't come. I'm pretty sure Jon wished he could come up with something else to do, also. Then Jodi, a friend of mine from the meditation group who had recently finished drywalling a shed at her house, suddenly offered to come help with her husband, Kim.

Now, I could see volunteering for a wall raising or a plaster party, but I had never, ever imagined that anyone would volunteer to come help us drywall the ceiling. I hadn't even been able to find a laborer who wanted to do the job for money. This was what I would call a good friend. And sure enough, they drove up at 8:30 on Saturday morning ready to work.

Jon had given me a run-through on the basics of drywalling while we covered one wall of the tool shed. It was much like the jigsaw-puzzle work I had done on the gable ends, measuring the shape of an area (with any luck, a square or rectangular area, but often a rhomboid) and cutting a piece to fit.

The goal of covering an area with drywall is, of course, to cover the area with as small gaps as possible and have the edges of the boards end over a piece of wood, so they can be screwed into place. After that, the seams and screws have to be taped for strength and covered with a layer of soft, wet gypsum "mud," so the wall ends up relatively smooth. Drywall doesn't burn, so by covering a wall with it seamlessly, we would help prevent fire damage to the house.

Jon fitted both of our power drivers with tips made especially for drywall, with a Phillips head in the center and another circle flaring outside the driver head. When I pushed a screw too far into the drywall, it broke through the surface of the protective paper, and thereby lost its strength to support the board. The screwdriver tip allowed the screw to dimple slightly into the paper, but not break it. The indent into the paper was so the head of the screw could be covered later with gypsum to smooth out the wall.

Most people then spray a gypsum texture onto their drywall, but I didn't think that look would blend with this earthy house. Instead, my ceiling would be covered with reed matting, which would not only look great, but cover all imperfections in our work.

Most of my framed interior walls would likewise be covered with drywall and then burlap soaked in a clay slip. I had heard about this technique at the workshops, and it seemed like an easy wall covering that would cover imperfections and blend with the earthen plasters. Also, if I later decided that I'd like to apply clay plasters over the burlap, it would serve as a texture to hold the mud.

With this overview of drywall in my head, I welcomed Jodi and Kim on Saturday morning. Jodi, a vivacious bundle of energy, loves construction as much as I do. They pitched right in, donning their tool belts and climbing the twelve-foot scaffold perched inside the west end of the house. The scaffold was eight feet wide, so we could reach most of the highest areas from its platform. We put the special tips on our drivers and began covering the gable end with drywall.

This was when I realized that having walls plumb and square really cuts down on the drywall time. However, when one is dealing with a load-bearing top plate, one is not dealing with plumb and square objects. So each piece of drywall had to be measured as a rhomboid. Jon stood below, taking the measurements that were called from above and slicing the drywall with a sharp utility knife.

As we finished covering the gable end, another friend, Donna, called and asked if she could come help, too. So, by 10 A.M., we had five people working. As we moved onto the ceiling, we realized that we needed the strong-shouldered men below and the smaller women on the scaffold. It was cramped quarters up there and heavy work lifting the sheets of drywall from below.

Jodi and I became the team on the upper scaffold, while Jon and Kim cut and lifted sheets. Donna helped as she was needed, either by writing down measurements or as an extra hand to lift difficult sheets.

We propped two ladders against the north wall and measured for our first full sheet to fit along one of the sloping sides of the cathedral trusses. Each sheet would cover two truss spaces. The men decided they could easily slide a full sheet up the twenty-foot ladder and onto the scaffold, where Jodi and I would rotate it and slide it back down to them as they scrambled up the ladders on the north wall. Jodi and I called out our measurements to Jon.

"West eighty-nine and a half, east ninety and an eighth, top forty-seven and a half, bottom forty-eight."

At that point, Jon had to reverse the measurements, since the board would be flipped upside down. When it was cut, Kim slid it up the ladder to Jodi and I, who crouched on our knees and glided the board over our heads, then rotated it toward the side to be drywalled. As we slid it down along the trusses, Kim and Jon climbed the ladders against the wall and caught the lower edge of the board.

At this point, as we all balanced this heavy sheet over our heads and eyed our corners and edges, we gave each other a status report in strained voices, most of our energy in our arms. Usually it went something like this:

"I'm a half-inch short on the northwest corner, but perfect on the northeast."

"We're long at the bottom, can we push it up any?"

"I think if we slide it west a little, we could get some more room, but I'll need to shave this one corner."

"I'm too far over on the truss. The next sheet won't have anything to screw into; we need to move it west."

The board was then moved around until it rested in its most optimum location. Then the utility knife or shaver tool was passed to any place that was long until the board fit. Drywall chips away easily, so I had to remember that this isn't a piece of wood and couldn't be forced into position with a hammer. Otherwise, I'd have a messy hole in the board or a scrunched-up corner.

On rare occasions, the conversation went:

"Perfect all along the top."

"We're perfect on the bottom."

"Speak now or forever hold your peace!"

Silence.

"Okay, go for it!"

At which point we all raised our screw guns and let the 1⅝" drywall screws whir. The screws had to enter the drywall very near the edges, so the screw would secure into the thin edge of the truss. As if it weren't enough that the walls weren't square, a few of the trusses were about an inch off. We had to secure another 2 x 4 board to the side of them if the drywall wouldn't reach.

All in all, it was a good thing I intended to cover the ceiling with reed fencing, because none of the imperfections, where the drywall didn't meet or we cut a hole for a light in the wrong place, would show.

I was on the scaffold for about half the day, but Jodi was up there the whole time, from 9 A.M. to 5 P.M. when we finally called it quits. Each time I climbed down the ladder, my knees felt bruised and I couldn't imagine how her knees were holding up. At one point, I rummaged under the tarp by the trailer and came out with two pads that go beneath sleeping bags. With these on top of the truss platform, our knees had a little cushioning, but not much.

As the sun lowered toward the mountains and the light dimmed through the west windows, we holstered our drivers and decided that was enough for one day. I couldn't have been happier. We had made it across almost the entire vaulted ceiling. Only one more sheet width to go, and we'd have the loft beneath us instead of the scaffold.

What an incredible help everyone had been. I wondered if I would ever sacrifice a whole day to help someone out like that! Maybe now I would, knowing how much it meant to have them help.

The next day, Jon and I finished drywalling the ceiling with the boys' help, but my arms felt like lead weights and my knees felt like they'd been hit with hammers. I could barely muster the strength to push the screws through the sheets, but unfortunately I had reasons to keep pushing myself.

My big earth plaster party was in two weekends. So far, more than twenty people had signed up and I wanted to be sure to use every one of them to their maximum capability. The ceiling had to be completed, so I could move the scaffold outside the house. We could break it down into two five-foot sections and use it to reach the upper bales. Besides fastening the drywall sheets to the trusses, I had to tape and mud the seams in the drywall, then paint the entire ceiling black and staple the reed matting into place before I could devote the scaffold to plastering.

During the weekday evenings, I kept working on taping and mudding the ceiling with wet gypsum, which is finer and smoother than any cake icing I've ever dealt with. I usually worked until ten or eleven—past my bedtime. Since I get up at 5 A.M., I try to tuck in by 9:30 P.M. The boys would come out and say, "Mom, go to bed, it's late!"

Wednesday evening was my time to get away from it all and meditate, so I took a break, even though my mind was trying to tell me how much work I had to do and how I couldn't afford to take an evening off. I knew a little about my mental and physical limits by this point, and I knew not to push them too far, so I went to meditation.

On Thursday, the gypsum mud was dry. I set to work sanding it with a very fine, black mesh sandpaper made for that purpose. I marveled at how smooth the gypsum can become and how little humps and bumps can disappear, though I didn't take the time to make it very smooth. I now knew why houses are covered with white powder when the drywall crew is finished.

On Friday evening, I began painting the ceiling black with a long-handled roller. Jon had been reed-matting ceilings for more than ten years and he assured me that if you leave the drywall white, it will show between the reeds, but if you paint it black, it will disappear and look like a shadow. It was one more step, but I decided to do it right.

My work clothes were becoming quite decorative, I thought. They were coated with various layers of earthen residues, white stucco, daubs of Liquid Nails and other caulkings, four colors of paint from the symbols on the gable ends, and now white gypsum and black paint from the ceiling. I thought perhaps I should mount and hang my jeans on the wall after the house was completed, as a memory of each phase of construction, but Jon and the boys weren't supportive of this idea.

After painting the ceiling, my arms and shoulders felt like I had decorated the Sistine Chapel. I permitted them a few stretches and kept going on Saturday morning, anxious to apply burlap soaked in a clay slip to the west gable end and apply the reed matting. This was the final weekend before the earth plaster party.

On a lunch hour during the week, I had gone to a ceramics store and purchased a large bag of white clay and some gold clay. After mixing lots of white clay with a little gold and enough water to turn it into a thick pudding, it looked like gray sludge.

A little nervous about the result, I spread some of the goo onto my Levis and headed over to the trailer to dry it with a hair dryer. The result was actually very nice—a mild parchment color. I didn't know if the texture of my Levis was affecting the color, but I liked it enough to give it a try.

Using push pins, I fastened a sheet of burlap onto the drywall and cut it into the desired shape to fit the gable end. Climbing back down the scaffold, I drenched the burlap in the clay mixture and climbed back up. The burlap clung to the wall with ease, pulled and pushed to fit the area required, but it had shrunk slightly from the water. So, I cut my next piece larger than needed. I also took the bucket of clay to the top of the scaffold, so I wouldn't have to drip and slip as I climbed the ladder.

It really was a simple, easy process, though the color still looked like a darkish muck. I smiled on the assurance that I would wake up in the morning and see a light parchment color. My arms and shoulders were screaming for a rest, and the sun was lowering in the sky as I completed this phase. Several people who had seen my Web pages stopped by—one group from Montana and one lady from Boston—so I happily took a break and gave them tours. I climbed back onto the scaffold at the end of the day long enough to spread blue paint in the niche around the stained-glass window, then called it a day.

On Sunday, sure enough, I awoke to a lovely beige-gold west gable highlighted by the blue niche. I loved the slight texture from the burlap, along with the organic look of the clay. Now it was finally time for Jon and me to begin the process of laying reed matting over the blackened ceiling. I could hardly wait.

We tossed the rolls onto the top of the scaffold, then climbed up after them with a large box of staples and hand-staplers. I had painted the staples black on the previous day so they wouldn't show, and Jon had brought two T25 staplers with a rounded tip, which apply rounded staples that wouldn't crush the reeds. We worked into the evening as the ceiling slowly turned from black to gold.

For the next few evenings I needed to prepare for the earth plaster party by clearing out some of the clutter around the outside walls, moving the scaffold outside, and preparing food. I had almost thirty people scheduled to arrive on Saturday, so I would need lots of chopped straw to mix with the mud. I had chosen a very simple formula for my plasters—clay soil, straw, and water. Clay would give the plaster strength and hardness, while wet straw would bond the clay and keep it from cracking while it dried. But there would be no time to chop straw during the party. Since Zej wasn't working too many hours at the *Arizona Daily Star*, I asked him if he would chop a couple of bags of straw each day in Jon's old chipper/shredder.

As if the Universe enjoyed giving me a hard time before every work party, the chipper decided to die on Monday. Andrzej called me at the office to let me know. There had been no grinding or gnashing of gears, no laudable explosion; it simply died in its sleep one night and refused to start the next morning. Zej took it to the mechanic down the road who gave a dim prognosis; it was beyond repair. We were talking hundreds of dollars, or basically a new 5hp Briggs & Stratton motor.

At first I didn't worry, assuming I could simply rent one somewhere. But after six phone calls to various rental agencies and six messages telling me they didn't rent chippers, I began to worry. I decided to buy one. Price quotes of about $500 greeting me at each store I called.

Finally, on Monday evening, I phoned a friend who told me that Keely Meagan's pamphlet about earth plasters mentions a simple mulcher available from Sears for about $100, a Leaf Whacker Plus. On Tuesday, I phoned the Sears near my work to inquire. The garden department told me they could order one and get it in on Friday, the day before the workshop.

That was a little too close for comfort for me, but better than nothing. However, I was planning on taking all of Friday off work to premix plasters for the party, and this store was on the other side of town, where I worked. It would take at least two hours out of my day to drive there and pick it up, so I called the Sears that is closer to my home. The main lawn and garden salesman found a Leaf Whacker Plus in his system, but said his computer kept refusing the code. He would need to confer with someone who wasn't in his office.

By Wednesday morning, the salesman, who was not accustomed to ordering leaf mulchers in the desert, still could not find the proper code to place the order. I suggested he call a New England store where I was quite sure they ordered these mulchers all the time. I don't think he appreciated the suggestion because he never called me back.

Mildly crazed, I phoned back to the first Sears and asked them if Leaf Whackers really did exist and if they still could get one in by Friday.

He replied, "Oh, I know they exist because we have one right here on the floor as a demo."

"You do!" I exclaimed, "Really? May I buy it today?"

"Well, I'm not sure if it's all there, but I'll check and call you back," he replied.

For about five minutes, I barely breathed. When he did call back, he told me the Leaf Whacker Plus was all there, complete with owner's manual, and since they had only sold one in the last three years—to a straw bale builder, I figured—they would sell it to me.

"Oh, thank you!" I exclaimed. I could well imagine that the Spirit Beings in charge of this house construction were having themselves a good little chortle as I took lunch early on Wednesday and raced over to Sears.

They had probably taken bets on whether I'd find the only leaf mulcher in the Sonoran Desert!

By Wednesday evening, I was happily chopping straw into large black bags. The mulcher worked perfectly. It only weighed a few pounds, so it was easy to move around and conveniently chopped the straw straight into the trash bag.

After moving the scaffold outside the house, I stepped back inside and glanced up at the open ceiling. The rough textures and organic colors of the reeds, along with the burlap on the gable end highlighted by the blue niche around the stained glass, were breathtaking. With a mixture of elation and exhaustion, I could see the interior becoming more beautiful than I had ever imagined.

But I found it was better if I didn't really step back and look too often. My mind and body had this way of thinking it was close enough to done, so couldn't they relax now? Paradoxically, the closer I seemed to being done, the harder it was to keep pushing on. I did better if I just kept thinking about what I had to do each day and moving forward, one small step at a time, as I had done for the past year and a half.

*Chapter Twenty*

# PLASTER PARTY

*Up to a point a man's life is shaped by environment, heredity, move-ments and changes in the world about him. Then there comes a time when it lies within his grasp to shape the clay of his life into the sort of thing he wishes to be. . . . Everyone has it within his power to say, "This I am today; that I will be tomorrow."*

—Louis L'Amour

I HAD scheduled the plastering party for the weekend of January 27, 2001. Ever since starting work in the house, I had been looking forward to the day I could begin the earthen plasters—the one phase of construction that I had studied. It had been a very busy year and a half since I attended my first earthen floor workshop at Canelo in June of 1999, and many, many details had crowded the plastering techniques to the recesses of my mind. Now I began retrieving those memories.

I had attended another workshop on earthen plasters while I was wait-ing for my building permit to be approved in September of 1999. To help my fingers remember the texture of a good clay mixture—how it squishes between the fingers and sticks to the trowel but spreads smoothly into the crevices of the straw—the Steens invited me to sit in on a couple of additional workshops after we had moved into the trailer in the spring of 2000. That helped a great deal, because my fingers and my mind had been through many distractions since my first workshop.

The focus of one of the workshops had been using casein, powdered nonfat milk protein, as a strengthener and water repellent. Many years ago, casein was used to make glue and paint, since it mixed easily with water to form a sticky, milky gel that dried hard (for glue) and clear (for paint.) The only problem with using it as a waterproofing agent in plasters was that it was no longer readily available and had never been approved by the building department.

In the spring 2000 workshops, I heard that casein doesn't really hold up very well in wet weather and that lime plasters repel water much better. The straw bale listserv had carried on a long discussion about the use of lime plasters in the fall of 1999, the winter 2000 issue of *The Last Straw* newsletter had been dedicated to lime plasters, and the Steens' workshops had discussed mixing about 10 percent lime with earth plasters to make them more waterproof and very hard.

When Wayne Bingham, the architect who was living with the Steens at the time, stopped by my house in May of 2000, he had recommended that I mix lime with the earth plasters and then coat them with lime and sand. He told me of his travels through Europe, marveling at the beauty of the lime finishes on some of the older homes.

The first discussions that I had heard about lime involved slaking it, or mixing it in huge vats and heating it with water, to form a paste. However, this form was very caustic and seemed to involve more work than I cared to encounter. In April 2000 I had watched an expert from Germany apply lime plasters on the house of Matts Myhrman, the straw bale guru. He had mixed powdered lime with water and sand in a cement mixer—no slaking required. One of the workers had also mentioned to me that the powdered form of lime wasn't caustic.

So, many months before actually scheduling the plastering party, I had begun thinking about using 10 percent lime in my earthen plasters and finishing the whole house with a coat of lime. It looked like a lot of work, but back when I thought I wasn't going to build the porch, this had seemed like the most durable choice. I still wanted to test the idea.

We had just finished installing the roof as June approached, with the threat of Tucson's monsoon weather. Since I hadn't passed the necessary lath inspection to proceed with plastering the exterior walls, I decided simply to waterproof all the cracks and niches where the rain might soak down into the bales. I had seen what happens when bales get wet—strong golden straw becomes black powder as the bale disintegrates. This is the major fear of straw bale builders. However, if the monsoon rains only soaked into the side of the bales, they wouldn't penetrate more than an inch or two. Given our hot sunny mornings to dry out, the walls would survive. Or so I had hoped.

I had ordered a truckload of sifted clay soil from the Pasqua Yaqui Indians and had asked them to dump it next to my mound of mortar sand. I had purchased a forty-pound bag of Type S lime at the building supply store and scheduled my first plaster day for Saturday, June 3, more than six months before the plaster party. Jon was going to be in Mexico for the weekend and the boys were in Hawaii, visiting their father. I had wanted to do something that was safe, since nobody would be around if I hurt myself. Earth plasters had seemed the perfect task for that weekend.

The mercury was expected to hit about 105 degrees that day, so I started early, by 8 A.M. I had to attend a wedding by midafternoon and had no idea how long mixing plaster would take. Digging out my notes from many workshops, I found a basic formula for cob, the coarse earth plaster mixture of water, clay, and chopped straw.

As I raised my shovel toward the beautiful mound of auburn clay, I hesitated. Why would I want to waste this beautiful soil on patches that would never show? Why not use the soil from my own land, which was a powdery mix of clay and sand, crafted by Mother Nature in a light peachy beige? It was certainly worth a try for a batch or two, I figured.

After filling a white construction bucket with water and pouring it into the deep wheelbarrow, I added two pailsful of soil. The Steens had taught me to let the water soak naturally into the clay before mixing. Little bubbles rose to the surface of the water as this natural absorption took place.

After several minutes, I poked my finger into the cool, mushy mixture and determined it was ready to churn. I loved the slimy, primal feel of immersing my bare hands into the spongy mud and squishing around, searching for large rocks to eject onto the ground.

The mixture felt close to what I remembered from the workshops, although a little too sandy. Pulling my hands out and letting them drip for a minute, I noticed my bare skin beginning to show. That shouldn't happen. When the mixture has enough clay, it should coat my hands and not drip off. I added a small bucket of the Pasqua Yaqui sifted clay soil, testing it again, this time to my satisfaction.

I ripped open the bag of white lime powder and filled a quarter of a bucket, then sprinkled that over the water and watched it disperse. I wasn't sure if I was supposed to use 10 percent of the entire mixture, or 10 percent of the sand-clay portion. So I did somewhere in between all that.

A few lumps formed, which I broke up with my fingers. I stirred the whole mix around a few times. Then I mounded two buckets of straw on top. I jotted down my ingredients on a muddy piece of notepaper so I could re-create them on another day, or adjust as needed.

I folded the straw into the thickening earth mixture until I had a lumpy brown mass flecked with golden bits. Then, using whatever memory was stored in my fingertips, I determined that the mix was close enough to what I had felt at the workshops and began pushing it between the bales.

This initial patching needed to be done with hands, I recalled, not a trowel. It had to be smushed hard into the fibers of the straw and into the crevices between bales. In my case, it also needed to be angled out from the bottom of the bales to the meet the edge of the stemwall, so rain couldn't puddle on the lip of the blocks and soak the bottom of the bales.

First I dampened the bale wall with a hose and then, like a kid making mudpies, joyfully worked down the west and north walls, pushing and sculpting as I went. If the gaps were particularly large between the bales, I stuffed them with straw first and then pushed the plaster over the loose strands with determination until it stuck and stayed. I remembered to always push upward, but I also sloped the clay down and outward, so rain would flow away from the bales. A piece of metal lath wrapped around a small 2 x 4 served as a shaping tool to rub away uneven areas of straw and angle the bales into the window bucks.

Early in the day, I noticed that the skin over an old blood blister on my right forefinger was scraped away and raw. I also detected a new sore on the palm of my right hand and a round dark blister on my middle finger. They were both black and dirty, but not too sore, so I decided there was no sense cleaning them now: I had hours of muddy work yet before me.

I really didn't remember my hands being sore when I had worked previously with plasters, but today they seemed to cut easily and the straw felt very abrasive. I figured I'd have to toughen them up if I were going to cover all these walls!

The temperature was climbing rapidly and I couldn't bear the blazing hot sun on the south side of the house, so I stayed on the north wall. Filling a bucket with water, I dunked my hat and blouse in water and proceeded around the stemwall and up the walls, delighting in the cool mud on my hands and the speed with which my work progressed.

By the end of the first batch, my hands were tender and painful. I washed them off and mixed my next batch with the hoe to give them a rest. In my gardening box, I found some cotton gloves to protect my hands for the rest of the project.

As I worked around the north side of the house and onto the east end, my hands continued to ache. Removing the gloves and glancing at my fingers, I saw a series of black dots on my fingertips where there had been holes in the gloves. Hmmm. The blister on my middle finger was larger. All the sores ached, but the center of the largest circle was strangely numb. I knew I didn't have blisters on the ends of my fingers, so something was damaging my skin. Probably the lime.

But, it didn't hurt all that much and I wanted to finish up the batch of plaster before I got ready for the wedding, so I continued. When I am engrossed in a project, it's hard to get me to rest.

As the sun moved across the top of the sky toward the west, the east end of the house fell into shade and it was very important that I fill the gaps in that wall. Our prevailing wind, bringing rain, came from the east. Retrieving a pair of rubber gloves from my gardening basket, I placed them over my increasingly damaged fingers. These should do the trick, I figured. Climbing the A-frame ladder with my mini-bucket of mud plaster, I proceeded to fill in the gaps and dents in the upper bales. The wheelbarrow reached empty just as the east end was completed.

With a glowing sense of accomplishment, I viewed my work and began rinsing my tools under the hose. My hands felt much better since I had protected them with gloves. After a quick dip in my wading pool to cool down my overheated body, I jumped in the shower.

While applying my makeup and fixing my hair, I noticed that my hands looked pretty grizzly. The skin was red and my fingers were swollen. My fingertips were covered with even more black dots. Yes, it must have been the lime. Well, in the future, I would wear gloves the whole time.

When I arrived at the wedding, my friends looked aghast at my hands and immediately poured me a bowl of ice water. The hostess, Susan, at whose home the wedding was taking place, ordered me to sit and soak until my hands couldn't stand it and keep soaking until the wedding began. These were obviously burns. She had burned herself several times and ice water always did the trick.

I had agreed to take snapshots of the wedding and soon got caught up in the excitement of the event. This was a good friend who had been single for more than forty years and met the man of her dreams only five months prior. She was glowing with joy, and my hands yearned to be snapping photos, not soaking in ice water, so I dried off my fingers and picked up my camera.

By 8 P.M. I could no longer hold the camera, nor bear the pain in my fingers. I could barely bend them. Susan sat me back down and brought me a new tray of ice. I couldn't tell which hurt more, the burn or the freezing. Susan kindly placed a phone call to the poison center, whose representative told me to go to the emergency room immediately and not attempt to treat myself; I had third-degree chemical burns. I had no medical insurance, so I wasn't going to consider that option. The burns didn't look so large that my immune system couldn't handle them, in my opinion.

I alternated my hands back and forth, in and out of the ice, until the wedding wound to a close and my body cried out for rest. I had a strong feeling that I should do something to neutralize the alkaline of the lime, so I stopped by a grocery store and picked up a jar of powdered iced tea, which contained tannic acid. Once home, I mixed it into a paste and spread the umber paste on my wounds. It stung terribly, and I rinsed it off quickly.

At 2 A.M. I awoke shivering and shaking, though I knew the desert temperatures were cause for sweat. After turning off my room fan, I retrieved two comforters from the boys' beds and piled them on me. Finally warm, I fell back asleep until the early morning. The pain in my swollen hands woke me at dawn. Taking six ibuprofen, I fell back asleep for a few more hours, convinced that my body needed rest.

When I finally rose and realized there was no way I could go to the lumber store, nor work, for I could barely bend the fingers of my right hand, I began to worry. What had I done? What should I do now? Somehow, I didn't feel that the ice water was doing enough. It numbed the pain, but maybe I should be covering the burns with aloe. I had heard that this plant was grown for radiation burns and I had one growing in a pot. Should I soak or apply ointment and bandages?

Opening my natural healing book, I read the paragraph on burns. "If the burn is yellow or black, then it is a third degree burn. Do not immerse it in ice water. Go to a physician. These burns should not be treated at home."

Why wouldn't someone just tell me what I could do if the burns were small and I had no insurance? I needed a hug and some good advice! Jon was out of cell phone range, so I'd have to figure this one out myself. Calming myself, I sat on the sofa and said a prayer for healing and help.

Within five minutes, I heard a knock on my door—a very rare occurrence in the open desert. Rudy, my neighbor with the horses, hadn't stopped by in months. My other close neighbors, Laura, the nurse, and her housemate, Sage, had moved out the week before. Opening the door, I was greeted by Laura's smiling face.

"Hi!" she chirped. "I came back to pick up a few things. I wanted to give you my new phone number."

Remembering that she was a nursing student, I showed her my hands. Within a few minutes, she had called a doctor who worked for the poison center and received some great advice on what to look for in alkaline burns. Were my nails numb? No. That was good. Alkaline numbs nerves and can get trapped under the nails. Was the old skin on my hands peeling off? Yes. That was good. Did the burns look infected? Not overly. Good. That was the main danger.

Laura had my hand slathered with Neosporin and wrapped in gauze bandages within the hour. Warning me of the many dangers of alkaline burns, she made me promise to unwrap my hands in the morning and go to a doctor if they weren't healing. I promised—if I could figure out how to unwrap my right hand with my left.

Monday doctor appointments are far less expensive than Saturday night emergency room visits. I thanked her profusely and spent the rest of the day napping and watching TV. Any ideas I had of working on the house were long gone. I just hoped I'd be able to work by the following weekend.

Monday morning, I sent an e-mail to work that I had done something really stupid to my hands and I would be in late. I felt better when Jon returned from Mexico and helped me unwrap the bandages. He determined that I was healing quite well, though admittedly he was used to having cuts all over his hands. My hands looked well within the normal range, as far as he was concerned. I still saw no reason to go to a doctor.

After coating the cuts with more aloe and Neosporin, Jon rewrapped the bandages. I gulped down more painkillers, herbs to boost my immune system, and just about every other herb and vitamin I could find, then headed to work. I couldn't type or write very well, but somehow I'd get through the day. If I stayed home, I'd be too tempted to work on the house.

Each day my hands improved dramatically and by the following weekend, I was back at work to finish the plasters, with three helpers who were visiting Tucson from Alaska. We all wore thick rubber gloves and kept a bucket of vinegar-water nearby!

Mixing several wheelbarrowsful of my evolving formula of earth, lime, water, and straw, we spent the day filling in the remaining holes on the south and east sides of the house. It was delightful to have some help and see how much more could be accomplished by three people than by one. The day sped by, my hands didn't hurt, and by sunset the house was ready for the summer thunderstorms—well, as ready as it was going to get.

I had done little more with plasters on my house since that first painful experiment. Since it took me the entire summer to finish mounting the doors and windows and lathing them all, those patches of earth-and-lime plaster were put to the test. We had up to sixty mile per hour winds on occasion with torrential rains that pounded on the straw and flooded across the rocky desert soil, but the plasters held and the bales stayed strong and golden.

Every now and then after a summer rain, I would stick my fingers into the damp bales to see how far the moisture went. It often went as far as I could feel, but by the end of the next day, it was largely dry. Thank goodness for our dry climate, I thought. That was about when lightning struck the saguaro.

As the rains were subsiding in September, and I was framing interior walls, Jon and I went to visit some friends I had met at the first Steen workshop, Michelle and Bill Campbell. They had hired Jon as their consultant, and we had all become good friends.

On the outside of one wall, Michelle had an orderly row of samples of various earth plaster mixtures—with lime, asphalt, and rice paste. When blasted with a hose, the asphalt mixture had held up the best by far, she said. It felt strong and sturdy to touch, whereas the lime felt crumbly. That was very interesting for me to see and consider. Asphalt had been the base mixture of adobe bricks for years. Since the Campbells' walls would be exposed to the weather, they were considering using asphalt emulsion mixed into the earth plasters. It would be much easier than lime, also.

All these mixtures and options were swimming in my brain, and I wasn't sure which direction I wanted to turn. But just after that, in October, I got the word from the building department that I could apply earthen plasters with no stabilizer, as long as I built the porch. I decided that was what I wanted to do.

I had run the gamut from learning about casein to lime formulas, the possibility of asphalt or no stabilizer at all, and now someone else suggested I should put cement into the first two layers of my plasters, since the house was load-bearing. This would help hold up the walls so they wouldn't settle and crack the plasters, he said.

With that suggestion, I felt totally confused. One of the reasons I liked straw bale construction was because the earthen plasters used minimal cement. From my house, I could see a mountain peak that used to be called Twin Peaks. The other peak was now leveled from cement mining and the remaining peak was on its way down. I wanted to know that I was not contributing in any great way to the demise of the mountains. And using components from the earth that I could apply myself was one of the main reasons I had wanted to build this house.

Now I was learning that earth plasters really don't hold up in weather unless they are coated with lime, but lime weakens the clay mixture so the plaster wouldn't be as strong for load-bearing houses. Lime is strictly for shedding water. Casein was good for the interior, from all I could gather, but not that useful on an exterior wall that will take weather.

Asphalt likewise sheds water, but I wasn't sure it made the plasters stronger. I hadn't even studied rice or wheat paste!

Here I thought I was heading into the easy part of construction with something I had already studied and it was turning into the most bewildering stage. Earth plasters must still be in the pioneering stage, I thought, and I might have to gather as much information as possible and just make a decision to the best of my ability.

Jon agreed that the house had further settling to do, but he had never heard of combining cement and earth plasters before. But then again, he usually worked with concrete stucco on his houses; earthen plasters were new territory for him.

My instinct back in October was that I should build the heavy porch, drywall the ceiling (which would also add a lot of weight), give the house several weeks after that to settle, and then use thick earthen plasters with no stabilizer. If they cracked, then I would mend them.

The more I sat with that decision, the more I liked it. I tend to like the simplest solutions. I sealed up the straw around the bathtub and behind the hot water shed on the east wall with a thin mixture of mud plaster, minus the lime and admired its strength. Jon recommended that I always seal the straw with some type of plaster before covering it with anything else, just to keep rodents and bugs from nesting there in the future.

I rubbed my hand over the wall often, as if to communicate with parts of my Being that bypass my brain, and to confirm that this was what I wanted to do for the house. It was.

When my parents arrived for Thanksgiving, my father offered to help with the construction while he was in town. By then, I knew that my time for earthen plasters was finally approaching. I was eager to test some plaster formulas without lime, so I suggested that we begin on an exterior wall.

First, we unrolled some roofing paper below the wall to catch any waste that fell, so we could reuse it. Then, we dampened the wall with a hose and smushed in a thin layer of clay slip to bond the clay and straw as far into the wall as possible. The clay slip was a mixture of about one part water to one part clay.

Then we mixed the thicker plaster. Pouring a bucketful of water into the wheelbarrow, we added Pasqua Yaqui clay and let it soak until the clay was soft enough to mix. About three buckets of clay gave us a nice chocolate-shake sort of mixture. When we dipped our hands into it, they stayed coated with rich brown—no skin showing through. If it coated my hands, then it would coat the straw.

For the mix, I decided to use the Pasqua Yaqui sifted clay soil; the earth from my land was too sandy. I added three buckets of chopped straw to our clay mixture, enough to make it thick and pliable. After dampening the wall with a hose, we pushed this mud mixture into the straw with our bare hands.

Dad had to leave after this first coat, so I continued into the late afternoon, building out the coat with a wooden trowel or float and leveling some of the unevenness of the bales until the wall looked relatively smooth. The plasters were almost two inches thick in some areas by the time I declared myself to be done. I had been taught never to use a metal trowel until the final coat because the metal pulls the clay to the surface, leaving a smooth finish. This is good for the end result, but not optimum for sublayers; those should be left rough for future bonding. A wooden float will leave a rougher surface, flecked with straw.

When I was satisfied with the smoothness of the wall, I ran a metal trowel over the plasters, smoothing them as much as possible. However, when the clay is wet, it doesn't get really smooth. The following morning, when the plasters were tacky, Jon and I went over the wall again with metal trowels and smoothed it to a beautiful sheen.

The plaster dried from a rich chocolate brown to a lighter sienna color in about a week, with flecks of straw throughout. I passed my fingertips over its surface every time I entered the house, feeling the hardness of the wall and admiring its rustic natural tones. No man-made finish that I had ever seen could come close to the natural beauty of this clay mix. There were some tiny hairline cracks, but nothing that bothered me in the least.

As January 27 approached, it looked like I'd have at least twenty-five people for my earthen plaster party. With any luck, we could coat the entire house in one day. Jon told me I was dreaming, but I thought it was quite possible. At any rate, it never hurts to plan big. I even cleaned up the bedroom so we could move indoors if we had time.

Several weeks ahead of time, I began sending mental requests to the Universe for a nice, warm, sunny day with highs at least in the upper sixties. This would be a very standard sort of Tucson winter day and wasn't beyond the realm of possibility. We had to work on the north side of the house, so I didn't want it to be too cold. I reserved a large mortar mixer from a nearby rental company and set up two scaffolds to plaster the upper bales. Jon said he would bring his scaffold, also, so we would have three.

With one week to go, the weatherman was calling for cold rain on Saturday, the plaster party day—probably snow in the mountains overnight. It reminded me of the weather that made me reschedule my wall raising; it never rains or snows in Tucson until you schedule a parade or a straw bale party!

This time, I had the porch for protection, and I knew that if I changed the date I'd lose a bunch of people, so I didn't. Rain or shine, the party would go on. After spending the early part of my week chasing down the Sears leaf mulcher when the chipper/shredder broke, I prepared the outer walls by covering all exterior electrical outlets with duct tape and taping large sheets of plastic over the windows. Pulling everything away from the walls, I unrolled roofing paper along the ground beneath the walls, to catch the mud drips.

The weather report still called for weekend rain on Friday. I took off work and spent the morning roofing the corner areas of the porch. Those hadn't been done yet, and I figured we might need as much protection as possible. This was superwoman work—up and down the ladders with large sheets of metal, marking them and then cutting them with a small-toothed blade in my saw and ear plugs in my ears. Then back up the ladder with the angled sheet and my screw gun to secure it to the blocking. I whipped through the work, realizing how much I had learned in a year and how much more confident I had become on ladders and beams.

By noon, I picked up the large mortar mixer and hauled it home behind my trusty little truck. I spent the afternoon mixing huge batches of mud while Zej chopped straw with the leaf mulcher. From the earthen plaster workshops I had attended, I had learned that it's hard to mix mud fast enough to keep up with a big crowd of plasterers.

The mortar mixer was a big, upright bin with heavy, metal paddles powered by a gas engine. It took both my weight and Zej's muscles to tip the bin onto its side, chain it in place, and scoop the mud into a low plastic tub. Towing the tub around the house, we made large piles of mud on every side, then covered them with roofing paper so they wouldn't dry out before the party.

Before sunset, I had three batches, equal to nine wheelbarrows of mud, placed around the four walls of the house. The interior of the house was clean, with the oak table waiting to serve drinks and lunch to the group. A line of trowels and gloves lay on the small table by the front door. I felt ready.

I camped in the loft of the straw bale house that night. I had moved my mattress up there to protect it from the rats under the tarp, and I found I preferred sleeping up there to the cramped trailer where the boys often stayed up late. About three in the morning, I woke to hear the wind rattling the new roofing on the porch. I hadn't finished fastening the upper edges of the metal sheets.

The storm was moving in, just as predicted. I tossed and turned the rest of the morning, while my mind buzzed with details, and I awoke with the dawn. Glancing out the window, I saw gray clouds to the east, but I heard no rain pattering on the roof. Maybe the weather reports would be wrong, as they had been for my wall raising

As I strolled outside, the air felt chilly and damp. My breath formed misty clouds around my face as a light drizzle coated my bare arms. Like it or not, it was raining. A cold wind blew in from the south, where the clouds hung dark and threatening around the base of the mountains. My fingers were frozen by the time I made it over to the trailer. The temperature must have been somewhere above freezing, for it was raining, but not by much.

Jon pulled in about 7 A.M. We soon began erecting tarps over the mortar mixer and clay pile. After yesterday's experience, I didn't want to shovel wet clay all day, that was for sure. Damp clay is heavy enough and wet clay would be beyond what I wanted to imagine. My lower back felt sore just thinking about it.

Jon had been an accomplished Boy Scout, erecting tents on cold, rainy evenings, so he knew just what to do, bracing and securing the tarps in the increasing wind and drizzle. While he was pounding poles and stakes into the ground, I was wondering whether I was crazy to think about plastering on a day like this and whether I should call everyone and cancel. Who in their right mind would volunteer to stick their hands in cold mud when they could be at home eating popcorn and drinking hot chocolate?

I was also thinking about heading inside for a nice, warm breakfast with hot tea, but before I could act on any of my thoughts, a truck pulled up the driveway. I had told people to be here at 9 A.M., rain or shine, and I got what I asked for! Out stepped Dyer, the engineer from the University of Arizona who had worked all three days of my wall raising. It was like seeing an old friend: a full year had passed.

As we were chatting, Frank, the former landowner, drove up in his van. Then my friend Ken, who had offered to take pictures, arrived, along with Marilee, her husband, and daughter. No matter the weather, the party was on. We gathered under the porch and while Jon and Dyer began mixing some clay slip, I gave a short explanation to the others.

I just told them that after the clay slip was blown onto the straw, we needed to cover it with a thick coat of mud that would seal up the straw, fill in the dips, and cover the humps. Since it was so cold, I recommended that we use trowels and gloves to apply the mud, rather than bare hands.

Then I told them that this wasn't a dainty little pat, pat of mud onto the straw, it was a firm upward push with the palms of the hand or the float, as if releasing old, pent-up hostilities. If people wanted, they could even throw mudballs from a short distance onto the straw and then smooth the surface over. Whatever method each person preferred, the object was to mash the mud firmly into the straw, forming a tight bond, and then end up with a smooth outer coat. I didn't care if the house had some humps, since it was a straw house, but we could try to fill in the major valleys and level off peaks.

I asked them to leave the lathed areas around the windows and doors for Jon and me. Metal lath is just too sharp, and I didn't want to see cut hands. I put a bucket of warm water and a towel inside the house so people could rinse their cold fingers. I also set up a big tub of hot water for cocoa and tea with an extension cord.

With all that said, Jon and Dyer had mixed up a bucket of clay slip— about one part clay and one part water. This would be even better than dampening the bales with a hose, because we could blast clay-water several inches into the bales. This would give the thicker plasters a good bond

*I'm cold and I'm muddy, but this is my idea of a great party!* Photo by Ken Ramey.

with the straw. Pouring a little of the screened mixture into a stucco hopper, which was connected to Jon's compressor, they began blowing the slip into the straw walls. Since the wind was whipping in from the south, the north wall was sheltered. It also needed the most work.

Several others had now joined us—another friend, Lynn, and her husband, Jim, who were beginning their own straw bale house; as was a new friend Tim and his son, from down the road. Two architecture interns who had heard about the plaster party through the Women Builders group; a woman named Amanda who had been helping the Steens with some of their projects, and another woman, Leigh, who was eager to "get dirty!" Paul, a friend from the meditation group, also arrived, ready to pitch in.

After giving them a brief demonstration, they all took over, finding places around the house, digging into the mud and spreading it around. I reminded a couple of people to push upward when the mud kept falling to the ground, and that was about all I had to say from there on out. The plasterers formed groups, some on the scaffold and some below. Usually one person shoveled mud up onto the scaffold, too. Everyone worked happily and cooperatively. Business seminars that want to teach teamwork should hold mud-plastering parties.

Jon and Dyer had almost the whole house covered with clay slip by now, and Jon had begun trying to spread the earth mixture over the metal lath. It didn't work. The thick mat of straw kept the mixture from pushing into the lath. We decided to make a different mixture using sand instead of straw. That would push through the lath to bond into the straw and then we could cover it with the clay-straw mix.

Paul worked with me as we tossed buckets of water into the top of the mixer. The rain had subsided to a drizzle and the tarps were perfect protection for the whole mud-mixing area. Paul and I alternated tossing shovelsful of clay into the top of the bin, giving it a stir, and testing how it coated our hands. When satisfied, we began piling in buckets of chopped straw and letting the mixer churn. As we poured the glop into a big black bin and began pushing it around the house, we were confronted by a phenomenon strange in Tucson—mud puddles.

Now, I had clearly requested seventy-degree, sunny weather for this day. I know perfectly well that God had heard my request, so I was wondering why She felt the need to slap us with a huge storm—just about the worst weather Tucson ever gets. Perhaps She heard my request for a mudfest and decided to join in the fun.

We slipped and slopped our way through the slime as we deposited mounds of muddy straw into the most needed areas around the house. At first people said the mixture was a little thick, so I lessened up on the amount of straw, but then they said it was too thin. Finally we came up with the perfect formula that spread smoothly and clung tenaciously to the straw when Zej and his friend, Don, blasted it in the form of mud balls.

The weather warmed slightly and the rain stopped. I was hoping that everyone was having some kind of fun. I couldn't tell, except that nobody was complaining. To me it was all fun, but then it was my house and my entire Being was bonded to the job. I don't have a good frame of reference for what it was like for someone else. I was so busy mixing mud and answering questions that I barely had time to notice what was going on. It looked like everyone was doing a great job, though. Each time I glanced down the north wall, more and more was covered with beautiful, dark mud.

At about 11 A.M., J.J. came out of the trailer to remind me to order pizza. He had a date to go to a military ball that night and needed to pick up flowers and his tuxedo that day, so he was going to be the lunch delivery person. He had no desire to cover himself with mud right before this big event, and I didn't blame him.

We all paused for a group photo before lunch. The entire north wall was done by then, along with most of the east end, and that was by far the largest part to be covered. Paul and I were having a hard time mixing mud fast enough to keep up with everyone, so we found some volunteers to stagger their eating while keeping the cob mixing.

It took everyone some time with a bucket of warm water to get their hands clean enough to eat pizza. It's not easy to snack during a mudfest, because cleaning up is so much work. It's not even that easy to catch a drink of water without drinking mud. And it's a good thing I had a working toilet in the straw bale house, or the trailer would have had a trail of clay across the carpet.

I was tired and happy to turn the clay-shoveling job over to some other people and have my first food of the day. At the wall raising, everyone had lounged over lunch and many left soon afterward, but at this party people ate standing, chatted briefly, and headed right back to work.

The sun was peeking through the clouds now and the temperatures were hovering in the fifties. We only had a little work on the south side and the west wall to go. I could hardly believe the incredible progress and the energy everyone was putting into completing the task.

With overwhelming joy and relief, I watched the west side of the house turn brown as the group focused their energy on the last patches of naked straw. By 3:30, the exterior walls were completely covered with a thick

*A lasting memento from the many kind friends whose hands shaped the plasters on my walls.* Photo by Ken Ramey.

layer of earthen plasters. Discussion turned to the wonderful sculpting that could be done with earth plasters.

I wanted a handprint from everyone. Since the lath area around the windows and doors wasn't completed, we decided to make a row of handprints above the stemwall on the west end, near the front entrance. Jon smoothed out the mud as much as possible with a metal trowel and one by one, we all pushed our hands into the freshly mixed earth. I beamed with joy to have this memento of these wonderful people who had toiled all day to accomplish this amazing task despite the cold and the rain.

We had had enough for one day. I gave everyone big, muddy hugs and thanked them from the depth of my heart for all their hard work. After they drove away, I took a long, hot shower in the trailer, trying unsuccessfully not to cover the bathroom with flecks of mud as I undressed. I can't remember when a hot shower had felt so luxurious! My arms and legs ached, but most of my pain came from my hands; my knuckles were swollen and the skin on my fingers throbbed from the constant scraping of straw and mud.

I wondered how all the others were feeling as they headed home to hot showers. Were they tracking mud through their houses and smiling at the layers of mud in their hair? Would this day be a fond memory? I hoped so, once the mud was rinsed off and the sore hands healed. It certainly was for me.

Hobbling back toward the straw bale house in clean clothes, I stopped and stared. In one whirlwind day, the walls were covered with mud. Everything else around the place was coated, too: caked trowels, buckets, gloves, and pieces of roofing paper lay scattered around the yard. The scaffolds were encrusted with muddy straw, but beneath my fatigue, I was ecstatic.

I would spend the next day and several evenings filling in holes and smoothing the surface with a metal trowel as it became tacky. I would spend many days after we had moved into the house sculpting window and door moldings out of white or colored clay. The red tape holding up the plastic over the windows looked nice. Perhaps I would find some red clay. Maybe I'd find another sacred symbol to shape on the wall by my meditation area, too.

For right now, I would rest.

## Chapter Twenty-One

# MUD AND MORE MUD

*The best way to realize the pleasure of feeling rich is to live in a smaller house than your means would entitle you to have.*

—EDWARD CLARKE

As I slipped back into my mud-plastered work clothes the day after the party, I thought of stories I had read about people who have had near-death experiences in which they flew freely among the stars as spirits and then groaned as they had to slide back into their heavy, cumbersome bodies. Fighting back tears of fatigue, I went to work.

I spread mud around the windows and doors, realizing my deadline for completion was one month away: the end of February 2001. Before I could pass my final inspections, I needed to install the cupboards and sinks in both the bathroom and kitchen, fasten all the electrical fixtures, outlets, and switches, cover the interior walls with either drywall or mud, and build the earthen floor. I could never do that in four weekends, but I estimated that I could finish in six or seven.

So far, I had received no summons in the mail from Kathy and I knew that if I received one now, the house would be done by the time the court hearing arrived. If I walked into the courtroom saying that I had returned the trailer and my intention all along had been to return it, the judge was bound to take a softer look on my side of the story. I could almost smile at the situation now. This trailer was so decrepit beneath its new paint that I never dreamed I'd be going into a court battle over it. But then again, I never imagined half the things that life had brought me.

The work seemed endless and the nights were very cold. My hands were sore from continual rubbing against caked mud, but I kept going, filling and smoothing some of the work done at the party. I soon realized that it would be impossible to finish the entire exterior, and since that wasn't necessary for my final permit, I moved to the interior of the house. I could dampen, smooth, and sculpt the exterior plasters later.

Though I complained about the weather, the plasters dried beautifully with only a few hairline cracks, and I knew I had the cold, damp weather to thank. Plasters that dry too fast in the heat of the summer often leave large cracks.

Several people who had missed the party came to help the following weekend, among them a man named Erik, referred from the Steens. He was traveling around the West looking for work in alternative construction. He said he was a skilled carpenter and would trade a place to sleep and some food for work. Normally I am hesitant about accepting help from complete strangers, but I needed help so I gave him directions to the house.

He drove up in a white truck in the late morning. He was a large man, full-bearded and full-bodied, with rosy cheeks and soft eyes. His worn Levis and T-shirt blended well with the rest of the muddy work crew. Handing him a trowel, I showed him to a pile of mud in the bedroom and demonstrated the basics for applying it.

The sun shone warmly that day, and the pace of work was slower than the previous Saturday. We chatted over sandwiches at lunch and took more time and care shaping the interior walls.

When everyone (except Erik) said good-bye that day, the walls of the main room and bedroom were completed, with only the sunroom, loft, and kitchen areas left to cover. Erik pulled his bedroll out of the truck and said he'd be fine to sleep on the ground next to the house. He didn't even have a tent.

He was a pleasant fellow, and as the days progressed I became more comfortable with him around. He would talk on and on about any and every esoteric subject to anyone who would listen. Often, he would find the boys to be a captive audience as they sat affixed to their computer screens. He ate heartily of anything I placed before him and moved his sleeping bag under the porch only when it began to rain one night. I had made him a smooth place in the straw bale bedroom, but he wouldn't use it.

When I asked him what had prompted him to begin traveling, he dodged the question. When I asked him where he was going next, he said he never knew. And when we watched a sentimental movie on Saturday evening, his body shook. I couldn't tell if he was laughing or crying, but Jon said his eyes were filled with tears as he gathered up his bedroll.

Erik was an experienced carpenter and since we still needed to dry-wall the wall between the bedroom and bathroom, and the tall walls that divided these rooms from the main room, he took on these tasks.

I could tell he wanted to stay to see the house to completion, but I needed some time alone. All these work parties and a continual stream of visitors, along with the hard work, were pushing me to the brink of collapse. I missed the quiet days of the summer when I worked by myself with only the birds and the wind for conversation. I explained this honestly to Erik and he understood.

Erik stayed until Friday, drywalling every day while I went to the office. On his last day he taped and mudded all the joints. I never really said good-bye to him; when I returned home on Friday evening, he was gone. I was sure he had been a gift from God—they come in all shapes and sizes and often when I least expect them. He had saved me an immense amount of work and by doing so, lifted my spirits so that I could proceed.

Before beginning the earthen floor, the interior wall of the sunroom needed to be coated with mud. Two volunteers, Christine and Patrick, arrived to help in mid-February. After showing Patrick how to mix mud and getting Christine started on spreading the clay, I decided to finish mudding the exterior door bucks, which were wood covered with paper and metal lath. The mud would have to stick upside down in the top of the doorways and I wasn't sure how that would go. I figured I'd begin it early in the day, when I was feeling energetic and patient.

With the help of a metal trowel, I found that a thin clay-sand mix did indeed stick into the lath upside down in the top of a doorway. I had to use very small amounts of mud on my trowel and spread it carefully. I could hear Patrick and Christine chatting and having a good time, so I kept working on the doorways while they mudded the sunroom.

As I completed the area around the back door and moved over to the bedroom door, I stopped into the sunroom to see how things were going. They were doing fine, despite frustration at getting the mud to stick in the lath areas, but there was a very strong odor coming from the room.

"I think your cats have used the mortar sand pile as a bathroom," Patrick suggested.

"Oh, no! Ugh!" I commented. "I just hope it smells better when it dries. I guess we had better start filtering the sand and picking from the top of the pile."

"I tried getting shovelsful from all over and deep inside the pile, but it all smelled."

At least it was the sunroom, not the main room of the house, I thought, trying to stay optimistic. We would need lots of sand for the earthen floor too, but the floor would be well coated with linseed oil. I hoped the oil would cover any smell. We worked through the day, coating the sunroom wall and door bucks until every bit of straw in the walls, inside and out, was covered with mud. The smell lessened each day until I could barely notice it.

Now on the weekends, I could begin the floor, the final major phase of the house. During the weeknights, I could install outlets and do other small jobs. The earthen floor needed to be the very last phase of construction because it would be relatively fragile and shouldn't have scaffolds or ladders digging into it or hammers dropped on it. For the floor, I would need to build the gravel subfloor to an inch below the final floor height. Then, I would lay long, thin redwood strips over the gravel and fill them with a mixture of clay and sand, instead of clay and straw. Sand would make the floor stronger than straw and assist in drainage if the earth beneath the floor became wet. When those layers of clay dried, I would soak the floor with linseed oil mixed with turpentine until it became hard and shiny.

My earthen floor workshop at the Steens had been more than a year and a half ago and my notes were barely legible. I had also purchased their small booklet entitled *Earthen Floors*, reread the earth floor portion in my Earthship books, *The Straw Bale House*, and any other information I could get my hands on.

I arranged for three days of vacation, Monday through Wednesday, February 19 to 21, to begin working on the subfloor. This wasn't something I was looking forward to since, it would involve many, many wheelbarrowsful of gravel. I wasn't sure how my back would hold up, but my money was tight and the labor companies in town wanted $15 an hour for someone to help me, so, as with many other phases of this house, I decided to do it myself.

On Monday, I began by clearing everything out of the bedroom and main room, then scraping the surface gravel into big piles. I had filled the floor with leftover concrete mix way back when we were building the stemwall. The sand had by now settled to the lower layers and the large gravel had risen to the surface. The house construction had added another layer of chopped straw, drywall screws, broken nails, and probably a few pencils and screwgun bits.

Jon recommended I remove this top layer and begin fresh. He lent me two scraping tools that looked like wide hoes. Turning the blade around on one of them, I set up one to push the gravel and one to pull it—push-me, pull-yous, I called them.

I then proceeded to scrape or push about two inches off the top of the floor, shovel it into wheelbarrows, and take it out of the house, dumping it where I figured my future driveway would be. Of course, since the layers were possibly full of nails, that might not have been a good idea. But again, as with many other phases of the house that were new to me, I didn't think of that until after the deed was done.

The weather cooperated with me beautifully. A very slight chill in the air kept me from getting too hot while I huffed and puffed in and out of the house. The desert was serene and quiet with only the birds in the nearby trees and saguaros to cheer me on and my two cats to play with the bits of gravel as they fell from my shovel. Alien Kitty had now grown to a huge Alien Cat. He was definitely of the big-boned variety, but there was also plenty of cat food padding beneath his fluffy peach fur.

We also had a new kitty, Ashley, who had wandered across the desert and made herself at home last September. So much for my vow of taking in no more cats to feed coyotes. At least both these cats had come from the desert and hopefully knew how to survive. I was happy for some more female energy around the site. Ashley was about half the size of Alien, dainty and feminine, with a solid gray coat and piercing gold eyes. Alien learned to play gently with her and the two of them had a great time darting all over the construction zone, hiding under tarps and jumping out at my rapidly moving legs as I passed by.

A truckload of AB gravel mix arrived about 4 P.M., dumped in a big pile on the northwest corner of the house. AB mix is sand and gravel mixed with clay soil as a binder. It is intended as a sublayer for driveways, packing down very hard and solid, which is why it is also a good base for earthen floors.

The pile looked very big, and I hoped one of the several people who said they might help on Tuesday would show up the next morning. I couldn't quite imagine shoveling it into the house by myself, one wheelbarrow at a time. After the scraping, I had five or six inches to fill up in most of the floor. From past experience with concrete, I knew how big a wheelbarrow feels when one is filling it up by shoveling and how minuscule the same load seems when dumped into a large area. I decided not to think about that as I spent the evening catching up on laundry, getting groceries, and writing my journal.

Tuesday dawned with high clouds and cooler temperatures. I had to rise early to get J.J. off to school, so I began shoveling shortly after dawn. After a few wheelbarrows, I figured out exactly how many shovels (eighteen) I could push up the ramp and into the house without spilling. Much of construction work is great for building muscles—pushing long screws, lifting heavy objects, hammering, prying—however, much of the work isn't great aerobic exercise. But this day I got a workout worthy of any fitness instructor. Actually, I think they should include pushing wheelbarrows up ramps as part of a great gluteal workout. I could feel the burn in the back of my thighs as I chugged up and over the doorways. Then all those other muscles came into play as I crouched down, wrapped the arms of the barrow over my biceps, and lifted with my legs.

I found myself huffing deep, oxygenated breaths as I got this routine into a rhythm that carried me through the morning. I told myself that after every three wheelbarrows I would take a break, stand up and stretch backward to ease my back, and smooth out what I had done. Sometimes I did and sometimes I forgot as my adrenaline took over. It was slow going, as I had suspected, and nobody showed up to help. Preparing a subfloor probably rates at about the same level as drywalling a ceiling on the scale of construction work excitement.

Every now and then I thought of giving it up and calling for a laborer to come out the next day at $15 an hour, but then I realized if I did that it would set me back a day and therefore a weekend. I was hoping to have the entire subfloor done by the time Jon showed up on Saturday, so he could help me with the mud. I needed my third vacation day to tamp the subfloor and lay in the redwood strips. So, I kept chugging, reducing the shovels per wheelbarrow load to seventeen, then sixteen, and fifteen by midday as my strength waned.

Andrzej woke up around noon and came out to help. He had fresh energy and with two wheelbarrows, the work progressed much faster—well, twice as fast. The clouds thickened as the day progressed and a cold wind blew in from the south. Jon phoned to let me know it was supposed to rain the next day. I didn't want to shovel gravel in the rain, so we kept going. I have no idea how many wheelbarrows of gravel I pushed that day—fifty? sixty? seventy?— a great many, filling the entire day.

As the twilight dimmed around seven, we had all the ramps pulled out of the house and Zej dumped the last couple of loads over the threshold. A day that I had dreaded was successfully completed and I was still standing and walking. I thanked both Andrzej and my back.

On Wednesday, my body creaked as I rose from bed, and I spent a long time sipping my tea after J.J. went to school. I was very hungry and ate a full breakfast, plus some chocolate ice cream leftover from the night before. Lately I had been augmenting my largely vegetarian diet with the richest and most delicious ice creams I could find, so I didn't lose too much weight. Not only was I losing weight, but I was turning fat into muscle. Hard physical work does have its bonuses. I know I had never been stronger. Most of my clothes had room to spare. My stomach and legs were much firmer then they used to be, although I've always been fairly strong. I had passed my fiftieth birthday over the summer and barely noticed. At least, it sure didn't bother me to be fifty. Nobody could say I was growing old and bored, stuck in some unsatisfying routine—my life was exactly where I wanted it to be. Well, almost—I still had to keep pushing toward that final occupancy permit.

While I lingered over breakfast, I imagined the pleasant years ahead when I could plant my garden, add some rainwater collection tanks, fine-tune the earthen plasters, and fill the house with cozy, eclectic furniture. Part of me enjoys being a hermit, bumbling around my garden, cooking and reading as I listen to great music, letting the chaos of the world pass me by. Now I would have the perfect environment for that.

The sugar and chocolate from the ice cream hit my bloodstream and jolted me from my reverie, back to the job at hand. Today's task shouldn't be too hard, I surmised. I'd have some time sitting in the truck while I picked up the tamper, a special tool for compacting the AB mix, and then more time sitting in the truck as I returned it. Laying the redwood squares shouldn't be that hard, either.

As I drove to the rental store, I wondered how hard it would be to use the tamper. I soon found out! The first dose of reality hit as two large men loaded the tamper in the back of my pickup and said, "You better have some help unloading this thing. It's really heavy."

I hadn't thought of that. The vibrating compactor looks like a very heavy-duty upright vacuum cleaner with a gas motor instead of a bag of air on top and a thick metal plate below instead of a brushed roller. It was made to tamp down gravel, which is very hard to compress, so of course it was heavy. Zej was at home, sound asleep. Nine A.M. to him is like 3 in the morning to me. Waking him up and asking him to lift heavy objects might not be a good idea—we might both end up with bad backs.

As I drove home, I formed a plan to back the truck up to the remaining pile of AB gravel and slide the tamper out of the truck and down the pile. To my delight, as I got to the site, I saw that the gravel did reach up to almost exactly the height of the tailgate. I was able to tug the tamper to the tailgate and let it slide. It ended up all cockeyed at the bottom of the pile, but at least it was cockeyed at ground level.

Before attempting to move it farther, I went into the house with a hose and dampened all the AB mix. This was supposed to make it pack much harder. Going back to the gravel pile, I turned the compactor as upright as possible, pulled back the choke lever, and tugged on the starter cord.

The machine rumbled its way forward, compacting and vibrating the already firm desert as we chugged our way up the ramp and into the sunroom. The compactor had a natural forward motion, but not much maneuverability. When we got into the sunroom, I let it pulsate its way across the gravely mix, leaving a smooth, well-packed trail behind. This tamper was pretty fun.

As it reached the corner, I had no room to turn it and I couldn't back it up, so I let it bash into the stemwall for a few moments before I gave up and hit the power switch. After several corners, I learned to anticipate the edge of the floor, go around to the side of the machine, and tug on the handlebars at each side. This made it turn a little better, but there was still no way to reach the extreme corners of the room. Those areas I could compact the old-fashioned way, by jumping up and down.

A couple of times it hit wet spots and bogged down with gravel and mud stuck to its bottom. I'd simply stop it, tilt it backward, scrape it off, and begin again, letting it shudder and shake its way around the floor until the whole place was very smooth.

Now, I just had to get it back into the truck. It was now about eleven and the skies were getting black with thick, threatening clouds. A few sprinkles danced on my bare arms. It was almost late enough to wake up Zej, but the truck was still backed up to the gravel pile, and I had some strong boards that I'd been using for ramps into the house, so I decided to try it on my own.

Balancing two strong 2 x 10 boards as a ramp up the gravel to the tailgate, I revved the motor and once again compacted a trail across the desert from the back door to the gravel pile. Without hesitating, I tilted the tamper back and let it shudder its way up the boards. The boards responded by gradually shaking apart, one to either side of the tailgate. As I was within a foot of the tailgate, the compactor fell between the boards and slid sideways down the pile.

Well, that went well, I thought. We almost made it. With a few adjustments this is very possible.

This time, I angled the boards toward each other slightly, so they would hopefully pulsate toward each other instead of apart. Revving the engine again, I chugged across the pile and back up the boards. For some reason, the boards again began to vibrate apart, but I was too fast for them. This time I made it up onto the tailgate, where the whole truck began to dance with the machine. Quickly, I turned it off and pushed the tamper into the truck bed, safely secured with bungie cords.

Heavy raindrops splattered on the windshield as I drove back to the rental store, but I felt quite proud of myself. Let the rains do what they may, I was ready to work indoors, on schedule. I had the afternoon to lay and notch the redwood strips. No more wheelbarrows!

I had decided to divide the floor into large squares made with wooden slats. These would look like the grout of large tile and also give me some hope that the floor would end up level. Jon had reminded me that since the slats were going right into the floor, I should make them out of either treated lumber or redwood, so they wouldn't bring termites into the house. Of course I chose the redwood. Then Jon told me that regular redwood is full of knots and very warped. Clear redwood would make a much more beautiful floor, though it is expensive. At least I didn't need much of it. Several weeks prior, I had ordered five sixteen-foot 2 x 6 clear redwood boards and had them ripped into twenty one-inch strips. They were now stacked neatly in the sunroom, waiting for me.

After a quick lunch, I laid the redwood boards beside each other on the floor of the living room. I needed to notch them every three feet, so they would fit together in squares, log cabin style. This was expensive redwood and I didn't have extras, so I measured and cut very carefully, then positioned them in neat squares throughout the main room and bedroom. My back creaked and groaned when I stood up at the end of the day, but the squares were all in place and I was ready to begin mudding the floor that weekend.

When Jon arrived on Saturday, he was limping from a very sore knee—most likely tendonitis. His right knee had been sore for months, but now it was inflamed. He would need to rest it and see a doctor. The boys and I would have to roll wheelbarrows of the mud into the house ourselves.

I felt mellow that day. So much difficult work was behind me now that I felt relieved. At the same time, the weather had turned springlike with highs around seventy and lots of sunshine. Wildflowers were awakening in bursts of color all over the desert. There were even patches of my favorite golden poppies peeking out from the desert sands. Birds chirped and flitted around the house, enjoying the weather, too.

Jon worked on doorknobs and installed my gorgeous Mexican sink with the dolphin into the bathroom vanity, along with a real faucet that turned on and off smoothly. The cold water in the kitchen sink of the trailer had now become almost impossible to turn off once it was on, and vice versa, so we didn't use it much. In the trailer bathroom, there was a leak in the trap under the sink, so we used a bowl in the sink and rinsed it down the tub. New fixtures would be a delight!

In order to keep the earthen floor from cracking too badly, we needed to fill the redwood squares in two, half-inch layers. I hoped to do one layer this weekend and one the next, which would be the first weekend in March. Then I wanted to coat the whole floor with a very thin layer of gold clay and silica sand. In my test samples, I had discovered that linseed oil turns the earth pitch black, and I didn't want a floor that dark. If I put a thin layer of gold and white clays mixed with sand, I could end up with a rich brown floor instead. After that was done, I could begin applying layers of linseed oil and tell Kathy to come get the trailer by the middle of March, if all went as planned.

*Patrick and Christine help me build and smooth the earthen floor.*

J.J. and Zej helped the first weekend. I enjoyed working with them and getting them out in the sunshine, away from the virtual land of Everquest. I realized that filtering cat poop out of the sand pile wasn't the most glamorous job to offer them, but they proceeded with their usual sense of humor. They took turns shoveling the filtered sand, clay, and water into wheelbarrows and mixing it with a hoe, then pushing it up the ramp and into the house, where I scooped and smoothed it into the redwood squares as they mixed another batch.

Though this was a lot of work, my joy at seeing a floor appear carried me through. The following weekend, Christina, one of the architect interns from the first mud party, came to my aid. She was a delightful person from Connecticut who loved the work and found it a great way to use up some of her excess energy. Patrick, my sand-filtering expert, also arrived to do the heavy mixing while Christina and I smoothed the upper layer of mud.

We had a pleasant day, chatting freely and playing some lively CDs that Patrick brought. The weather had turned cooler, with highs in the fifties. But with the French doors open into the main room of the house and the low rays of the late winter sun shining through the large windows of the sunroom, the house stayed cozy. The passive solar design was working, and my house was coming to life.

Gas and electric prices were rising, and I knew that soon all my hard work would be paying off. Not only that, but the sunroom was going to be a beautiful glass room with an aviary, water fountain, and lots of plants. It would make a dramatic entrance to the house and a pleasant place to sit and read, or simply sit.

The second layer of the floor cracked, as had the first, and the clay pulled away from the redwood as it dried—just as I had expected. The cracks were actually lovely and I wished there were some way to preserve them, but instead I made a thin mixture of clay, water, and silica sand, poured it over the squares, filled in the cracks, and took the floor level right up to the top of the redwood.

Finally, a week later than I had expected, on Saturday, March 17, I applied the top coat of white and gold clays mixed with silica sand and a few handfuls of finely chopped straw to the bedroom floor. It went on very easily with a small metal trowel over the semidried upper layer of brown clay, and it also cracked as it dried.

In my test samples, small cracks had disappeared when I applied linseed oil, so I went ahead with the application of the oil. I had always told my friends that I would begin the earthen floor on the area under the bed and by the time I got to the living room, I would know what I was doing. Well, that became partly true, I began under the bed.

The oil darkened the gold clay into a medium brown color, just as I had hoped, but the cracks still showed. I scraped off the top layer and began again, applying the fine gold clay in several thin layers until no cracks were visible.

I began the living room area by again applying several coats of the final gold clay and silica sand, smoothing the final layer with a sponge trowel to make sure no cracks appeared, and trying to smooth all the bumps made by the trowel. This took many more hours than I had imagined. Days dragged into another week as I applied the clay, let it dry, watched the cracks appear, then applied another coat, let it dry, then cleaned the clay off the redwood strips, mended areas that had pulled away from the boards, and finally was ready for the linseed oil.

Each evening, I applied a new layer of oil, thinning with more and more turpentine as I went, but now the trowel marks on the top surface of the clay were showing more than I had hoped they would. The oil soaked into the clay for the first few coats, but the upper layers took days to dry. Even then, they still felt sticky. I really wasn't pleased with the floor.

Finally, I realized that I needed something shinier and stronger as a top sealer of the floor. I examined floors wherever I went. One day Jon and I had lunch at a sandwich shop with dazzling tile floors.

"That's Arizona Sealer, from Border Products," Jon said. "It's the hardest, shiniest thing around."

Of course, I was on the phone with Border Products the next day. They said the sealer was a solvent-based acrylic. That sounded like a possible solution—at least it wasn't a water-based product. So I bought a gallon and covered a bit of the floor in the bedroom closet.

It dried within a day, shiny, smooth, and hard. Cautiously exuberant, I covered the entire closet floor and waited another day. The results were still great after only one day of drying. Completely relieved, I bought two gallons and a lambswool applicator to do the entire floor.

There were many areas where the linseed oil had formed a thick, wrinkled coating, so I scuffed my feet over as many of them as I could find to break it up, then swept the floor with a hard, stiff broom to remove it. Joyfully, I spread the Arizona Sealer over the whole floor after work one evening and then slept in the trailer because the aroma was too strong for me to breathe.

While I still didn't dare step back and realize that I was just about done with the house and Kathy hadn't sued me, I could feel the joy beginning to bubble inside me. Much as I had felt the weight of the house crushing down on my shoulders when I began this project, I now slowly began to feel the load lifting.

The following evening, the floor was shiny and gorgeous. It was not tile smooth, but it had an amber beauty in the textures of the clay that reminded me of brown marble, if such a thing exists. Finally, I smiled with satisfaction and marveled at the magnificence of an earthen floor, with its variations and friendly softness—so different from concrete or machine-crafted floors.

Chapter Twenty-Two

# HOMECOMING

*It is my right to be uncommon—if I can . . .*
*To dream and to build, to fail and to succeed . . .*
*to think and act for myself . . .*
*and to face the world boldly saying,*
*"This, with God's help, I have done."*

—DEAN ALFANGE

THE desert was aflame with orange poppies and purple lupine as I completed the floor. Palo verde trees were bursting into cascades of yellow
blossoms, and the weather suddenly warmed into the eighties. Long-
legged jack rabbits and smaller fluffy bunnies scurried across the desert,
nibbling on the many green plants that had sprouted from the abundant
winter rains. I'm sure every valley waterfall was overflowing as it cascaded
over the red rocks into delicate streams. It had been too long since I had
hiked into the mountains.

A few March days had pushed into the lower nineties, but the house
had stayed in the midseventies with no cooling used. When the nights
dipped into the upper thirties again, the house stayed cozy warm. And
when the winds howled outside, there wasn't a shudder from these sturdy
walls. This was one solid house.

While I had been oiling the floor and letting it dry, Jon had been
installing the electric circuit breakers and kitchen cupboards. We had
bought the cabinet skeletons with no doors, which cost me about $600
instead of $6,000. I would make doors for them later, hopefully out of
saguaro ribs. We needed only the base cupboards with a plywood coun-
tertop and the kitchen sink for the final inspection.

While the floor dried, I had spent several delightful evenings tiling the
bathroom shower with my colorful Mexican tiles. Patrick, bless him, had

come almost every Saturday to do whatever needed to be done—build stairs to the exterior doors, drywall closets, and any bits of carpentry that we had neglected until the very end. He was an immense help.

Both Patrick and Jon were lifesavers, for I was out of money and out of time. I had a mortgage waiting at less than 7 percent if I could get my final permit and close on the loan by the end of March. My payments would be about $400 a month—just about what I had anticipated. I would be able to repay everything I had borrowed and still have a little left to buy a sofa. The kitchen cabinets had gone onto Jon's credit card.

I phoned for my final permit on March 27 and took a day off work. I tried not to be nervous, telling myself that anything the inspector might find, we could fix. While I waited, I applied burlap in clay slip to the east gable end in the loft. This work was just as messy as it had been on the west gable, but it kept my mind and my hands busy. In the early afternoon, I heard the inspector's truck drive up and stop.

As calmly as possible, I rinsed my hands in a nearby bucket of water, dried them on my shirt, and went downstairs to greet him. It was the same man who had given me such a hard time at my intermediate inspections, but I shook hands with him as with a long, lost friend.

Walking around the house, he still had that same amused smile on his face as he asked me about the plasters and the earthen floor. I assured him I wasn't going to leave the walls brown forever. He poked a polarity tester in every single outlet to see if they worked and peered under the sinks to see if we had raised the in-line vents above the drains. We had.

He told me that I was supposed to have sanitized kitchen counters instead of plywood, but I told him the plywood was coated with two layers of urethane sealer. He said that was okay. Becoming quieter, he unrolled the plans and scrutinized them.

"Did you get an insulation certificate for the ceiling?" he asked.

"Yes, I have it in the trailer. Would you like to see it?"

"Yes."

I scurried over to my files in the cluttered trailer and brought the certificate to him.

After glancing at it he said, "Okay, you're all set then." He scratched his initials on the inspection sheet next to the final permit and handed me a green card for the electric company.

"Thank you," I said, almost stunned. "Thank you very much."

From the sunroom door, I watched him climb in his truck and drive away. I waited until he was down the road out of earshot before I let out a big "Yahoo!"

*My inspection card with a list of all twenty-four
inspections. It now hangs on my wall in a golden frame.*
Photo by Rick Peterson.

Walking back to th inspection sheet, I brushed my fingers lightly over
his initials, making sure they hadn't vanished. I stared at the sheet for a
few minutes, trying to absorb the reality that there would be no more
inspections.

The house was built; I had made it. My mind wasn't prepared to have
passed an inspection on the first attempt. My thoughts and emotions stumbled over each other. Graduation day had arrived and this was now my
home, not a construction site; no more deadlines. I could sleep late on Saturdays, bake cookies and real meals in my new kitchen.

I should call Jon and tell him the good news, I thought. The boys
would be excited to know that we could finally move out of the trailer!
I could call Kathy and tell her to come get the trailer, and I could call
the mortgage company—and then, after all the little details were finished,

I would have a big party for everyone who had helped build this house, for it had not been built by one person.

Later. My knees grew weak as I sank into a nearby chair, letting tears silently flow. Now, I could cry. Tears of fatigue streamed down my cheeks, and tears for all the fears I had faced without crying. Tears for all the days nobody had shown up to help, and tears for the days when I wanted to spend time with my boys but couldn't. There were tears for all the things that could have gone wrong and tears of self-pity for the days I had worked so hard, when other people were lounging by their pools. Then there were just tears . . .

As all the tears cleansed my Being, a peace radiated through me. The tears turned to those of joy that I had done it despite all the pressures, tears of relief that Jon had shown up to help and guide me, tears of amazement at all the other people who had come to help, tears for all the miracles that made the impossible possible, tears of relief that the strain was behind me now and I had this wonderful house.

As my eyes dried, the late afternoon sun shone through the windows, bathing the mudded walls in a golden hue. The earthen floor sparkled in the sunlight. The spiral staircase wound gracefully into the loft where the boys would sleep. It took a little imagination to see the elegance and charm that this house would become with a light gold clay slip covering the brown mud and raw drywall, bamboo lining the curved wall around the staircase, Mexican tile touches here and there.

The house and I were bonded for life. It was a reflection of me, as I had made all these choices for its construction and colors. I knew every bump and crack in the bales, its weak points and strengths, its beauty and dark corners. My Spirit lined the walls and crevices; my love of the desert was reflected in its Soul. I was sure it had one.

Yes, it had cost many more thousands than I had imagined and had taken much longer than I had planned. It was good that I didn't know all this at the beginning or I would have been twice as scared to build it. But now, I had an elegant home that I would be proud of forever, with a mortgage I could afford. The utility bills would be negligible for the minimal heating and cooling required. I would install a solar hot water heater as soon as I could to minimize the electric bills even further. One of my next projects would also be large tanks to collect rainwater for the garden.

The house would return all my work many times over. Its sturdy walls would shelter us from the extreme heat of the summer and the cold winter nights. Its porch would protect us from the baking sun and driving monsoon rains. Looking at it in my future days, I could recall the memories of how it was built, bit by bit, weekend after weekend, while my romance with Jon blossomed. A smile crept across my face as I remembered our many days of work sprinkled with kisses and laughter.

If I built it again, would I change anything? I couldn't tell yet. The loft and the porch had been expensive, requiring carpentry skills beyond my abilities and using more lumber than I liked. I had sworn that I would never build two stories in the desert heat, because it's too hard to keep the upstairs cool. I would soon find out how true that is, even with all our insulation.

The high ceiling had been difficult, but it gave the house an elegant style. The spiral staircase took up a great deal of precious room, but it was lovely. Doing it again, I might build a one-story house with a room for the boys on one end. On Kauai, we had built a large room with a folding divider-wall in the center. This way the boys could have a playroom when they needed one, or privacy if that was what they preferred. If the boys were younger, I think I definitely would do that—maybe put a porch on part of the house and mix asphalt emulsion in with my plasters to waterproof them where there was no porch.

A larger one-story home would have meant less specialized carpentry and less lumber but also a larger foundation, more days of wall raising, more days of mudding, and more earthen floor. The labor and costs might well have evened out. However, this house had a charm that had captured me from the moment I saw the floor plan on Wayne's worktable, and it still enthralled me. Despite its difficulties, I had made it through to the final permit, and I couldn't be happier. No, I decided, at this point I had no regrets.

What an amazing, challenging, soul-searching, exhausting, adventurous project it had been! I doubt if any period of my life will be richer or more fulfilling. I stood now with a strength and confidence that I'm not sure I really understood. My muscles had grown along with my inner strength.

I had learned to treat lime with respect and build doorways straight and plumb, so the doors will fit snugly and open smoothly. Even straw bale walls need to be fairly straight if the roof is going to fit. I had learned to use screws wherever possible, not to change the plans without talking to the inspector, and to buy two measuring tapes so I don't spend half the day looking for one. I learned to clean up after every job and put every tool in its place, for there is a black hole to which tools can depart, much the same as ballpoint pens.

I learned to make my plumbing connections far enough apart so I can cut them out and replace them, if I ever need to, and to note the difference between hose threads and plumbing threads. I learned to use Super Glue to close up the cuts on my fingers, Bag Balm to protect my hands from the dry air, vitamin E oil to repair my hands after a day's hard work, and to drink water constantly. I had made friends with mud.

I had developed great respect and a little jealousy for the people who do this every day for a living, from the concrete specialists to the electricians. It's hard physical and mental work, but it's great fun to breathe the fresh air, flex the muscles, and create beautiful homes. I had begun a new life with the texture I had been seeking. All the hard work had balanced very nicely with my office job, to the point where I became more content even when I had to sit in the office, knowing how much sun and exercise I would get on the weekends.

Not only had I made friends with mud and straw, but I had met a wide range of people with a genuine enthusiasm for alternative building. They were wonderful people from all over the world who help each other build houses for the joy of it, asking nothing in return. May I become one of them as I move into my future.

I had also seen the delight in peoples' eyes as they viewed this simple, earthy home and couldn't help but run their fingers over the earthen plasters and smell the straw. There is something friendly and familiar in curved lines, irregular walls and organic materials. I hoped my house would speak to everyone who entered of how they could do this themselves, if they so chose.

I had learned that our houses are very complex; I agree with Thoreau. Now I understand why they are so expensive. As I had faced detail upon expensive detail, I kept asking myself if I could do without this or that. The answer was usually, not unless I absolutely have to. And yet, by insisting on all these comforts, I was pushing the construction to the limits of what an unskilled person could accomplish on his or her own.

All those details have become what we consider necessities—lights that go on and off at the flick of a conveniently located switch, heating and cooling systems that maintain a comfortable temperature at all times, tight seals on everything to keep the weather and bugs away, faucets that deliver just the right temperature of water on demand, roofs that don't creak in a high wind, a foundation that would survive floods and tremors, and septic systems that flow smoothly, among many others. At least now I would always notice and truly appreciate these "necessities" that so much of the earth's population lives without.

The inspections added to all the stress and complexity, of course. They made me feel like I was back at school where there was a major test at the end of each chapter. Every little requirement of all twenty-four inspections made the house almost impossible to complete without professional guidance. But the inspections kept me from making major mistakes, also. There is a reason behind each inspection, I learned—they aren't just created to torture the homebuilder, although they sure have become intricate.

I would, of course, want insurance on the house, as well as my mortgage, both of which were dependent on the series of inspections. Insurance companies and banks need to know the house is built to certain standards before they put their money against it. I often felt as if some of the details of each inspection should be a homeowner's choice rather than a requirement, however. But then again, when I am building so a mortgage company can resell the house if I default on payments, I'm not building solely for myself.

One of the main gifts of this house to me, besides its warmth and protection, has been the change its construction brought about in my thought processes. The project was so enormous and unfamiliar, and I had so much at stake, that failure wasn't an option. The only way I found to survive was to look no further than the coming weekend. I was always planning for the upcoming phases of the house, but I didn't allow myself to question whether I'd be able to accomplish them; I simply moved forward with as much certainty as I could muster that when the time came, the solution would be there.

Somewhere in the process, I changed the chatter in the recesses of my mind from fears and imagined doom to creative thoughts. Every time I felt my mind slipping into worry, I would switch the background conversation to thankfulness for the solutions and completions that were about to happen. I visualized the house completed, with bright tile and cozy earthen plasters, down to the smallest detail.

To assist myself in making this transition to positive thinking, I often imagined that there was, indeed, a Spirit Committee assigned to overseeing the construction. Their jobs as angels and guides were at stake if the project failed, so we were all working together. I was their liaison at the job site, doing the grunt work. Instead of worrying, I just sent out requests for guidance, imagined that they were sharing the burden, and let part of my mind step back and watch it all happen. And, as in so much of our lives, many imagined opportunities for failure never occurred.

Most of all, as I lived in the present moment of each weekend, not bothering to worry, but enjoying the beautiful desert and the joy of creating, I lived with a new intensity and joy. I loved my moments of building and woke on Saturday mornings eager to dive into the day's activities. Well, most Saturday mornings. Giving up television and social engagements in the evenings was no sacrifice, not even close. There will be plenty of time for those in my future, if I choose them.

I had taken a blind step off a cliff in faith, not knowing exactly how the house was going to be built, but certain that if I didn't take the first few steps, I'd never experience the last few. I had landed in a more magnificent place than I had ever imagined. I am still in awe of the amazing process that unfolded before me.

Never had the project stopped for lack of money. The ebb and flow of money became another form of creative energy, often used to make me change a decision, such as the design of the house, or step across the boundaries of my fears, as on the roof. But even though the house was way over budget, when I really needed to pay for something, the money was there.

As I faced each weekend with new challenges, my mantra became "I can do this. It's been done before by many people; it can't be that hard." And by the end of each weekend, the task was done (or at least half done, for it always took longer than I thought).

My house also led me to Jon. With him on the other end of the phone or by my side, I knew I wouldn't make major mistakes and I didn't have to spend hours reading how-to books. That was an invaluable load lifted from my small shoulders, as was his physical help with the difficult jobs. How I would have made it through the house without him, I don't know, and fortunately I don't have to find out. He was one of the miracles that my house brought to me. With him as a partner, I not only learned to build, but to give and receive love freely, openly, with passion and joy, but without clinging. May I remember this long after the house is completed.

May I also remember some of the other lessons from this project: to live simply and think of the whole planet as I make my decisions. May I remember to live without worrying, enjoying the present, planning for the future, and bringing only the lessons from the past.

May I seek beautiful things to create and selfless deeds to give, knowing that anything is possible and any limitations I see are only figments of my fears. May I remember that my fears may be overcome; I am larger than they are. May I notice the songbirds and sunsets that come to celebrate my days. May I remember to pause and join in the celebration. May I give and receive love with friends, cats, angels, trees, houses, myself, and loved ones with my heart wide open and my feet securely planted beneath me. May I remember to ask for help when I need it.

May I remember all this every time I look at my beautiful house. May I remember not only how I built the house, but how the house built me.

*Ta-da!* Photo by Jon Ruez.

# RESOURCES

## Books and Articles

Chiras, Daniel D. *The Natural House: A Complete Guide to Healthy, Energy-Efficient, Environmental Homes.* White River Junction, Vt.: Chelsea Green, 2000.

Eisenberg, David. "Sustainability and the Building Codes." Paper presented at the Building Environment and Thermal Envelope Council (BETEC) Emerging Technologies Symposium, Sustainable Building Envelope Materials, Washington, D.C., 1997. (Other articles by David Eisenberg available at www.dcat.net.)

Hemp, Peter. *Plumbing a House.* Newtown, Conn.: Taunton Press, 1994.

Ireton, Kevin, ed. *Foundations and Concrete Work: The Best of Fine Homebuilding.* Newtown, Conn.: Taunton Press, 1997.

Lacinski, Paul, and Michel Bergeron. *Serious Straw Bale: A Home Construction Guide for All Climates.* White River Junction, Vt.: Chelsea Green, 2000.

Meagan, Keely. *Earth Plasters for Straw Bale Homes.* Santa Fe, N. Mex.: Keely Meagan, 2000. To order, contact Keely Meagan at keelymeagan@hotmail.com or P.O. Box 5888, Santa Fe, NM 85702.

Myhrman, Matt,s and S. O. MacDonald. *Build It with Bales: A Step-by-Step Guide to Straw-Bale Construction,* 2d ed. Tucson, Ariz.: Out on Bale, 1997.

Reynolds, Michael. *Earthship,* 3 vols. Taos, N. Mex.: Solar Survival Press, 1990.

Steen, Athena Swentzell, Bill Steen, David Bainbridge with David Eisenberg. *The Straw Bale House.* White River Junction, Vt.: Chelsea Green, 1994.

Welsch, Roger. "Baled Hay." In *Shelter.* Bolinas, Calif.: Shelter Publications, 1973.

## *Journals and Web Resources*

*The Last Straw Journal.* HC 66, Box 119, Hillsboro, New Mexico 88042. Phone: (505) 895-5400; E-mail: thelaststraw@strawhomes.com; Web site: www.strawhomes.com.

**www.ahouseofstraw.com.** The Web site I constructed to document the building of my house. Includes photos.

**www.dcat.net.** The Development Center for Appropriate Technology (DCAT) site contains straw bale building-code information and articles by David Eisenberg.

**www.greenbuilder.com.** A directory of builders, consultants, architects, and experts by state and country, plus many other resources for sustainable building.

**www.eren.doe.gov/buildings/documents/strawbale.html.** A report on straw bale homes by the U.S. Department of Energy.

**www.moxvox.com/surfsolo.html.** An extensive list of links to straw bale Web sites (including sites with information on building codes).

**www.caneloproject.com.** Bill and Athena Steen's Web site, with information on their workshops and ongoing projects.

**http://solstice.crest.org/efficiency/strawbale-list-archive.** The straw bale e-mail discussion group archives, indexed by subject. To subscribe, send an e-mail with "subscribe strawbale" in the subject line to: strawbale-subscribe@crest.org.

# Other Recent and Related Books from CHELSEA GREEN PUBLISHING

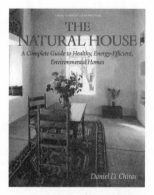

THE NATURAL HOUSE
A Complete Guide to Healthy, Energy-Efficient, Environmental Homes

*Daniel D. Chiras*

paper • 8 x 10 • 480 pages
• b&w photos • appendices
• index • ISBN 1-890132-57-8
• $35.00

This exciting book, written by a veteran author who himself lives in a straw bale and rammed-tire home, takes the reader on a tour of thirteen natural building methods, including straw bale, rammed earth, cordwood masonry, adobe, cob, Earthships, and more. You'll learn how these homes are built, how much they cost, and the pros and cons of each method. A resource guide offers contacts and resources for every region.

In a writing style that is clear, engaging, and fun to read, the author shows how we can gain energy independence and dramatically reduce our environmental impact through passive heating and cooling techniques, and renewable energy. Chiras also explains safe, economical ways of supplying clean drinking water and treating wastewater, and discusses affordable green building products.

While Chiras is a passionate advocate of natural building, he takes a careful look at the "romance" of these techniques and alerts readers to avoidable pitfalls, offering detailed practical advice that could save you tens of thousands of dollars, whether you're buying a natural home, building one yourself, renovating an existing structure, or hiring a contractor to build for you.

## About the Author

Dan Chiras holds a Ph.D. in biology and teaches courses on sustainability at the University of Denver and the University of Colorado. He has published five college and high school textbooks as well as books for general audiences. Chiras is an avid musician, organic gardener, river runner, and bicyclist who lives with his two sons in a passive solar/solar-electric home in Evergreen, Colorado.

paper • 8 x 8 • 128 pages
• color photographs
• ISBN 1-890132-77-2 • $22.95

In the past two decades, the bale-building renaissance has attracted some of our most gifted architects, artisan builders, and craftspeople. The hands-on process of constructing walls with a completely natural substance has appealed to both very experienced builders and those who find this to be a uniquely accessible form of creating shelter. The characteristic thick walls and wide windowsills of straw bale houses, the possibility of incorporating curves and even arches, and the rousing experience of family "wall-raisings" have become well-known. Combined with older styles of plastering and earthen floors, these very contemporary buildings have a timeless quality that's easy to recognize yet hard to achieve with conventional manufactured materials.

Athena and Bill Steen, co-authors of the original *Straw Bale House*, have now created a book that celebrates in gorgeous color photographs the tactile, sensuous beauty of straw bale dwellings. Their selection of photos also demonstrates how far bale building has come in a very short period of time. Along with handsome homes, small and not-so-small, this book shows larger-scale institutional buildings, including schools, office buildings, the Real Goods Solar Living Center, and a Save the Children center in Mexico.

In addition, this book includes an introductory essay by the Steens noting key lessons they have learned in years of building with bales: insights into the design and construction process, and critical advice about features that ameliorate the impacts of moisture, weather, and wear-and-tear over time. Each photograph is also accompanied by narrative text highlighting a given building's special features and personal touches.

### About the Authors

Athena Swentzell Steen grew up in Santa Fe and at the Santa Clara Pueblo, building with natural materials from an early age. Bill Steen is a photographer and collaborative builder especially interested in combining building techniques with community-enhancing approaches to design. Athena and Bill live in Canelo, Arizona.

**Chelsea Green Publishing • Books for Sustainable Living**

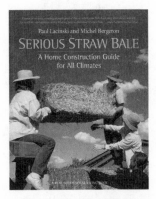

paper • 8 x 10 • 384 pages
• 8 page color-section
• b&w photos • illustrations
• index • ISBN 1-890132-64-0
• $30.00

Bergeron and Lacinski's new book is the first to look carefully at the specific design considerations critical to success with a straw bale building in more extreme climates-where seasonal changes in temperature, precipitation, and humidity create special stresses that builders must understand and address. The authors draw upon years of experience with natural materials and experimental techniques, and present a compelling rationale for building with straw, one of nature's most resilient, available, and affordable byproducts.

For skeptics and true believers, this book will prove to be the latest word.

• Thorough explanations of how moisture and temperature affect buildings in seasonal climates, with descriptions of the unique capacities of straw and other natural materials to provide warmth, quiet, and comfort year-round.

• Comprehensive comparison of the two main approaches to straw bale construction: "Nebraska-style," where bales bear the weight of the roof, and framed structures, where bales provide insulation.

• Detailed advice-including many well-considered cautions-for contractors, owner-builders, and designers, following each stage of a bale-building process.

This is a second-generation straw bale book, for those seeking serious information to meet serious challenges while adventuring in the most fun form of construction to come along in several centuries.

### About the Authors

Paul Lacinski is a partner in Green Space Collaborative, an environmental consulting firm offering integrated project management and innovative design services. He lives in Ashfield, Massachusetts. Michel Bergeron is a founding member of Quebec's legendary ecological design-build firm, Archibio. He lives in Montreal.

THE HOUSE THAT JACK BUILT
# TREEHOUSES

DAVID PEARSON
A REAL GOODS SOLAR LIVING BOOK

paper • 8 x 8 • 96 pages • color photos • b&w illustrations • index
ISBN 1-890132-85-3 • $16.95

## Circle Houses: Yurts, Tipis and Benders

The House That Jack Built series continues its exciting exploration into innovative housing styles with a foray into the world of portable houses. *Circle Houses: Tipis, Yurts, and Benders* looks at mobile homes from three wildly different cultural perspectives, each of which has increasing relevance in our contemporary world. Lots of color, great stories, and just enough how-to information to get you in trouble! This is a book that is guaranteed to stimulate your imagination.

paper • 8 x 8 • 96 pages • color photos • b&w illustrations • index • ISBN 1-890132-86-1 • $16.95

The first book in The House that Jack Built series, *Treehouses* introduces homemade buildings from all over the world, from tipis to treehouses to houseboats. Edited by David Pearson, best-selling author of *The Natural House Book* and *The Natural House Catalog*, these delightful books of practical inspiration will appeal to both dreamers and doers.

Treehouses are the epitome of fantasy. In this book, you will get enough practical information to get started, and enough inspiration to last a lifetime. Drawing from real projects from around the globe, the book features twenty distinctive tree dwellings. Each is a masterwork of inventiveness, due in part to the uniqueness of the respective settings, but also to the outpouring of creativity that accompanies the challenge of living in trees.

Beautiful color photographs portray finished projects and the construction process. Pragmatic tips and tricks provide less experienced builders with the confidence to begin designing their own treetop retreats. A how-to section illustrated with line drawings and easy-to-follow instructions gives even weekend carpenters enough information to complete a simple project. The extensive resource section offers places to visit, both real and virtual.

Thanks to Julia Butterfly Hill, who lived in a redwood tree for two years to protest logging practices in the California, treehouses have lately been prominent in the news. Their appeal is timeless. To live in the trees is to reside in a state of natural splendor. David Pearson, one of the pioneers in the natural building movement, captures the combined spirits of innocence and daring in this awesome little book.

Maybe the "house that Jack built" will become the house that you build!

## About the Author

London-based architect David Pearson is author of *The Natural House Book, The Natural House Catalog,* and *Earth to Spirit: In Search of Natural Architecture.*

**Chelsea Green Publishing • Books for Sustainable Living**

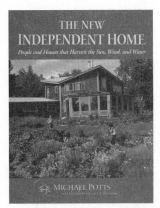

paper • 8 x 10 • 400 pages
• 16 page color-section • b&w photos
• index • ISBN 1-890132-14-4
• $30.00

Michael Potts's 1993 book, *The Independent Home*, has become one of our best sellers and is flagship of the series of popular Solar Living Books, produced in association with Real Goods. Because of its impact in bringing the almost unknown promise of solar energy to thousands of readers, one longtime observer of energy trends described the publication of the original Independent Home as "the most important event in the solar industry in more than a decade."

In this newly revised and expanded edition, Potts again profiles the solar homesteaders whose experiments and innovations have opened the possibility of solar living for the rest of us. Potts provides clear and highly entertaining explanations of how various renewable energy systems work, and shows why they now make more sense than ever. He is a brilliant guide to the stages of planning and design faced by everyone who seeks to create a home that reconciles the personal and global dimensions of ecology.

Over the past five years, the concept of an "independent" home has evolved beyond the energy system to encompass the whole process of design and construction involved in planning a renovation or new home. Independent homes are homes with integrity and personality. Traditional-style dwellings are now being built with natural materials, such as straw bales and rammed earth, and combined with state-of-the-art electronic technologies for harvesting free energy from the surrounding environment.

Potts writes lucidly about homeowners some would consider to be the lunatic fringe, and others would regard as among the only sane people on the planet. This movement for self-reliance is an important trend that will continue to surprise and delight us as we approach the inevitable dawn of the Solar Age.

### About the Author

Michael Potts is a freelance writer, networker, computer applications designer, and director of the Caspar Institute in northern California. He and his family have been building their own innovative, low-impact, off-the-grid home for twenty years.

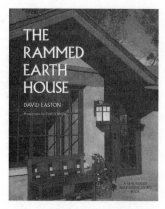

# THE RAMMED EARTH HOUSE

DAVID EASTON

Photographs by Cynthia Wright

paper • 8 x 10 • 288 pages
• 16 page color-section • b&w photos
and illustrations • resources
• index • ISBN 0-930031-79-2
• $30.00

Humans have been using earth as a primary building material for more than ten thousand years. As practiced today, rammed earth involves tamping a mixture of earth, water, and a little cement into wooden forms to create thick, sturdy masonry walls. Earth-built homes offer their inhabitants a powerful sense of security and well-being, and have a permanence and solidity altogether lacking in so many of today's modular, pre-fabricated houses.

## About the Author

David Easton has led the revival of rammed earth in this hemisphere. He makes his living as a builder in northern California.

## The Rammed Earth Renaissance

video • 45 minutes • ISBN 0-9652335-0-2 • $29.95

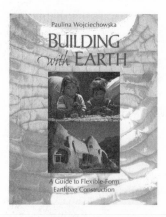

Paulina Wojciechowska

BUILDING with EARTH

A Guide to Flexible-Form Earthbag Construction

paper • 8 x 10 • 192 pages
• b&w photos and illustrations
• bibliography • resources
• index • ISBN 1-890132-81-0
• $24.95

Building with Earth is the first comprehensive guide to describe the re-emergence of earthen architecture in North America, where adventurous builders are combining timeless forms such as arches, vaults, and domes with modern materials and techniques. Using inexpensive, recycled or salvaged polypropylene tubing or textile grain sacks, even relatively inexperienced builders can construct an essentially tree-free building, from foundation to roof.

This book will take you "back to the future" of natural building, which lies in the merger of ancient architectures with cutting-edge earth-based techniques now being researched for their potential in building durable dwellings in the Third World, off-the-grid dream homes in exotic locales, and even structures on the moon!

## About the Author

Paulina Wojciechowska was born in Poland and spent her formative years in Afghanistan and India. After studying architecture in Great Britain, she traveled to the United States and Mexico to study "natural," "alternative," and indigenous building methods. She apprenticed with Nader Khalili at the California Institute of Earth Architecture (Cal-Earth) as well as Athena and Bill Steen at the Canelo Project.

# Put $50 out there and just see what comes back from

# *the Invisible Universe*

THE INVISIBLE UNIVERSE is a virtual and virtuous "place" for people who want to be on the leading edge of sustainable living. For a $50 membership fee (annual), you receive the following benefits:

Midwest Renewable Energy Association

1. A free book. (Our selection will change from time to time, but at the moment new Denizens receive *Slow Food: Collected Thoughts on Taste, Tradition, and the Honest Pleasures of Food*, a $24.95 value.)

2. A free trial subscription to (your choice) *Natural Home Magazine*, *Mother Earth News*, *Permaculture Magazine*, or *Resurgence Magazine*. A value of up to $25.

3. A one-year membership in Co-op America, entitled to their full benefits, including a copy of their indispensible reference *The Green Pages*. A value of $30.

4. Free admission to Convocations, festivals that celebrate sustainability. These carry a dollar value of $25, but how do you really attach dollars to learning and fun?

5. The Hub enewsletter and *The Junction*, Chelsea Green's print newsletter.

6. Access to the unpublished Invisible Universe Web site, where Denizens are encouraged to mount the soapbox, show off, or just noodle around.

7. A free gift anytime you visit the Solar Living Center or Terra Verde. Just identify yourself as a Denizen of the Invisible Universe and show them your invisible membership card.

8. Free shipping on all Chelsea Green books— for Denizens only!

## Co-op America
building an economy for people and the planet

*...and much more*

The HUB

---

This is the club for people who don't join clubs, an organization for people who prefer exclusivity with a common touch. To learn more or to join the Invisible Universe:

**CALL us toll-free at 1.800.639.4099**
**VISIT our Web site www.chelseagreen.com**

CHELSEA GREEN PUBLISHING CO.

the invisible universe

# CHELSEA GREEN

Sustainable living has many facets. Chelsea Green's celebration of the sustainable arts has led us to publish trend-setting books about organic gardening, solar electricity and renewable energy, innovative building techniques, regenerative forestry, local and bioregional democracy, and whole foods. The company's published works, while intensely practical, are also entertaining and inspirational, demonstrating that an ecological approach to life is consistent with producing beautiful, eloquent, and useful books, videos, and audio cassettes.

For more information about Chelsea Green, or to request a free catalog, call toll-free (800) 639-4099, or write to us at P.O. Box 428, White River Junction, Vermont 05001. Visit our Web site at www.chelseagreen.com.

Chelsea Green's titles include:

*The Natural House*
*The Straw Bale House*
*The New Independent Home*
*The Hand-Sculpted House*
*Serious Straw Bale*
*The Beauty of*
  *Straw Bale Homes*
*Building with Earth*
*The Resourceful Renovator*
*Independent Builder*
*The Rammed Earth House*
*The Passive Solar House*
*Wind Energy Basics*
*Wind Power for Home &*
  *Business*
*The Solar Living Sourcebook*
*A Shelter Sketchbook*
*Mortgage-Free!*
*Stone Circles*

*Gaia's Garden*
*The Neighborhood Forager*
*The Apple Grower*
*The Flower Farmer*
*Breed Your Own*
  *Vegetable Varieties*
*Keeping Food Fresh*
*The Soul of Soil*
*The New Organic Grower*
*Four-Season Harvest*
*Solar Gardening*
*Straight-Ahead Organic*
*The Contrary Farmer*
*The Co-op Cookbook*
*Whole Foods Companion*
*The Bread Builder*
*The Village Herbalist*
*The Pesto Manifesto*
*Secrets of Salsa*

*A Cafecito Story*
*Believing Cassandra*
*Gaviotas: A Village to*
  *Reinvent the World*
*Who Owns the Sun?*
*Global Spin:*
  *The Corporate Assault*
  *on Environmentalism*
*Hemp Horizons*
*This Organic Life*
*Beyond the Limits*
*The Man Who Planted Trees*
*The Northern Forest*
*The New Settler Interviews*
*Loving and Leaving the*
  *Good Life*
*Scott Nearing: The Making*
  *of a Homesteader*
*Wise Words for the Good Life*